Phryne

Also available from Bloomsbury

Female Mobility and Gendered Space in Ancient Greek Myth
by Ariadne Konstantinou
Revisiting Rape in Antiquity: Sexualised Violence in Greek and Roman Worlds
edited by Susan Deacy, José Malheiro Magalhães and Jean Zacharski Menzies
Women in Ancient Greece: A Sourcebook by Bonnie MacLachlan
Women's Life in Greece and Rome: A Source Book in Translation
by Maureen B. Fant and Mary R. Lefkowitz

Phryne
A Life in Fragments

Melissa Funke

BLOOMSBURY ACADEMIC
LONDON • NEW YORK • OXFORD • NEW DELHI • SYDNEY

BLOOMSBURY ACADEMIC
Bloomsbury Publishing Plc, 50 Bedford Square, London, WC1B 3DP, UK
Bloomsbury Publishing Inc, 1385 Broadway, New York, NY 10018, USA
Bloomsbury Publishing Ireland, 29 Earlsfort Terrace, Dublin 2, D02 AY28, Ireland

BLOOMSBURY, BLOOMSBURY ACADEMIC and the Diana logo
are trademarks of Bloomsbury Publishing Plc

First published in Great Britain 2024
This paperback edition published 2025

Copyright © Melissa Funke, 2024

Melissa Funke has asserted her right under the Copyright,
Designs and Patents Act, 1988, to be identified as Author of this work.

For legal purposes the Acknowledgments on p. x constitute
an extension of this copyright page.

Cover design: Terry Woodley
Cover image: Franz von Stuck, *Phryne*, 1917, oil on canvas. Gift of Dr. Anna Berliner,
public domain, 62.9. Portland Art Museum, Portland, Oregon

All rights reserved. No part of this publication may be: i) reproduced or transmitted
in any form, electronic or mechanical, including photocopying, recording or by means
of any information storage or retrieval system without prior permission in writing
from the publishers; or ii) used or reproduced in any way for the training, development
or operation of artificial intelligence (AI) technologies, including generative AI technologies.
The rights holders expressly reserve this publication from the text and data mining
exception as per Article 4(3) of the Digital Single Market Directive (EU) 2019/790.

Bloomsbury Publishing Inc does not have any control over, or responsibility for,
any third-party websites referred to or in this book. All internet addresses given
in this book were correct at the time of going to press. The author and publisher
regret any inconvenience caused if addresses have changed or sites have
ceased to exist, but can accept no responsibility for any such changes.

A catalogue record for this book is available from the British Library.

A catalog record for this book is available from Library of Congress.

ISBN: HB: 978-1-3503-7187-3
PB: 978-1-3503-7191-0
ePDF: 978-1-3503-7188-0
eBook: 978-1-3503-7189-7

Typeset by RefineCatch Limited, Bungay, Suffolk

For product safety related questions contact productsafety@bloomsbury.com.

To find out more about our authors and books visit www.bloomsbury.com
and sign up for our newsletters.

*For Audrey and Dorothy, the original dreamgirls.
I'm lucky to know your stories.*

"Not as she is, but as she fills his dream"
Christina Rossetti, "In an Artist's Studio"

Contents

List of Illustrations	viii
Acknowledgments	x
Note on Translation	xiii
Introduction	1
1 Mnesarete to Phryne	23
2 Phryne the Artist's Model	51
3 Phryne on Trial	79
4 Phryne's Afterlife	103
Conclusion	143
Notes	147
Bibliography	171
Index Locorum	183
Index	187

Illustrations

1. Bronze statuette of Aphrodite Anadyomene, 1st–2nd century CE, Metropolitan Museum of Art (2021.40.56) 53
2. Aphrodite of Knidos, Copy of Praxiteles; restorer: Ippolito Buzzi (Italian, 1562–1634), Musei nazionale romano di palazzo Altemps (8619). Photographer Marie-Lan Nguyen 65
3. *Praxiteles Giving Phryne his Statue of Cupid*, Angelica Kauffman, 1794, oil on canvas, courtesy of RISD Museum (59.008) 108
4. *Phryne seduces the philosopher Xenocrates*, Angelica Kauffman, 1794, oil on canvas, private collection. Photographer Andres Salvador 109
5. *Phryne Tempting Xenocrates*, Simon François Ravenet, the Elder, after Salvator Rosa, 1770, engraving, courtesy of Harvard Art Museums (R9422) 110
6. *Phryné*, Gustave Boulanger, 1850, oil on canvas, courtesy of Van Gogh Museum (s0456S1996) 113
7. *Phryné devant l'Aréopage*, Jean-Léon Gérôme, 1861, oil on canvas, Hamburger Kunsthalle (HK-1910) Photographer Popszes 114
8. "Standing Female Nude," featuring model Marie-Christine Leroux, Gaspard-Félix Tournachon (Nadar), 1860, salted paper print from glass negative, Metropolitan Museum of Art (1991.1174) 117
9. "Phryne before the Chicago Tribunal," Bernhard Gillam, 1884 June 4, political cartoon from *Puck* 15 (378), restored by Adam Cuerden, Library of Congress (AP101.P7) 119
10. "Phryné suppliante," zinc cut-out, courtesy of Musée de Châtellerault (2007.0.8) 122
11. Sibyl Sanderson as Phryné, image from *Saint-Saëns* by Lucien Augé de Lassus, 1893 125

12 *Phryne at the Poseidonia in Eleusis*, Henryk Siemiradzki,
    1889, oil on canvas, Russian Museum (Ж5687) — 129
13 *Phryné*, José Frappa, 1903, oil on canvas, Musée d'Orsay
    (LUX 1235) — 131
14 *Phryne*, Franz von Stuck, 1917, oil on canvas, courtesy
    of Portland Art Museum (62.9, gift of Dr. Anna Berliner) — 132
15 *Phryne*, Antonio Parreiras, 1909, oil on canvas — 133
16 Poster for *Altri Tempi*, 1952, starring Gina Lollobrigida, directed
    by Alessandro Blasetti, Società Italiana Cines — 135
17 Poster for *Frine, cortigiana d'Oriente*, 1953, starring
    Elena Kleus, directed by Mario Bonnard, Zeuss Film — 137
18 Poster for *La Venere di Cheronea/Aphrodite, déesse de
    l'amour/Aphrodite, The Goddess of Love*, 1957, starring
    Belinda Lee, directed by Fernando Cerchio and Viktor
    Tourjansky, Rialto Film — 139

Acknowledgments

This project is the result of a long process that goes back to my earliest days in graduate school; it owes a great debt to C. W. Marshall, who allowed me to write a master's thesis on the women featured in Alciphron's *Letters of Courtesans*, which first introduced me to the phenomenon that is Phryne. Toph has been a teacher, a mentor, a colleague, and most importantly, a friend, a model of scholarly generosity whose fierce support is the reason I am a Classicist. Ruby Blondell, my PhD supervisor, helped me refine my thoughts on fragments, their contexts and transmission, which has been so important to my understanding of Phryne and what we know about her. Ruby's work on Helen of Troy and the other "bad" women of Greek antiquity has been a guiding light for this project.

My home institution, the University of Winnipeg, has supported this work, most of all by providing me with a research assistant, the talented Bourke Karras, who collected and sorted through every possible mention of Phryne in ancient Greek literature. I also thank audiences in Bogotá, Colombia and at Dalhousie University in Halifax, Canada, for listening to the papers that gave rise to this project and offering helpful insights that have shaped its final form. Naomi Campa has been a sounding board extraordinaire about the citizenship status of women in Classical Athens (even if we have not yet quite agreed about the finer details). I am immensely grateful to the reviewers at Bloomsbury for their feedback on this project and the guidance of Lily Mac Mahon and Zoë Osman through the process of publication.

I am especially grateful to have a group of supportive colleagues in my own department and at my institution who have lent books, talked through ideas, and offered their wisdom throughout my writing process. Two in particular, Alyson Brickey and Carla Manfredi, provided encouragement and clarity in moments when my own thoughts were too tangled to commit to the page. I have been blessed with a department that supports their junior colleagues unwaveringly, which has meant more than ever as we have all faced an avalanche of unpredictability since the onset of the Covid-19 pandemic in March 2020. Peter Miller has guided me through the labyrinth of finding grants and teaching releases, while Conor Whately and Melanie Racette-Campbell are stalwarts who don't mind a colleague popping in unannounced with the most random of questions. Our students at University of Winnipeg are a constant source of joy and hilarity (and more than a little racket emanating from the lounge beside my office). The teams at Peopling the Past, the Women's Classical Caucus, and the Women's Network are colleagues who make our field a better place and who have shown me the wonderful things that can come from collaboration.

This particular project was conceived of during the first Covid-19 lockdown in spring 2020 and much of it has been written at home, beginning when my daughter was six years old and making her own way through Zoom schooling and the challenges of being away from routine and friends. I am forever indebted to the wonderful group of neighbors who entertained her and kept an eye out for her while I was writing in the home office (the whole Harvard Gardens gang but the Hemmerlings in particular). I would also not have maintained my equanimity on heavy research and writing days or after endless Zooms without their encouragement, typically offered around the firepit at all times of year (even at -30 Celsius!). My ringette teams (both the Honey Badgers that I played with and the SWRA Under 10 Fury that I coached) provided just the right distractions in the final stretch of work on this project, and especially to the Fury, your hard work and unstoppable spirit have been my inspiration this year.

On the note of support and encouragement, I would be remiss not to mention my boisterous and loving family, and given the theme of this book, the women in particular. To every one of my aunties (outlaws included), my mom, Karen, and my sisters, Kelly and Kirstin, there is nothing I do that hasn't been shaped by you and your unwavering love. To Misha, my best girl, my own golden flower, thank you for your charming chatter as you created art beside me in the home office, your understanding when I needed quiet time to work, and the sunshine you bring to my life everyday. To John, who has kept the home fires burning time and again whenever I can't walk away from writing or need to go away to a conference or visit an archive, and is very good at feigning interest in the ancient world when I need to talk through an idea, this book is your accomplishment as much as mine. You are steadfast in all the ways I need. And finally to my dedicated writing companion, Rasputin, who never leaves me alone with my thoughts and knows more about fragmentary Greek literature than any dog should.

Note on Translation

All translations of Greek and Latin are my own. I have endeavored to provide transliterations of individual Greek terms where possible. In transliterating names, I have opted for the most common spellings over perfect consistency.

Introduction

At some point in the first half of the fourth century BCE, a Boeotian girl by the name of Mnesarete came (or more likely was brought) to Athens and began to participate in the sex trade there. By the third century BCE, that girl, now known to the Greek world as Phryne, had become (in)famous, a symbol of the elite culture of Athens. By the second century CE, she was synonymous with the city itself, and her name alone was sufficient to invoke the cultural heights of what was considered to be Athens' golden age. In between these moments, we have nothing left but fragments, short anecdotes passed on and on again in literary compendia that tell the story of a witty and beautiful woman who amassed great wealth, associated with some of the most well-known historical figures of ancient Greece, and herself held great influence. They create an image of a life that is glamorous and titillating, yet they also hint at the tenuous position of a foreign-born sex worker in a society structured to privilege male citizens above all others. Stories that at first glance seem to highlight Phryne's place in Athenian high society and the power of her beauty upon closer inspection reveal the danger of being a prominent woman in that city during the fourth century.

Phryne, the ultimate fragmented dreamgirl, is therefore an ideal case study for examining several aspects of ancient Greek social and literary history as no single ancient work devoted to her alone or featuring her as protagonist survives, yet she has had a significant cultural footprint both in antiquity and in the modern world. First, the bits and pieces that comprise her presence in ancient cultural artefacts are representative of the presence of women in ancient Greek history generally. So rarely do they feature as major players in historical narratives that we are left to piece together scattered anecdotes and material evidence to build a fuller image of what their lives may have been like or what cultural impact they may have had. Much of this is filtered through women's relationships to the men around them and distorted through stereotypes based on gender. Because stories about Phryne and her demimonde circulated over and over again for hundreds of years, we can use her as an example to trace this process of filtering, in order to see how a life can be reduced to anecdotes that are in turn reassembled into what appears to be a fulsome narrative. By interrogating that larger narrative with an eye to gender and social status, we can better understand Phryne as a social-historical figure. Although in the case of Phryne it may not be possible to get a clearer image of the woman behind the dream, we can use such a process to better discern the contours of lives like hers through cautious speculation.

This same process of tracing Phryne's presence in ancient Greek literature from her own lifetime through to the Roman Imperial period also provides a means of thinking about how the city of Athens shifted from a cultural powerhouse to a focal point of nostalgic reminiscence: how is a real city turned into a literary dreamscape? The famous *hetairai* of Athens, some historical and some fictional, or in the case of Phryne, a combination of both, present a similar paradox: they are typically foreign-born women who would have been politically powerless during their own lifetimes, yet they came to embody Athens' intellectual legacy in later Greek literature.[1] The stories about Phryne are so deeply rooted in the Athenian milieu that investigating her role in these narratives allows for a similar consideration of the evolution of Athens' place in Greek literature from the Hellenistic period onward. How did a city with waning political and economic influence amass that much cultural capital and become a focal point of later literary obsessions? Looking at how Phryne was transformed from powerless immigrant to potent symbol while considering how Athens became a similarly powerful signifier allows me to take a broader perspective on what remains of her biography, as I examine the literary processes of building larger narratives through the circulation of anecdotes and quotations.

Finally, we can combine these two approaches (tracing Phryne's sources and considering the place of Athens in Greek literature) to think about how, in the case of all of the *hetairai*, but especially in the case of Phryne, the female body became a site for the nostalgia characteristic of Greek literature of the Imperial period. The literature that discusses the grand *hetairai* pairs their beauty with their wit, as though one cannot exist without the other, and although their appearances are rarely described in any detail, the reader is nevertheless encouraged to visualize these beautiful bodies, turning them into vehicles for the re-visioning of Classical Athens. Phryne is ideally positioned for this discussion, as she left not just a literary footprint, but a visual one too, as a possible model for the famous Aphrodite of Knidos. In fact the connection between Phryne and its sculptor, Praxiteles, is one of the major themes in the literature about her. As a result, many of the stories about her center on her great beauty and as these stories were passed on over time, the emphasis on the power her appearance held over others grew, with the result that it became central to her reception in a variety of post-Classical media.

Because of Phryne's gender, occupation, and the literary reimagining of fourth-century Athens, our sources for the most part treat her as a cipher, meaning information on her lived reality is scarce and must be gleaned from them with caution. The authors who have preserved the remaining fragments that comprise our evidence for her (primarily Athenaeus, but also Plutarch and Pausanias among others) are mostly interested in her beauty and the men with whom she associated. Those that assume her voice, either in reporting her witty repartee or authoring letters attributed to her, use her voice to reinforce the fictional world they have created. For this project, that means that I am less interested in writing a traditional biography with a tidy chronological narrative, but rather my goal is to assess the evidence for Phryne as a set of smaller narratives, themselves composed of fragmented anecdotes, to consider how they work together to create the illusion of a complete life story. Any discussion of the historical Phryne is used here to better understand how Phryne the dreamgirl came to be, and as with any dreamgirl, we must constantly be aware that the nitty gritty of her actual existence has largely been elided by what she means to those who paint, sculpt, and view her image, and especially to those who write and read about her.

Phryne's Stories

The stories about Phryne share a few key themes, some of which are common to most of the named Classical *hetairai* (e.g., greed and over-indulgence), and others which are unique to her alone (public nudity). They are largely preserved for us in texts that were assembled from the first century BCE onward by authors from the Roman Empire like Plutarch and Athenaeus who were mining the literature of Alexandria and Athens for anecdotes and quotations to underpin their own nostalgic programs. The following is an overview of the contents of these stories, and an attempt to put them into some coherent sequence, with an acknowledgment, however, that any tidy narrative that they may seem to form is entirely illusory.

Phryne,[2] according to our stories, was not always Phryne, but rather a Boeotian girl from Thespiai named Mnesarete, whose pallid complexion eventually earned her the nickname Phryne, meaning "toad" (Plut. *Moralia* 401a).[3] She may have had humble origins (Timocles the comic poet jokes that she was once a caper-gatherer, fr. 25 K-A), but soon enough reached such a point of great fame and wealth that the comic poets of Athens could make fun of this too.[4] In fact, Phryne, along with many of her prominent colleagues, earned a reputation for being money-hungry, so that the comic poet Anaxilas could compare her to Charybdis, saying that she gulped down ship-captains along with their ships (fr. 22 K-A). But like her other *hetairai* counterparts, this greed was always paired with a quick wit that could be used to get the better of her male clientele and the notable men Phryne was associated with, as when she asked a man named Moerichus for a *mina* (roughly one hundred *drachmai*) when he wanted to sleep with her. When he replied that she had only charged a foreigner two gold staters just the day before, she told him to wait around until she was in the mood, and then she would accept the lower fee (Ath. 13.583c).[5]

Her appeal to an elite clientele also places Phryne alongside many of the most notable Athenians of the fourth century BCE. Among the philosophers, artists, and politicians she was associated with was her lover Hypereides the orator. A noted anti-Macedonian leader with a notorious taste for *hetairai*, he was said to have defended Phryne in court when Euthias, one of her former clients, brought her up on charges of impiety, specifically improper behavior at the Lyceum, introducing a new god, and forming unlawful religious groups. In this we see the downside of Phryne's notoriety in Classical Athens, a place where the wives and daughters of male citizens ideally had no significant public presence. Stories that feature this trial are almost entirely focused on its supposed conclusion: an acquittal brought on by

Hypereides' sudden removal of Phryne's dress to reveal the beauty of her nude body (Plut. *Moralia* 849e).

It is the overwhelming beauty of her naked body that became a hallmark of many of the stories about Phryne and also connected her to even more prominent figures, among them the painter Apelles and the sculptor Praxiteles. Despite some anecdotes suggesting that Phryne was cautious about revealing her body in public (Ath. 13.590f), the story of her nudity in the courtroom seems to have inspired later tales of her nude appearance at the festival of Poseidon at Eleusis.[6] There she is said to have removed her clothing, undone her hair, and walked into the sea in front of a crowd of onlookers; Apelles was said to have been inspired to create his "Aphrodite Rising from the Sea" from this sight (Ath. 13.591a).[7]

Praxiteles, too, was said to have used Phryne as his model and in these stories we can see the beginnings of Phryne's long-lasting impact on art history and its relationship to the female nude. Many of the anecdotes and poems connecting the two tell of her modeling for the Aphrodite of Knidos, the first monumental female nude sculpture in the ancient Greek world, while also linking the *hetaira* and the sculptor romantically. In addition to the statue of Aphrodite, Praxiteles was also said to have created two other images of Phryne, one a sculpture placed alongside images of Eros and Aphrodite in her hometown of Thespiai and the second a golden image of Phryne which the people of Thespiai dedicated at Delphi (Ath. 13.591b). The connection between the sculptor and his model inspired further elaborations from quite a few poets of epigrams and the fictional letter-writer Alciphron, all of whom imagine the sculptor creating his works as gifts of love for Phryne, describing her as not simply a muse to the sculptor, but an embodiment of erotic love itself.

In these stories, Phryne's notoriety and beauty are entangled to such a degree that they are ultimately inseparable. Her fame and access to elite clientele come largely from her beauty, but the way that she uses the social and economic capital that her appearance accrues is what makes her infamous. In stories of Phryne later in life, she makes her reputation into a lucrative source of income, claiming that it allows her to sell her "dregs" (*truga*, Plut. *Moralia* 125a). Even more so than the other grand *hetairai*, she seems to have accumulated a significant fortune, so large that after Thebes had been sacked by Alexander the

Great in 335 BCE, Callistratus records that she made an offer to rebuild its city walls, with the stipulation that they bear an inscription reading "Alexander razed them, but Phryne the *hetaira* put them back up again" (Ἀλέξανδρος μὲν κατέσκαψεν, ἀνέστησεν δὲ Φρύνη ἡ ἑταίρα, Ath. 13.591d=*FGrH* 348 F 1). As Kapparis notes, this conditional offer likely bears a wry note of bitterness: Thebes had destroyed the walls of Phryne's hometown of Thespiae twice at this point. Even in stories such as this one that seem on their faces to be typical examples of the wit so commonly attributed to the *hetairai*,[8] we see a Phryne who plays with and builds on her own personal brand of infamy so that Phryne the individual is inseparable from Phryne the icon.

That melding of woman, image, and anecdote is indeed the hallmark of the stories about Phryne. With the exception of the brief mentions of her origins, the Phryne that remains to us in these stories is larger-than-life: a stunning beauty whose appearance we can claim to know from endless copies of a monumental statue, a woman of great wit whose intellect is apparent through devastating snippets of repartee, and someone whose public presence in her own time was incendiary.

Athens the Literary Dreamscape

The stories about Phryne that I have just summarized cannot be fully appreciated without considering their setting, Greece in the fourth century BCE, and especially the city of Athens. By the time the stories I have referenced here began circulating in earnest in the third century BCE, Athens had lost a great deal of its political and economic sway in the ancient Mediterranean. At the end of the fourth century, in parallel with the rise of Macedonian power in mainland Greece and the end of the city-state as the dominant organizing principle in the Greek world, Athens' fortunes had waned significantly. Although the Athenian leader Lycurgus had worked hard to bolster Athens' financial situation and military forces, the Macedonian general Antipater dissolved the democracy in 322 BCE after Athens lost the Lamian War alongside the Aetolians and the Thessalians.[9] This loss also signified the end of Athenian maritime power in the Aegean. Notable figures like Hypereides, so famously associated with Phryne in the courtroom anecdotes, fled the city, while others, like the prominent orator Demosthenes, took their own lives rather than face the prospect of Macedonian retribution.

Political life in Athens after this time was unstable, especially after the death of Antipater (one of Alexander's generals who had assumed rule over Macedonian holdings in Greece), the execution of the popular Athenian leader Phocion, and the short-lived restoration of democracy in 318/17. The subsequent installation into leadership of Demetrius of Phaleron saw the wealthy portion of the population become wealthier and increasingly supportive of the Macedonian occupation. This segment of the population did however continue to support artistic work, particularly the plays of Menander, whose plays more often than not supported the status quo.

At the same time as Athens' political and economic prominence was disappearing, Alexandria was becoming one of the preeminent cities in the Mediterranean under the rule of the Ptolemies. Following in the footsteps of earlier Macedonian rulers like Archelaus who had courted prominent playwrights and philosophers in the late fifth century, the Ptolemies set about turning Alexandria into an intellectual center. Many circumstances were in their favor: political stability in Egypt; the great wealth accumulated from Alexander's conquests; and the long-established intellectual tradition, particularly connected to the written word, already present in Egyptian culture.[10] As mainland Greece became less central to the Greek world and traditional patterns of performance began to shift, a new literary and dramatic canon took shape that allowed writers, readers, and audiences to take part in Greek identity regardless of where they were geographically. Alexandria, along with other cities like Pergamon, hosted collectors and scholars who worked extensively with this newly formed canon, some of whom analyzed the earlier works of Homer, the lyric poets, and the Athenian playwrights in great detail. Others, however, used this canon as raw material to create new literature and new genres.

Because third-century figures like Apollonius of Rhodes and Callimachus, the authors who were expanding on pre-existing genres or inventing new ones, were also scholars, they used their extensive knowledge of genre, history, and detail to create intricate reimaginings of Classical Greece while turning to the broader Mediterranean context. Those Alexandrians interested in comedy largely concentrated their work on Classical Athens and particularly on the comedy of the fourth century.[11] Because that comedy was very much rooted in Athenian culture and its social structure, the new works produced in Alexandria by figures like Machon, himself a comic playwright in the Athenian tradition, recreate that Athens, with emphasis on its notable personages, especially the *hetairai* and their clientele. As the fascination continued over several generations, each new iteration of a comic Athens gradually turned the *hetairai* and other denizens of their world into stock characters inhabiting a stage set that resembled Athens. By the time that Aristodemus was composing his *Geloia Apomnemoneumata* ("Comical Recollections") in the second century BCE,[12] the Athens he featured so prominently had mostly left the domestic and political milieu of late fourth-century comedy behind in favor of a demimonde in which the social rules of historical Athens were suspended or even turned upside down to favor the witty women at the center of the anecdotes he related. In the fashion of true nostalgia these vignettes could never represent that city faithfully, nor did they intend to. The authors who recorded the comic vignettes featuring the *hetairai* were harnessing the cultural capital of Classical Athens to draw attention to their literary artistry; mimesis of the past only served to draw attention to discontinuity with it.[13]

Several hundred years later, beginning in the late first century CE, authors writing in Greek from various parts of the Roman Empire turned back to Alexandria and through it to Classical Athens for their own elaborate displays of learned nostalgia, many of which were therefore also deeply rooted in fourth-century comedy. Authors like Plutarch, the late first-century/early second-century CE Boeotian, and Athenaeus, the late second-century CE writer from Naucratis, plumbed the Alexandrian works of Machon and Aristodemus for the anecdotes they included in their more fulsome compendia. Alciphron, the third-century CE writer of fictional letters, then animated those anecdotes in missives claiming to be written by several of the historical *hetairai*, including one notable example voicing Phryne's desire for Praxiteles to which I will return in detail in Chapter 2 (*Letters* 4.1). The Athens depicted in all of these Imperial-era works is a fictionalized playground for authors using Greek literature and language to claim some kind of Hellenism amid the ongoing cultural fission and fusion of the expanding Roman Empire.[14] Due to its central role in the development of philosophy and oratory, Classical Athens was an "intellectual home" for educated people throughout the Roman Empire,[15] thus to write about it offered both cultural capital and a blank canvas to the authors who set about fictionalizing it.

Accordingly as I look at Phryne's presence within it, I explore the literary dreamscape that Classical Athens became starting with the Alexandrian scholar/authors, not as a weak imitation of the original, but as a space of creation and self-fashioning for each author that took it up.[16] As with my interest in Phryne herself, the historical reality of Classical Athens is of less importance to this discussion than the processes that shaped the versions of it at that were produced at different points in history. Here I am most interested in how cultural capital is accrued to people, places, and eras, particularly through the formation of literary genre and canon, and consequently how each generation of authors and artists to revisit Phryne's stories makes use of it.

Literary Fragments: Creation and Circulation

The reasons why later authors chose to fictionalize Classical Athens in particular are as challenging to articulate as it is to assess the accuracy of their nostalgic portrayals of the city in that period. These fictions were clearly useful to their creators in navigating their own times and places.[17] Yet the authors I will focus on here, Machon and Aristodemus from Hellenistic Alexandria and Plutarch, Athenaeus, and Alciphron from various parts of the Roman Empire (among other authors of their periods) are so varied, both temporally and in ethnic identity (where it can be securely ascertained), that their Atticizing must be understood as multivalent. What all of them do have in common, at least when they relate anecdotes about the *hetairai*, is a shared set of sources that follow a relatively clear path from the courtrooms and stages of fourth-century Athens to Alexandria to the expansive world of the Roman Empire as well as their desire to show mastery of those sources. Some authors seem to have had access to Classical works in their entirety, while others were working from excerpts. Here, I trace the literary journey of the *hetairai*, and Phryne in particular, from legal speeches in fourth-century Athens to Imperial fictions.

Female sex workers, especially those foreign to the city, loom large in Athenian legal oratory from the Classical period, especially in speeches from the mid-fourth century. Typically they are portrayed by speakers as a danger to the status of not only other women, but also the status of all legitimate citizens of Athens.[18] They are used to impugn the reputations of the men associated with them and become anti-symbols, embodiments of all that was opposite to civic ideals. Mere association with *hetairai* signified that a man had abandoned proper democratic values, as we see in *Against Timarchus* (42) or *For Phormio* (45), so that sex workers became a trope in legal oratory by the mid-fourth century. They were also relatively easy targets because they could not claim Athenian identity and its attendant protections, regardless of their origins.

Being such a significant presence in public discourse led the collective cultural footprint of the *hetairai* to expand on the stage in the latter half of the century. *Hetairai* are only mentioned briefly a handful of times in Old Comedy from the fifth century and early fourth century, as lusty, deceitful, and excessive drinkers, but it was in plays from the mid-fourth century on that they were first portrayed as characters onstage. Several of these plays feature ridiculous caricatures of real-life *hetairai*.[19] Typically, these female sex workers are depicted as being drunken and greedy, with regular comparisons of the women to consumable goods like food. In the plots of comic plays focused on myth, *hetairai* are still present and sometimes mentioned by name. In Timocles' *Orestautocleides*, the comic playwright offers a lengthy list of real-life elderly *hetairai* who play the Furies to Autocleides' Orestes, including Phryne, a passage I will consider at length in Chapter 1.

With the shift into more situational comedy around 340 BCE, as typified by the plays of Menander, the more generic stock character of the *hetaira* appears. The *hetairai* in these plays, now entirely fictional, were sometimes portrayed in a more sympathetic light and described as, for example, "wise" (*sophē*), "honorable" (*semnē*), or "urbane" (*asteia*).[20] Some plays even bear names such as *Pornoboskos* and *Korinthiastes*, which mean "procurer," and thus likely featured sex workers in prominent roles.[21] Recognition plays, in which the true identity of a character is revealed over the process of the play, were also popular at this time, so the virtuous pseudo-*hetaira*, soon to be identified as a true citizen woman, also debuted on the Athenian stage. In these later plays, sex workers are still placed in opposition to citizen wives in terms of legal status, but in keeping with the socially conservative plots of many of these plays, especially those of Menander, they are no longer quite the venal images of excess from both mid-fourth-century comedies and oratory.

Examples of the *hetaira* with a heart of gold from Menander's plays include Habrotonon from *Epitrepontes* and Chrysis from *Samia*. Menander often used the generosity and kindness of the sex workers in his plays to contrast with the poor behavior of his male citizen characters, which is not to say that a character like Habrotonon was portrayed as an ideal woman, but simply that her behavior, when compared to the foolishness of Charisius, the young citizen man in love, stands out as loyal, generous, and clever. Chrysis, the eponymous woman from Samos in *Samia*, is particularly kind-hearted, wet-nursing a neighbor's baby after her own has died.[22] Much of the comical misunderstanding in this play revolves around the fact that Chrysis has been entirely faithful to her client, Demeas, while he accuses her of the opposite. The other kind of sex worker that appears in Menander's plays is the pseudo-*hetaira*, an as-yet-unrecognized young citizen woman who is on the brink of taking part in the sex trade, without having actually done so. This character type typically appears only briefly on stage if at all, in keeping with her true citizen identity, and as such is not as richly characterized as her non-citizen colleagues. When the pseudo-*hetaira*'s true identity is discovered, she takes on the role of proper wife, and strengthens the web of social connections so key to Athenian status. Overall, the late fourth-century comic *hetaira* reinforces the identities and statuses of others in a gentler way than previous iterations from both comedy and oratory.

One of Menander's contemporaries, Lynceus of Samos, himself a comic poet who produced plays at Athens, seems to have been one of the first authors to combine the *hetairai* of the stage with the historical *hetairai* in the genre of the witty anecdote, possibly building his comical stories out of a small set of actual occurrences.[23] He compiled a collection of gossipy stories called *Apomnemoneumata* ("Memoirs"), in which he related several stories about the comic poet Diphilos and his companion, the particularly witty *hetaira* Gnathaina. These anecdotes in turn seem to have set the standard for further stories about affairs between various poets or artists and foreign-born *hetairai* in which the women are typically portrayed as just as clever and quick-witted as their lovers if not more so, exercising the power of rhetoric over their prominent male companions in place of actual political power.

As the literary culture of Alexandria developed at the turn of the third century BCE, so did its theatrical culture. Under the Ptolemies, the city celebrated its own Dionysia (while Athens adapted its own version). Comedies in the style of Menander seem to have been quite popular and Alexandria was home to several of its own comic playwrights, including Machon, who had come to the city from the area around Corinth and worked in the mid-third century.[24] In addition to producing plays in the style of fourth-century Athenian comedy, Machon also composed a book of anecdotes, written in iambic trimeters to connect them directly to comedy, called *Chreiai* ("Anecdotes").[25] These short scenes were humorous retellings of the lives and deeds of the Athenian *hetairai*, their lovers, and other members of their demi-monde like parasites. Based on the fragments of Machon's collection that remain, it seems that he must have consulted the gossipy anecdotes of Lynceus' *Apomnemoneumata* and condensed them even further to suit the concision required of his genre. The characters in Machon's work move freely through Athens, interacting with notables of all kinds and often subverting the power of the elite with wit alone.[26]

In the third and second centuries BCE in Alexandria, the fascination with the *hetairai* did not abate and they continued to be associated with comedy, as scholars and authors with an interest in one often had an interest in the other. Machon worked with Aristophanes of Byzantium, the noted literary scholar and head of the Library, whom he taught about comedy, and who then wrote his own treatise on *hetairai*. By this point, Classical Athens was the focal point of such collections, with the *hetairai* presented as stock characters in a comical demi-monde, constantly besting their powerful and prominent clients, but for the most part insulated from the concerns over political status that informed so much of the comedy of the late fourth century.[27] Thus by the time that Aristodemus was assembling his own collection of anecdotes featuring *hetairai* in the second century, the *Geloia Apomnemoneumata* ("Funny Recollections"), the conventions of this literary sub-genre were already well-established and the anecdotes had likely circulated many times.

An important, if unanswerable, question that remains about these collections is how much of their contents were innovations or augments to the traditional stories about the *hetairai* and how much was simply reworked or even quoted from previous collections, going all the way back to Lynceus' late fourth-century collection. Since we have the most fulsome evidence of Machon's work, we can see several instances when he takes the raw material of fourth-century comedy and adapts it for his parodic needs, highlighting the wit of the *hetairai* in particular. This suggests that Machon at the very least selectively edited the stories of the *hetairai* that he included in the *Chreiai* with an eye to this emphasis. What we can establish is that later authors turned back to the Alexandrian treatises I have just discussed as well as to fourth-century comedy when they wanted to talk about *hetairai* and in doing so recognized the interrelation of the two genres.

It is also likely that some of the fragmented portions of comedy we find in Imperial literature may have survived only in the Hellenistic collections of anecdotes and not as full plays. While it is probable that the scholars at Alexandria would have had access to the scripts of many of these plays, simply due to the comprehensive nature of the Library, as time passed the overwhelming emphasis on epic and drama in combination with the privileged status of Menander's plays in both scholarship and performance meant that there would be fewer copies of other comic scripts from the fourth century in circulation.[28] At the same time, there were also many epitomes, hypotheses, and collections of excerpts from longer works being produced at this time to satisfy an increasingly literate populace's appetite for Greek literature and drama, meaning that many readers only ever encountered many works in shortened or fragmented forms as the influence of Alexandrian scholarship saw drama move "from stage to page."[29]

Thus when authors writing several centuries later in the Roman Empire wanted to reimagine a comical or nostalgic version of Classical Athens, they were turning to an already fragmented set of sources. When it came to the *hetairai* they depicted, they were working with portrayals of women that had already been carefully curated to emphasize their wit; even more so than in the Classical and Hellenistic literature I have discussed here, the *hetairai* in literature from this period are cultural agents whose cleverness is constantly on display, "the pulsating heart of Athens' vast cultural archive."[30] The *hetairai* and Phryne as the most prominent among them offer an excellent metaphor for understanding the process of fragmentation that Classical Athens and its literature underwent in the transition from the Hellenistic period to the Imperial period. The intentionality of this process means that the fictionalized version of Athens along with its fictionalized inhabitants were subjected to a slow and careful process of selection that was governed by a set of generic expectations. It is therefore not sufficient to think just of the content of each of the fragments I will encounter in this process of piecing together the ancient evidence for Phryne or only of what its original author was trying to communicate. All of the fragments that will be considered in this book survived through a very intentional process which must be accounted for, so if we want to understand how Phryne's story was shaped over time, we must consider how each of these fragments functioned within its new context and how the later authors who have preserved them were using them. We may even consider such fragments to be their own genre of literature, given the very intentional process that selected and preserved them in other works.

In thinking through the impact of fragmentation on Phryne's narrative, I am influenced by Camelia Elias' idea of the coercive fragment. According to her conceptualization of the ancient fragment, the fragment suggests a presupposed whole "from which the fragment has been coerced into detachment."[31] Fragmentary texts can be approached by considering what is missing or by assuming that they are complete in the reader's imagination; they are always in flux.[32] Navigating Phryne's stories means dismissing that presupposed whole and embracing the flux that characterizes her anecdotes. The Phryne of one source is often different from the version in the next and the variation in her depictions is often a function of how her narrative was reimagined from fragmentary material.

The task for the reader of the fragments that preserve Phryne's stories is therefore to engage with each source that mentions her in its original context (e.g., the fourth-century comedies) while also considering the process by which it was preserved. Looking to an Imperial source like Athenaeus or Plutarch entails a consideration of authors like Machon and Lynceus as key links in the chain of transmission. Because of the process I have described here, each repetition of these anecdotes, as they were carefully selected and inserted into a new context, created a new instantiation of Phryne, each time adapted to the requirements of that new context. As Hannah Čulík-Baird explains in the introduction to her book on Cicero and his use of Latin poetry in his own works, even when an author who is citing or quoting another's work intends to be faithful to the original, the undertaking itself "*necessarily introduces variations and distortions.*"[33] Even if the content itself within the anecdotes and quotations that mention Phryne managed to survive without distortion, the selection and reproduction of each one to suit new contexts bring different aspects of her to light and so the Phryne that appears in each has been shaped according to the needs of each author that takes her up.

For these reasons, Phryne's narrative and our understanding of the woman herself will always be incomplete and so it is specifically because of this fragmentary state that a figure such as Phryne invites the reader or spectator to, if not fill in all that is missing in pursuit of an impossible state of completion, imagine her in a more fulsome fashion than that in which the ancient sources have actually presented her. As I shall illustrate with my discussion of the various versions of Phryne from antiquity to the modern era, it is the fragmentary state of her remnants that offers enough space for each new creator, genre, or era to adapt her story and find new meaning from it.

Nostalgia and Fictionalizing

The Imperial author who preserves the vast majority of the fragments on Phryne is Athenaeus, a second-century CE author from Naucratis in Egypt who collected a vast and eclectic body of knowledge in his work *Deipnosophistai* ("The Learned Banqueters"). Fifteen books (out of as many as thirty) and an epitome survive, portraying a dinner party that lasts several days, hosted by Larensis, a Roman. Building on the long tradition of sympotic literature, which extends at least as far back as Plato's genre-defining dialogue with its roots in the poetic traditions of the Archaic symposium, the conversation of the diners covers a wide array of topics, with special emphasis on food, drink, and in Book 13, women. In this work, Athenaeus draws on at least 1,250 authors, quoting some and offering tantalizing hints at the works of others, but his main sources are comic plays from fourth-century Athens.[34] Book 13, sometimes titled "On Women," is structured as an argument between Cynculus, a Cynic philosopher, and Myrtilus, a grammarian who is both comical and pedantic.[35] Cynculus, who is vehemently against Atticist education, presents his argument as invective against both the *hetairai* of Athens and against the type of scholarly culture that focuses on Classical Athens, exposing the *hetairai* and Athenian culture as commodities at the same time when he calls these women *megalomisthai* ("big earners," Ath. 13. 569a). Myrtilus, meanwhile, the very embodiment of Athenian-style *paideia*, emphasizes the glamorous liaisons of the *hetairai* with notable men, carefully using terms like *eromenai* ("beloveds") to describe them, which earns him the insult *pornographos* ("pornographer/one who depicts sex workers").[36] For Myrtilus, the *hetairai*, because of their association with notable figures of Classical culture, are a key means of transmitting that culture. Cynculus, on the other hand, turns to comedy, a genre notoriously unfriendly to sex workers, for many of his references to those women.

It is helpful here to consider why authors like Athenaeus, of various ethnic backgrounds and scattered around the Roman Empire, would have an interest in revisiting a fictionalized version of Classical Athens in their work. Tim Whitmarsh sees claims to "Greekness" on the part of Roman authors as a creative act,[37] which is bound up in the fictionalizing of Athens that the Imperial authors inherited from their Alexandrian predecessors. This creative act allowed Imperial Greek authors to place themselves beyond the contemporary real-world political influence of the Roman Empire. "Athens" was an idea that they all seem to have understood as possessing certain qualities, but that each author then reworked through creating new scenarios set in that city or by carefully selecting anecdotes and details that shaped the version of Athens they wanted to present (as in the case of Athenaeus). By reworking and therefore claiming that much-desired space in their literary endeavors, the Imperial Greek authors were also asserting their own cultural power via *paideia* (in the context of this historical period, "learnedness" that suggested its possessor had in-depth knowledge of Classical Greek literature, philosophy, and artwork and was in that sense a member of the civic elite).[38]

That they should turn to Athens to do so is no surprise, since it had occupied such a prominent place in the literary and educational canon for centuries by then. Texts like the plays of Menander were still in heavy circulation, as mainstays of school reading lists and stages throughout the Empire. Attic-style oratory was widely practiced and the Attic dialect of Greek was central to much new literature at the time, the result of generations of education centered on a "fare of Attic classics."[39] Athens was not only the space these authors sought to inhabit in their work, but it was already familiar territory to them. This deep familiarity and the well-established cultural currency that Classical Athens had accrued allowed the Imperial authors to treat it as raw material for their reimaginings, which in turn allowed for ever more innovative engagements.

Athens during that period (especially during the second century CE when Athenaeus was writing) had a resurgent intellectual life as Romans like Herodes Atticus and the emperor Hadrian were pouring resources into the city, particularly into buildings and cultural institutions that reflected its glorious past 500 years prior. Since the city remained a political non-starter, it offered open opportunities for wealthy Romans to inscribe their nostalgic yearnings onto the remains of the Classical city.[40] Thus while the Classical city was being reimagined in literature, it was being rebuilt in-situ.

We may think of all of this work, both on the page and in the real world, as characterized by and motivated by nostalgia. Commonly understood as a longing for a past that is not entirely real, nostalgia is a quest that can never succeed: the past can never be fully rematerialized nor does a nostalgic version of it reward extended examination with an eye to accuracy. And so because the past must accordingly always be a space that requires a great deal of imagination in its recreation, I argue that Imperial authors like Athenaeus who were fictionalizing Athens understood the limitations of their nostalgic programs and turned to techniques like excerpting/quoting and allusion in order to replicate the transitory nature of nostalgia.[41] Fragments and their careful curation then become fictionalizing tools in the hands of Imperial Greek authors. To return to my previous discussion of how fragmentation entailed generating new versions of the original, I want to argue that this process was very intentional on the part of authors like Athenaeus, who were just as interested in creating as they were in recreating.

Yet for literary nostalgia to be employed effectively, it requires just enough vividness (*enargeia* in Greek) to conjure the past, even if only momentarily. *Enargeia* in literature elicits what Ruth Webb refers to as "the feeling of presence," in which the reader is transported to the past.[42] Due to the fundamental impossibility of ever fully describing a world (fictional, historical or somewhere in between),[43] the authors who do take up Classical Athens use various techniques to summon sufficient *energeia* to make their versions of that time and place compelling to an educated audience; their Athens is populated not by people as they were, but as they could have been. The *hetairai*, and Phryne especially, become an embodiment of that phenomenon in

Imperial Greek literature largely because of the carefully curated anecdotes that feature them, chosen especially for their concision and wit. Even more so than the men they are associated with, from whom cleverness is to be expected, their quick repartee in the anecdotes is evocative precisely because it transgresses class and gender expectations.[44] Laura McClure has addressed the *hetairai* in Imperial literature as a type of nostalgic fetish, which both conjures the loss of Classical Athens as a cultural center while offering it as a unified whole.[45] Thus in the brief anecdotes about them the *hetairai* manage to encompass the broader cultural trends relating to the city. In addition to their quickmindedness, the beauty of the *hetairai* further augments the sensation of *energeia*, as the reader is encouraged to envision them and their environs, even without detailed visual descriptions.

I would like to add to the conversation on *hetairai* and nostalgia for Athens by also considering the foreign origins of the most notable of the *hetairai* associated with fourth-century Athens. If, in Ewen Bowie's influential postulation, the fascination with and cultural sway of Classical Greece during the Imperial Period grew out of the political marginalization of Greeks,[46] then we must consider the ways in which those marginalized authors working in Greek claimed another politically marginalized group as symbols of the city on which they focused their nostalgic efforts. The journey of women like Phryne from courtroom spectres to comic punchlines in their own time, to protagonists of anecdotes, and finally to fragmented objects of fascination in their literary afterlives, helps us to untangle the many contradictions of the particular brand of nostalgia that was centered on Classical Athens, but most importantly it leads us to recognize the role of fictionalizing in that process. In the case of Phryne, that fictionalizing was an ongoing process that had already begun in her own lifetime in the courtrooms and on the stages of Athens and so from the time she became a public figure, "Phryne" was subject to constant renegotiation.

Modern Scholars on Phryne

By the time Imperial authors like Athenaeus were taking up her stories, Phryne was *the* preeminent *hetaira* in literature. Her name comes up again and again in all kinds of literature, from fictional letters to epigrams, where her beauty and nudity are the most common theme. Because of her prominent position in the literary record, Phryne has featured in many studies of the ancient Greek *hetairai* in literature; here I discuss the work of three scholars on Phryne in her literary context, all of whom have been highly influential on this project and whose work has proved essential as I dissect the themes at play in her depictions.

Despite not yet being the sole subject of a book-length study, Phryne has featured in many analyses of the ancient Greek *hetairai* collectively, notably Laura McClure's *Courtesans at Table* (2003), which takes up the *hetaira* as a cultural sign in Athenaeus' *Deipnosophistai*; indeed, much of my understanding of how Phryne is used symbolically is indebted to this work. The literary process that preserved stories of the *hetairai* from the fourth century onward is key to appreciating which details of their lives were preserved and how they were exaggerated or invented. An important means of doing so is using McClure's identification of the literary *hetaira* as a fetish as the framework of this investigation. If sexual labour is understood as a commodity, the work of the *hetaira* is to disguise this fact in addition to the use of her body as a means of earning a living; when *hetairai* appear in literature after the fourth century, according to McClure they are an artificial means of conjuring the past, and this artificiality is elided in a way that mimics the *hetaira* disguising her own labour.[47]

Others, most notably Patricia Rosenmeyer and Helen Morales, have looked closely at individual literary episodes with Phryne at the center. A common theme in these studies is the pretence of the literary *hetaira* and how it relates to the role of viewership in the ancient literature on Phryne. For Morales, one of the common themes in Phryne's narrative is the creation and reception of art. As the two main stories about her, the revelation of her naked body while on trial and the creation of the Aphrodite of Knidos, invite the reader to visualize her beauty, they do little to actually describe it, thus drawing attention to the idea of Phryne rather than actually conveying information on the woman herself.[48] Rosenmeyer takes a close look at Phryne's presence in the epistolary fictions of Alciphron, an author from the second century CE who wrote a collection of letters set in a Menandrian version of Athens. One of these letters, addressed to Praxiteles from Phryne, is an invitation to make love next to a statue he has sculpted of her, which Rosenmeyer understands as an inversion of the Pygmalion story in which the statue speaks back to its creator.

More importantly, Rosenmeyer remarks on how the process of visualization in this letter results in the triangulation of the relationship of Phryne and Praxiteles: it is no longer lover and beloved, but co-creators and their mutual creation.[49] In turn, the reader is encouraged to take part in the author's act of creation in visualizing and making the fictional letter "real." This project takes Morales' and Rosenmeyer's ideas about audience, viewing, and fictionalization and their relationship to Phryne as foundational to its examination of the visual aspects of her stories.

In addition to the work on Phryne I have just discussed, Madeleine M. Henry's *Prisoner of History: Aspasia of Miletus and Her Biographical Tradition* (1995) has provided a helpful model for my study in its careful dissection of the narratives related to Aspasia, the fifth-century BCE woman partnered to Pericles and associated with Socrates' circle. By assessing the ways that Aspasia's biographical tradition portrays her as a woman in the public eye, with an emphasis on generic convention, Henry clarified the ways that Aspasia's gender shaped the discourses around her during her own lifetime as well as in subsequent literary representations. Henry also identified the threads in Aspasia's narrative that connect her to the famous men with whom she was so often associated while exploring the unique position of that historical woman in her own time as I hope to do here with Phryne.

Using Henry's monograph as an example, I have sorted through the complex set of stories about Phryne, a woman equally as paradoxical and as public as Aspasia, and like her, a foreigner in Athens. Phryne, more than any other figure from Classical Athens, embodies the incongruity of what that city symbolized in the Hellenistic and Imperial literary imagination, and so this book will trace her presence in that literature with a focus on her transformation from real woman to literary character. Chapter 1 introduces the scant historical evidence remaining about her and considers her transformation from Mnesarete the Thespian girl to Phryne the Athenian *hetaira* with a social-historical focus on the status of foreign-born sex workers in fourth-century Athens and an examination of the relationship between oratory and comedy with regard to their portrayals of *hetairai*. Since much of the evidence I present here will be used in service of speculation, I use it to contemplate the possibilities for a woman like Phryne, rather than to recreate the realities of her life. Chapter 2 turns to one of the most celebrated stories about Phryne: her relationship with

Praxiteles and modeling for the Aphrodite of Knidos. Here I reflect upon how beauty and nostalgia are intertwined in Phryne's story and how the texts that preserve it invite the reader to gaze upon the past by envisioning her body. The famous statue of Aphrodite also allows me to consider Phryne's impact on ancient material culture and the part that nudity plays in shaping the depiction of her beauty.

In Chapter 3, I address the other story that has dominated Phryne's narrative: her trial for impiety and the infamous revelation of her naked body to the jurors. My discussion of this moment incorporates threads from the previous two chapters, as I look at Phryne on trial in the context of her status and occupation and compare her to other women on trial in the fourth century. I also consider her moment of revelation alongside other stories of Phryne being nude in public and how the literature that tells her story turns her into an object of broad public titillation. I argue that in her case, more than with any of the other famous *hetairai*, the visual component is central to understanding Phryne's cultural impact. My final chapter takes up Phryne's afterlife, that is, her cultural presence after antiquity. She appears in paintings, operas, cabaret revues, and films, among other media, often in ways that mimic and respond to her appearances in Greek literature. Here I consider how the larger themes present in the ancient stories (nudity and debates over public morality) have influenced her reception, but also how later standards of beauty and prurience have influenced depictions of Phryne and their consumption by the general public.

In sum, this book intends to bring together the various historical and literary threads that meet in the figure of Phryne. She is not just a sexy snippet or an "it-girl";[50] rather she is one of the few prominent women from that period whom we know by name. Because of her unique position as a woman who was notable in her own lifetime and who has amassed a body of heavily fictionalized stories about her that circulated after her death, Phryne enables us to understand better how women in ancient Greece can be transformed into sign and therefore how cultural capital could be accrued by historical female figures, and then once they became literary figures, how that capital could be accumulated by those who wrote and read about them alike. Through Phryne and her ongoing cultural presence, we can begin to understand how a biography can be assembled from a set of disparate, fragmentary sources and ultimately what goes into the making of an ancient Greek dreamgirl.

1

Mnesarete to Phryne

In the following chapter, I endeavor to trace the emergence of the figure known as Phryne and speculate on how a woman like her could have come to prominence in the context of fourth-century Athens. Because so much of our material on Phryne is concerned with her as a grand *hetaira* and ties that term directly to sex workers, a significant portion of the evidence I present here will necessarily apply more generally to the sexual labor of women in fourth-century Athens and as such is purely speculative in regard to the actual life of Phryne. I have chosen to include this portion of the book, which departs from the evidence that is directly related to Phryne, because despite Phryne's early days remaining largely unknowable, we do have a significant body of evidence that helps us better understand the lives of women who were like Phryne. Using as my examples women like Neaira, whose biography Apollodorus fleshes out quite thoroughly (if cruelly) in his accusations against her, I can think through the mechanisms that would allow a foreign-born sex worker to rise to notoriety. I do so with the intention of reengaging the literary version of the *hetaira* with the realities of sexual labor in recognition of the vulnerabilities of foreign-born women and sex workers within the political and legal systems of fourth-century Athens. We cannot begin to deconstruct the enigma of a figure like Phryne without considering the potential circumstances of her life and work since it is precisely those circumstances that brought her to wider attention within the Athenian context. There is much at stake when we insist on a complete separation of the literary *hetairai* from their real-life counterparts, least of all that it sorts ancient sex workers into hard-and-fast categories that obscure the complexities of that occupation and those women's lives.

Another intention in this chapter, therefore, is breaking down further the distinctions between groups of sex workers that scholars have conventionally been used to categorize these women. Although many scholars have questioned the utility and veracity of categories like *pornē* and *hetaira* over the last several decades (my discussion of the meanings and uses of these terms follows shortly),[1] when thinking of Phryne and her peers it is far too easy to disregard the actual labor involved in their occupation, thereby reifying those same categories. In focusing on the dreamgirls, we can skew and glamorize the real work of sexual labor.[2] With respect to the literary sources that recall the stories of the *hetairai* as well as the work of providing paying clientele with companionship, this process is of course by design. Both are invested in eliding the labor involved in sex work and presenting relationships between *hetairai* and their clientele as organic interactions between peers.[3]

Sexual Labor in Classical Athens and the *Hetairai*

When we turn to sources from the fourth century, it becomes apparent that despite carrying some sense of economic and social hierarchy, the terms *hetaira* and *pornē* were used rather flexibly. The following quote from *Against Neaira*, which offers a tidy categorization of the female sexual partners a citizen man might seek, has appeared time and time again in discussions of sex work in Classical Athens: "We have *hetairai* for pleasure, *pallakai* for the daily care of the body, and wives for producing legitimate children and to be faithful guardians of domestic matters," (τὰς μὲν γὰρ ἑταίρας ἡδονῆς ἕνεκ' ἔχομεν, τὰς δὲ παλλακὰς τῆς καθ' ἡμέραν θεραπείας τοῦ σώματος, τὰς δὲ γυναῖκας τοῦ παιδοποιεῖσθαι γνησίως καὶ τῶν ἔνδον φύλακα πιστὴν ἔχειν, 122).[4] The *hetairai* of the first category seem to mean sex workers more generally, i.e., women who are available for sex but not part of the household unit, while the other two categories concern ongoing relationships centered on the household; the categories themselves were quite labile in practice, but the distinction of relationships within the household and without can be helpful for thinking about how *hetairai* were conceptualized in fourth-century Athens.[5] Kate Gilhuly has argued that the categories offered here are less a reflection of real women's lives and more a commentary on Athenian male citizens;[6] the categories that are applied to female sex workers are best understood using their interactions with their male clientele as a framework.

Within the category of sex worker, especially in the ancient context, there is a great deal of variety and the expansive vocabulary applied to women participating in the sex trade supports that presumption. Before examining the most prevalent of these terms, however, it is necessary that I define sexual labor in the Classical Athenian context and in the context of my discussion of Phryne, especially as it applies to female sex workers. In endeavoring to offer some delineation of categories here, I acknowledge that they are ultimately quite flexible, and the women I will discuss could likely fit into several of these categories at one time or will have moved between them at various points in their lives. I also recognize that sexual labor as a concept is broad and multivalent and therefore open to a great deal of individual interpretation; what is seen as sex work by some is not seen this way by others. Many people, especially enslaved people, in ancient Greece undertook or were subjected to acts that we might classify as sexual labor but are not addressed here due to the focus of this conversation; I have no wish to elide their presence in the historical record. Thus I limit the following definitions for the purposes of this discussion to Phryne and her peers only. This delineation also confines my conversation to sex work that takes place in heterosexual contexts; equally I have no wish to elide the importance of same-sex desire in ancient sex work either. With all of these caveats in place, I consider sexual labor to be sex acts or companionship with erotic undertones that is compensated in some way (either with direct payment or through gift-giving). In the understanding I am working with here, sex workers are typically sought from sources outside of the client's household and while the relationship between a sex worker and her client may be long-lasting, she is not incorporated into his household as a sex worker on a permanent basis, although she may be part of a household with a client temporarily or may leave behind the status of sex worker upon incorporation into a household.[7] These sex workers may have been free or enslaved, engaged by a pimp or independent,[8] and are likely to have moved between these statuses at some point in their lives. We must also acknowledge that the categories applied to these women by later writers and then again by modern scholars may not reflect the ways they thought about and categorized themselves.

The Greek terminology applied to female sex workers can be confusing or even misleading due to its euphemistic nature. For example, throughout this book I use the term *hetaira*, which in its most direct sense simply means "female companion,"⁹ to refer to Phryne and her peers, whom I unequivocally identify as sex workers. I do this partially because that is one of the terms that is used often in oratory and comedy from the fourth century to classify women as sex workers and sexually suspect (whether the women mentioned in these sources were or were not actually sex workers is not as important to such labelling as the fact that these labels could inflict great damage on a woman's reputation).¹⁰ I also do this because the term *hetaira* as used in the Hellenistic and Imperial sources I discuss here unambiguously refers to sex workers. Although some scholars, especially Rebecca Futo Kennedy, have argued that the term as used in the fourth century could refer to unmarriageable women living outside of a traditional household headed by a *kurios*,¹¹ I use it here because in the sources that apply it to Phryne and her colleagues, it is employed specifically because of its association with sex work.

Hetaira has often been translated as "courtesan" in the past, but this translation can be challenging to untangle, as it has carried so many definitions across periods and cultures that its associations are wildly varied, although almost always connecting intellectual/artistic activity with sex work. Perhaps the most useful aspect of this term to my discussion is the suggestion that there is a fundamental unknowability of the women to whom it is applied.¹² Invariably, the term "courtesan" suggests a sense of glamor and eroticism that is appropriate to the way the term *hetaira* is used in Hellenistic and Imperial literary sources, but is not quite appropriate to its more pejorative uses in the fourth century. Some scholars, Leslie Kurke most notable among them, have threaded this needle by making note of the association of *hetairai* with the symposium, an elite male-centric drinking party that came into being in the Archaic period. For Kurke, at this earlier stage when the term first came into regular use, the *hetaira* is defined by a combination of economic and political factors, wherein she "embodies the circulation of *charis* ["gracious reciprocity"] within a privileged elite,"¹³ associated with gift-exchange (her means of earning a living from her clients) and a social circle separated from the mainstream of Archaic society. At this preliminary stage, there is already a blurring of the identity and status of *hetairai* within the aristocratic groups that such women circulate in, in which they can be treated as insiders or outsiders depending on the needs of the group, processes which Kurke views as ultimately supportive of elite status,[14] and which presaged the capricious way *hetairai* were often treated by their elite male clientele in the fourth century.

Another common way to define the *hetaira* has been placing her in opposition to the *pornē* (often pejoratively translated as "whore" and denoting a lower economic and social status), therefore focusing on status more specifically among sex workers as opposed to in broader society. While this distinction at first seems largely economic in terms of the *pornē*'s income (she is understood to be paid for her time and labor in a more direct and quantifiable fashion than the *hetaira*), the social status of her clientele, and therefore the *pornē* herself, is also understood to be well below that of the *hetaira* and her circle. In Anaxilas' comic play *Neottis*, produced sometime in the 340s, the distinction between the two categories is defined by comportment and therefore a performance of social class:

ἐὰν δέ τις μέτρια † καὶ λέγουσα
τοῖς δεομένοις τινῶν ὑπουργῇ πρὸς χάριν,
ἐκ τῆς ἑταιρείας ἑταίρα τοὔνομα
προσηγορεύθη. καὶ σὺ νῦν οὐχ ὡς λέγεις
πόρνης, ἑταίρας δ' εἰς ἔρωτα τυγχάνεις
ἐληλυθὼς ἄρ' ὡς ἀληθῶς· ἔστι γοῦν
ἁπλῆ τις;

And if she's moderate, saying that
she renders her services to those in need out of goodwill,
she is called by the name "*hetaira*" from her companionship,
and now as you say, you've fallen in love, not with a *pornē*,
but a *hetaira*, really: is she so straightforward?

fr. 21 K-A

This passage demonstrates that even though these categories can seem to be quite well-defined, like most binaries, there is a great deal of slippage between the two poles; the labile nature of these categories has also been remarked upon by many scholars interested in sexual labor who argue that their usefulness is limited.[15] In this discussion, I am mostly interested in the way any speaker or author wants to characterize the woman to whom he applies either term.[16]

The category of *pallakē* is another one that has been differentiated from *hetaira* in the past, but with which there is also a great deal of slippage. As with *hetaira* and "courtesan," this term has often been translated as "concubine," another word with a great deal of cultural baggage across its various applications. Morris Silver has argued that the institution of *pallakia* amounted to a quasi-marriage, with attendant legal recognitions,[17] while others have conceived of it as an option for women who were legally barred from becoming legitimate wives (due to foreign or enslaved status) but who were seeking a stable relationship and incorporation into a household.[18] Whether an official arrangement of legal consequence or simply ongoing cohabitation, *pallakia* does seem to have offered a measure of protection to women who entered into these relationships through incorporation into an *oikos*. In the cases of several of the women identified as *hetairai* in legal speeches (such as Neaira and Alke, both of whom I will discuss below), moving in with the men they were involved with did not necessarily mean leaving behind the sex trade or a clientele from outside of the *oikos* completely even though they were members of a shared household. Some of the live-in arrangements with clients/lovers were not intended to be permanent and so blur the lines of what could be considered sexual labor.

In the case of this discussion and keeping in mind the potential slippages between categories, it is best to consider the use of the term *hetaira* here as less of a useful social-historical category and more of a euphemistic label applied to women who evaded easy definition within their own time and who, because of the rhetorical and literary processes they were subjected to, were associated with both sexual labor and the elite circles of Classical Athens. Even Athenaeus, our great chronicler of all things related to the *hetaira*, includes a short discourse on the flexibility of the term from the dinner-guest Myrtilus, who states that actual *hetairai* are "women who have the ability to maintain a relationship without trickery" (τῶν φιλίαν ἄδολον συντηρεῖν δυναμένων, 13.571c), while "free women and girls these days call their acquaintances and friends *hetairai*" (καλοῦσι γοῦν καὶ αἱ ἐλεύθεραι γυναῖκες ἔτι καὶ νῦν καὶ αἱ παρθένοι τὰς συνήθεις καὶ φίλας ἑταίρας, 13.571d). After citing Sappho as an example of such a woman (hardly someone from "these days" as they were imagined by Athenaeus), Myrtilus goes on to address the euphemistic nature of the term: "And they also call the ones who receive pay '*hetairai*' and receiving pay for intercourse "being a *hetaira*," no longer recalling the word's origin," (καλοῦσι δὲ καὶ τὰς μισθαρνούσας ἑταίρας καὶ τὸ ἐπὶ συνουσίαις μισθαρνεῖν ἑταιρεῖν, οὐκ ἔτι πρὸς τὸ ἔτυμον ἀναφέροντες, 13.571d). The term as used in the Classical period, but especially in the fourth century is so intentionally slippery that her ability to elude definition is ultimately what defines the *hetaira*: "a hetaera remains a hetaera only so long as she can foil attempts to pin her down."[19] For this reason, whenever I refer to a social-historical phenomenon related to sexual labor, I will use the term sex worker, and when considering the literary version of Phryne and her peers, I will use *hetaira*.

Using Neaira to Understand Phryne's Origins

Turning to examples of real women, parts of whose stories have been preserved in legal speeches, can help us begin to understand the origins of someone like Phryne and how a woman like Phryne could have become so prominent in fourth-century Athens. What I offer here is largely speculative and so should not be understood as straightforward biography but rather a narrative that could apply to many of the women involved in the sex trade in Athens during Phryne's lifetime. The few facts that I am able to ascertain I will endeavor to signpost as clearly as possible.

One thing that we do know about Phryne's early life is her original name. Our sources agree that her given name was Mnesarete ("Recalling Virtue"),[20] and it does seem to have been common for *hetairai* to take on nicknames as they gained more prominence.[21] Another widely accepted fact is that Phryne was from Thespiai, so we can likely place her birth prior to the late 370s BCE, when that Boeotian city and its surrounding territory were heavily damaged by the Thebans as revenge for joining the Spartan alliance against them at the Battle of Leuctra.[22] As a young child, she could have come to Athens with her family as a refugee from the unrest in Boeotia, but it is unclear whether the Athenians actually welcomed fleeing Thespians due to a lack of evidence for the Athenians granting them citizenship as they had with the Plataians.[23] A statue of Phryne at Delphi was said to have been inscribed "Phryne the daughter of Epicles of Thespiai" (*FGrH* 405 F 1), suggesting that she retained some sense of connection to her Thespian family even as she became famous and wealthy in Athens.

Another path that could have brought Phryne to Athens was early involvement in the sex trade. The speech *Against Neaira*, one of our most fulsome accounts of a woman's life from the Classical period, narrates the career of a sex worker who was brought to Athens from Corinth at a young age and presents an example of how foreign girls and women involved in the sex trade made their way to Athens during the fourth century. While it represents the litigant's side of a court case over the citizenship status of a woman accused of sex work and therefore is likely exaggerated at some points and can be straightforwardly cruel to Neaira at others, a more sympathetic reading of the speech allows us to consider the way a child was commodified and then trafficked until she finally reached a point at which she was able to become a free inhabitant of Athens. Although it has been credited to the famous orator Demosthenes, the speech was possibly written by and certainly delivered by Apollodorus as part of an ongoing feud with Neaira's "husband," Stephanus, with its key argument being that Stephanus' marriage to a foreign sex worker had undermined democratic and religious standards in Athens (*Against Neaira*, 59.13).[24] Since the case centers on the status of Neaira and both her foreign origins and her occupation are discussed in detail, the speech offers an excellent opportunity for considering how both of these aspects of a woman's identity could affect her place in Athenian society. The trial itself took place in the late 340s,[25] meaning that even if Phryne and Neaira were not exact age-mates, the trial took place during the time that we can assume Phryne was active at Athens and so we can think of Neaira as a sort of peer for Phryne.

Neaira's story begins in Corinth, at a brothel operated by a woman named Nicarete, herself a freed slave. Apollodorus tells us that Nicarete had a special skill for identifying beauty in young children (the term he uses here is *micra paidia*, with the diminutive suggesting very young children, 59.18) and that she made her living by selecting and then training those children for the sex trade. It is clear from the speech that Neaira was enslaved at this point, as she, along with six peers,[26] was sold off later on (after the prime of her youth had been exploited by Nicarete, ἐπειδὴ τὴν ἡλικίαν ἐκαρπώσατο, 59.19). Her first venture into Attica came when she was still owned by Nicarete and came to take part in the Eleusinian Mysteries along with Nicarete and another sex worker, Metaneira, at the behest of Lysias, the famous logographer. At this time, the visitors from Corinth stayed at the home of a man named Philostratus and Apollodorus tells the jury that Neaira was earning a living with her body (i.e., taking part in the sex trade), despite being "quite young and not yet mature" (νεωτέρα δὲ οὖσα διὰ τὸ μήπω τὴν ἡλικίαν αὐτῇ παρεῖναι, 59.22). She stayed on in order to celebrate the Panathenaia with another client and dined and drank alongside many men, which Apollodorus characterizes as the actions of a *hetaira* (59.24). We are also told that during this period of enslavement, Neaira was presented to clients as a free daughter of Nicarete in order to draw higher fees (59.19).

Although none of our sources mention very much of Phryne's early life, beyond the comedian Timocles' joke that she was once a caper-gatherer (fr. 25 K-A) (which is either shorthand for poverty or perhaps a bawdy joke related to sex work), from this portion of Apollodorus' narrative we do see one of the ways that very young children, some of whom were Phryne's actual colleagues in Athens during their adulthood, were brought into the sex trade. In addition, we see how even enslaved girls and women working in what was most certainly a brothel could be presented to potential clientele as *hetairai*, with an emphasis on their supposed freedom being deployed in order to garner higher fees. In her youth and possibly even her childhood, Phryne could very well have been working in such a context and so already interacting with some of the most prominent and wealthy men in Athens.

If, however, we are to imagine that Phryne was enslaved at an early point in her life and then by the time she was an adult had ended up in Athens as a free woman, we should also consider by what mechanisms an enslaved foreign sex worker could become free.[27] Returning to Neaira's story, we see that one of the ways for a woman involved in the sex trade to be manumitted was through the intervention of wealthy clients. As is expected of a woman categorized in a legal speech as a *hetaira*, Neaira had ongoing relationships with several clients who maintained her financially by paying significant fees, although these would presumably go to Nicarete.[28] Later on, Neaira acquired two more clients, Timanoridas the Corinthian and Eucrates the Leucadian, who purchased her from Nicarete for thirty *minai* (59.29). This was a significant sum of money at that time, representing several years of income for a typical skilled laborer.[29] Neaira remained enslaved under this arrangement and was definitely at the disposal of the men who had purchased her (59.29),[30] but was now out of Nicarete's brothel and available exclusively to Timanoridas and Eucrates. Soon enough the men were ready to be married, and since it was no longer ideal that they be involved in this way with a sex worker, the two men made a new agreement with Neaira that she could purchase her freedom from them, for the price of twenty *minai* (again, this was still a significant sum).[31] The conditions for this deal included leaving Corinth and no longer working for a pimp. In order to raise the twenty *minai*, Neaira contacted a series of former clients from various city-states to collect enough money, which Apollodorus mentions she added to her own savings to make up the total sum (59.30). At this point, she made her way to Athens, and Apollodorus spends a great deal of the rest of his speech narrating her scandalous behavior there.

This portion of Neaira's story illustrates the vulnerabilities of enslaved sex workers during Phryne's lifetime and their reliance on wealthy clientele. It is possible to envision someone like Phryne, if enslaved, needing the charity of men she had been involved with to gain manumission. Even if never enslaved, a foreign woman in fourth-century Athens who made her living from sexual labor would have needed ongoing financial arrangements with men in order to have a stable livelihood and so would have needed to keep those relationships on very good terms. In some cases, as with Neaira, Timanoridas, and Eucrates, men were housing the sex workers they were in relationships with, either in their own household or a secondary one,[32] so the women in such situations were dependent on these men even for basic necessities. Until Phryne had accumulated enough wealth to be securely housed and funded independent of any individual man, presumably at a point well into her adulthood, she would not have been free from the whims of her clients.

Alke and the Socially Mobile Sex Worker

Another historical woman that we can turn to as a means of better understanding what Phryne's life may have been like is Alke, who features in a speech by Isaeus, *On the Estate of Philoctemon*. The case in question dealt with a dispute over the estate of a wealthy Athenian (Euctemon) who had passed away at the age of ninety-six, but whose sons from his first marriage (Philoctemon among them) had predeceased their father. Euctemon had two surviving sons from his second marriage, but the concern is that they were not born to an Athenian wife, but rather to Alke, at one point a sex worker; a secondary concern is that Euctemon was not in fact their father, but that it was a freedman named Dion. This trial took place in 364 BCE, so it is earlier than Neaira's, yet it still offers us a narrative of how a sex worker moved in and through Athenian society in the fourth century.

Although the speaker at no point labels Alke a *pornē* or a *hetaira*, she is described as being in situations that clearly point to sexual labor and the speaker emphasizes her enslaved status. His introduction points to Alke being a sex worker at some point in her life, since she was purchased as a young child (Isaeus uses the diminutive *paidiskē*, "young girl" (Is. 6.19), suggesting pre- or early adolescence, as with Neaira when she was purchased by Nicarete). She was employed in a brothel of some kind at the Piraeus operated by a freedwoman associated with Euctemon, where she worked until she aged out of the sex trade (Isaeus says that she was "quite old" (*presbutera*, 6.19), when she left).[33] The speaker claims that it was during her tenure in the Piraeus home that she gave birth to the children under dispute in this speech. After reaching an age at which she could no longer be a sex worker herself, Alke was then dispatched by Euctemon to take care of another home/possible brothel in the Kerameikos (6.20). Here the speaker alleges that Euctemon effectively abandoned his own legitimate marital household to live in Alke's home, where he was then persuaded to introduce her boys into his phratry as his own children (6.21).

Allison Glazebrook points out that Alke, particularly in comparison to Euctemon's legitimate Athenian wife, moved around Athens and its environs quite freely, meaning that she was able to assume a place in new and shifting social networks. Given the importance of one's social connections in a city like fourth-century Athens, this meant that her identity also shifted with each move and so was fundamentally unstable.[34] Since the Peiraeus and the Kerameikos were both on the periphery of Athens proper, attracted transient populations, and were also entertainment districts where one might expect to find sex workers and brothels, we can suppose that most of the girls and women who took part in the sex trade in Athens would have moved through those spaces at some point, with their movement through them tied to their social mobility.[35] Like Alke, they may have taken part in the sex trade from a very young age (the common thread from Neaira's story as well) and later aged out of directly selling sex, while still remaining involved in the sex trade. As women like Alke moved through their careers and through Athens itself, their statuses would often shift, some becoming free like Neaira, others entering long-term relationships and even forming households with clients, and some becoming the employers of other sex workers. These changes, however, would not be predictable and varied from woman to woman, and were typically contingent on the men with whom they were associated. Being a sex worker in fourth-century Athens would have meant both freedom and a tether for a woman like Phryne.

Alke's case, while illustrating the spaces in which sex workers could be expected to circulate, also identifies Athenian spaces in which enslaved sex workers were most definitely unwelcome. By setting up an approximation of an *oikos* with Euktemon, Alke assumed an identity that should not have been available to her (wife) and then doubled down on that claim by having him introduce her children into his phratry, by extension claiming that she was a citizen wife. Since the household and its formation around marriage between an Athenian man and an Athenian woman was central to claims of citizenship in the fourth century, women involved in the sex trade, foreign women, and enslaved women (some of whom, like Alke, were all three) were not welcome as central members of an *oikos* and their attempts to define membership in that household were in that sense against the law. Alke, however, seems to have been very committed to this new but fraudulent identity, attending the Thesmophoria, a women-only festival of Demeter and Persephone that was meant to be limited to married women of Athenian descent (6.50). Her presence there is mentioned by the speaker as the most shocking of all of her actions and continues the pattern in this speech of placing an enslaved foreign sex worker in opposition to a free, respectable Athenian wife.

Like that of Neaira, Alke's presence in a household represented a threat to the very foundations of Athenian society. But this characterization of her behavior as fraudulent and harmful does not mean that we cannot use her story to imagine other possible narratives, in which women involved in the sex trade set up their own households independent of the expectations and strictures that shaped the lives of citizen women. Whether or not Alke set about doing so with dishonest designs, she had children and lived in a household with a man who acted as (and may have been) their father despite Alke having been a sex worker from a very young age. Although likely still enslaved at that point, when she moved to the Kerameikos and began running her own establishment, she was not entirely under the control of a *kurios* as many other women would have been and it does not seem as though Euctemon took on such a role in the new household they formed together.

Using Alke's story, we can envision the parts of Athens that Phryne may have spent time in, as well as identify the social spaces in which she would not have been welcome. We can also think of how some sex workers were able to access a kind of freedom to move through the city and associate with different circles because their lives were not expected to adhere to any standard pattern. In Phryne's case, we can imagine her life in establishments like the one that housed Alke from early on and we can see her circulating through places like the Peiraeus or the Kerameikos before reaching a certain point of affluence that allowed her to set up her own household and live life as an independent woman. Both Neaira's and Alke's stories are instructive as we think through the possible origins of a figure like Phryne, allowing us to peek behind the curtain of nicknames, anecdotes, and glamor that obscure the labor of the *hetairai* to see more clearly that many of Phryne's peers, if not Phryne herself, were at some point in their careers in the sex trade heavily exploited and in many cases enslaved. Of particular note is that both Alke and Neaira began sex work as very young girls who had been especially chosen for the task.

Metic Women and Sex Workers

Another way of considering Phryne's Athenian life and her potential vulnerability is to think of her position as a foreign woman in a society that prized citizenship and local identity above all. Since she was from Thespiai and not Athenian (even if born there to Thespian parents), Phryne would have fit into the category "metic," from *metoikos*, suggesting one who lives alongside another, and in the Classical Athenian context, a resident who was free but excluded from the privileges of citizenship. In the fourth century, metics (foreigners who had been resident in Athens for a certain amount of time, children of metics upon reaching adulthood, and newly freed slaves) were expected to register with a magistrate (the polemarch) and with their deme of residence, as well as to have an Athenian sponsor known as a *prostates*.[36] All registered metics were required to pay a tax, the *metoikion*, which was twelve *drachmai* per year for men, and for women without a male authority figure (a husband, father, or son), six *drachmai*.[37] Given that women who acted as their own head of household were included as their own category in these laws and were assumed to be able to pay an amount that was not insignificant,[38] we can assume that there was a sizable population of metic women in fourth-century Athens earning reasonable incomes and not dependent on male relatives.[39]

Metic women and their labor were an important part of the Athenian economy during Phryne's lifetime. We know from both literary and epigraphic evidence that metic women in fourth-century Athens were vendors in the agora, wool workers, seamstresses, nurses, musicians, midwives, healers and priestesses, among other occupations in addition to the sex trade, and so metic women of all kinds were very visible in that society. Those who worked in public-facing occupations certainly faced reduced social status, which also meant that citizen women who worked outside of the home could be disparaged by being referred to as metics. In Demosthenes' *Against Euboulides* the mother of the speaker, Euxitheus, has been accused of being a foreigner simply because she sold ribbons in the marketplace (57.34) and served as a nurse (57.35). While many women associated with sex work were metics, the nexus of foreignness, independence, and the sex trade that *hetairai* like Phryne came to embody in legal oratory should be recognized as a discursive strategy responding to Athens' construction of citizenship more than a historical reality.[40] At the same time, as we think about Phryne in her historical context, we need to consider how her various identities would have influenced her experience of Athenian society.

We do not have any evidence that Phryne paid the *metoikion* (Athenian record keeping did not prioritize metics or women), but we can turn to yet another legal case that deals with metic status to speculate on her position as a foreign-born sex worker in Athenian society. Hypereides' *Against Aristagora* comprises fragments from two speeches given in trials that featured an accusation of *aprostasiou*,[41] a charge which seems to relate to a metic not paying the *metoikion*.[42] This case features Aristagora, a woman who could be categorized as a *hetaira*, formerly enslaved and then freed by the notable orator Hypereides (the same Hypereides who defended Phryne in her infamous trial) so that he could install her in his home in the Piraeus as his *pallakē* (Ath. 13.590c). (These aspects of Aristagora's story also offer yet another illustration of the shifting identity and status of the sex worker.) Hypereides had two other women housed in two other homes he owned in Attica, one of whom seems to have changed roles from being his mistress to becoming Hypereides' housekeeper, and he and Aristagora at some point had a serious falling out. In the case of Hypereides and Aristagora, the *metoikion* became a useful means for the orator to seek revenge on a woman with whom he had quarrelled. Because she had been part of Hypereides' household as his *pallakē*, Aristagora was not liable to register as a metic and pay the tax. Once she left his household, she was independent and needed to register. We can only speculate on the timeline between the end of their relationship and Hypereides' prosecution of her, but it is clear that the *graphē aprostasiou* was motivated by personal vengeance.

Aristagora's case shows how the laws of Athens could be used in order to exploit the legal vulnerabilities of free women involved in the sex trade and how their erotic entanglements with citizen men could offer protection and status while they were underway but then leave metic women exposed to serious legal challenges once they had ended. A metic *hetaira* living independently would most likely want to be registered and pay the *metoikion* if she was able to in order to avoid such prosecutions. One can also imagine the more prominent a woman was, the more appealing a target she would be to men with malicious designs. Such concerns applied to newly freed women as well as those who were considered foreign and so any independent, non-citizen woman in Athens was equally liable to prosecution on these terms if she did not follow the law. In Chapter 3, I will explore more fully Phryne's personal liability to prosecution as a metic woman, as well as her relationship to Hypereides, the prosecutor of Aristagora, however here it is sufficient to note that the combination of her notoriety in Athens and her metic status would have made her a tempting target for any man who wanted to do her harm and that her combination of foreignness and independence put her in danger from this kind of aggression.

Hetairai and Notable Men in Athens

None of our sources suggest that Phryne was an ongoing part of a household with any one man but it was clearly her association with prominent male

Athenians that brought her fame, so now I would like to turn to an examination of the kinds of men that she and her colleagues associated with in the fourth century. As with so much of the material that tells us about the *hetairai*, most of what tells us about the men that they were involved with comes from the Hellenistic period and so should be assessed critically. The pairing of *hetairai* with artists and philosophers in particular had become an important trope of the anecdotes circulating in the third century BCE and it should be noted that in texts like Machon's *Chreiai*, the pairings are just as likely to be suited to the type or content of anecdote being related as they are to be a historical reality.[43] Among the list of men who are named as having some kind of association with Phryne are two of the most famous artists from Greek antiquity, Praxiteles and Apelles (whose connections with Phryne I will examine in detail in the following chapter); political figures like Gryllion, whom we are told sat on the Areopagus but was a parasite to Phryne; orators like Hypereides (who features in the discussion of Phryne's trial in Chapter 3); and philosophers such as Xenocrates, who was head of the Academy in the late fourth century.

This list and the groups it represents are not unusual for the *hetairai* as described in Hellenistic and later literature. Other notable *hetairai* like Lais, the noted beauty, were also associated with Apelles and Xenocrates, as well as with Demosthenes the orator, but also with quizzical figures like Diogenes the Cynic, whose connection to a famously desirable woman like Lais was surely a great source of humor to later generations. Lais and the men in her circle provide a representative example of the kinds of distortions that were probably introduced by later authors seeking to link famous names with one another, find a suitable punchline, or even make someone famously interested in boys like Demosthenes seem acceptably heterosexual.[44] A careful accounting of the chronology of Lais' lifespan and those of her supposed lovers creates awkward pairings, placing some of them together when she was in her senior years and the men were very young. The patterns that emerge from assessing these combinations of *hetairai* and noted men from the mid-fourth century emphasize connections to political figures/orators, artists, and philosophers, but many of these relationships, attested only in Hellenistic and later sources, are best treated as convenient constructs that highlight generic expectations of the literary *hetaira*. Nonetheless, the relationships of *hetairai* from the mid-fourth century, as depicted in later literature, in some sense reflect historical circumstances in that they are different to those from after the Macedonian takeover of Athens, at which point more Macedonians and pro-Macedonian Athenians are paired with *hetairai* in our sources. When portraying *hetairai* from that period, even the later sources, shaped as they are by generic expectations, cede center stage to pairings like Lamia and the Macedonian general Demetrius *Poliorcetes* while disregarding philosophers and orators.

Since I will address Phryne's relationships with the orator Hypereides and the artists Praxiteles and Apelles in subsequent chapters, here I would like to focus on the connection between philosophers and *hetairai*, with a consideration of sources and genre. *Hetairai* appear in philosophical texts from the fourth century, with the most famous example being Theodote, who appears in Xenophon's *Memorabilia*, his collection of Socratic dialogues. In this text, Xenophon describes Theodote as a great beauty, who would "spend time with those who tempted her" (οἵας συνεῖναι τῷ πείθοντι, 3.11.1), and made her living from those who wished to become her benefactors (as Xenophon has her say, "If someone who is dear to me wants to do well by me, that's my livelihood," ἐάν τις, ἔφη, φίλος μοι γενόμενος εὖ ποιεῖν ἐθέλῃ, οὗτός μοι βίος ἐστί, 3.11.4). The exchange between Theodote and Socrates about how she earns a living and the role of persuasion in a *hetaira*'s relationships have featured prominently in scholarly discussions of how gift exchange partially defines the *hetaira* (especially in contrast with the *pornē*),[45] however their conversation informs my discussion because it puts a *hetaira* in friendly and clever dialogue with a philosopher, a precursor to the kind of repartee featured in the later anecdotes.

Other sex worker-philosopher connections from the fourth century include Aristotle and Herpyllis and Epicurus and Leontium. As mentioned above, Herpyllis seems to have been a sex worker who was brought into Aristotle's household after the death of his wife as a *pallakē*. Aristotle then made considerable provisions for her in his will,[46] while Leontium appears to have been a member of Epicurus' circle and someone who frequented his Gardens.[47] Because the philosophers, despite their connections to elite Athenians, were not truly part of mainstream society, they were not unlike the *hetairai*: often itinerant, taking on elite "clientele," and making their living from persuasion.[48] These connections are already highlighted in the conversation between Socrates and Theodote that Xenophon reports and then become the subject of later parody in authors like Alciphron, who writes a letter "authored" by the *hetaira* Thais to her lover, Euthydemus, in which she is trying to convince him to abandon his philosophical pursuits to spend more time with her. Here she tells her lover that she is as much a teacher as the sophist Euthydemus is following (4.7.6), and she accuses the philosopher of pursuing financial gain from her lover and his friends just as much as she does: "These things are nonsense and affectation and profiting from young men, you twit!" (λῆρος ταῦτά εἰσι καὶ τῦφος καὶ ἐργολάβεια μειρακίων, ὦ ἀνόητε, 4.7.4).

Lais, Phryne's peer and sometime rival (according to Athenaeus 13.588f), is the *hetaira* most often associated with philosophers. As early as the Hellenistic period, she is linked to Aristippus of Cyrene, a follower of Socrates,[49] while Imperial sources like Diogenes Laertius put her together with Diogenes the Cynic. Athenaeus even relates an instance when Diogenes teased Aristippus for paying for what he, a man notoriously disinterested in cultural standards for public behavior and even hygiene, received from Lais for free (13.588f). Pausanias links the Cynic and the *hetaira*, claiming they are buried near each other in Corinth (2.2.4-5).[50] The relationship with Diogenes epitomizes the interest of later authors in pairing *hetairai* thought of as beautiful and wealthy with men notorious for their disinterest in such things in order to contrast the two and set up either ridiculous scenarios or punchlines for anecdotes.

Xenocrates was a figure paired with both Phryne and Lais by Diogenes Laertius as a means of contrasting the physical temptations offered by *hetairai* with the intellectual life of philosophers, which reflects the Imperial tendency to depict the two groups as being in opposition to one another.[51] A student of Plato's who later succeeded Speusippus as head of the Academy from 339 to 314 BCE, he leaves behind very little work with which to assess his theories,[52] but we can assume he was chosen to play such a role as a prominent representative of one of the more conservative schools of philosophy in the fourth century. Diogenes Laertius portrays Xenocrates as so committed to the life of the mind that he rarely even left the Academy. According to the Imperial-era biographer, on one occasion, in order to test Xenocrates, Phryne came to him under the pretense that she was being pursued by someone. When the philosopher let her into his humble home, which only had a single couch, he allowed her to share it with him; the *hetaira* tried to tempt him but left untouched, telling anyone who asked that she had "left behind not a man, but a statue" (οὐκ ἀπ' ἀνδρός, ἀλλ' ἀπ' ἀνδριάντος ἀνασταίη, D.L. 4.2.7). Xenocrates' virtue was so powerful that in another version of the story, he was also able to resist Lais, equally as famous and desirable as Phryne, after his students had sent her to him (D.L. 4. 2.7). The fact that Lais can be swapped into the story in place of Phryne speaks to the genre of anecdote and how little it was interested in individuating the *hetairai*. These stories have a precedent in the work of Valerius Maximus, a first-century CE Latin collector of anecdotes. In explaining the continence of Xenocrates, he tells of Phryne, late at night at a party once much wine had been consumed by all, making a bet with some young men that she would be able to seduce the philosopher. He allowed her to get close and lay in his arms but went no further, so when the young men demanded she pay out, her response, as in Diogenes Laertius' version, was that she had made the bet "about a man ... not a statue" (*de homine ... non de statua*, 4 ext. 3a).[53]

From anecdotes such as these, we learn more about standards for the literary depictions of *hetairai* and philosophers in combination rather than meaningful details about any of the individuals involved. Nonetheless, given the amount of acclaimed philosophers present in Athens during Phryne's lifetime and the other high-profile men they associated with, we can assume that she would have encountered many philosophers in the circles in which she traveled, even if she never welcomed one as a client. Although none of our sources put her in conversation with a philosopher as Xenophon did with Theodote and Socrates, she is likely to have interacted with men like Xenocrates regularly. One can imagine the same wealthy young men who followed the philosophers seeking out the companionship of women like Phryne and some potential for conflict between the two groups over time spent with and resources spent on either group as we see in Alciphron's fictional letter. Yet it is the connections between the groups in literature that hint at potential real-life acquaintances. The *hetaira* besting the intellectual or the philosopher rejecting a great beauty makes for paradoxical comedy, but both groups were used in literature from the Hellenistic period onward as a means of poking at elite male Athenians because they were sought persistently by that group. Both philosophers and sex workers could move through different parts of society because of their flexible and shifting statuses (see my discussion of Alke above), with their ability to draw an elite clientele or circle of followers key to long-term success and independence from mainstream society. Consequently, while the anecdotes that began to circulate in the Hellenistic period may not be literally true, they point to real dynamics at play for both *hetairai* and philosophers, by which Phryne's own relationships would certainly have been shaped.

Phryne and Her Colleagues in Comedy

Although many sex workers largely operated outside of the boundaries of mainstream society, that same mainstream in fourth-century Athens was deeply intrigued by them and often sought to work through the complexities signified by their presence in that city. I have already discussed the ways that women like Neaira, Alke, and Aristagora were implicated in legal cases because of their outsider status. The use of women characterized as *hetairai* to strike at the men associated with them and to represent all that was opposite to Athenian ideals had become a common trope in legal oratory by the middle of the fourth century and therefore sex workers had become a significant presence in public discourse.[54] Their enlarged cultural footprint and association with prominent male citizens meant that they also became prime targets for mockery on the comic stage; the parallels between the courtroom and the stage as spaces for civic performance have been commented on by many scholars.[55] Plays thus repeated much of the rhetoric from the courtroom, often characterizing sex workers as a tempting evil, as in the following passage from Antiphanes' *Country-Dweller*:

ἔστιν δ' ἑταίρα τῷ τρέφοντι συμφορά·
εὐφραίνεται γὰρ κακὸν ἔχων οἴκοι μέγα

A *hetaira* is a misfortune to the one who supports her;
For he takes pleasure in having a great evil at home.

fr. 2 K-A[56]

While *hetairai* and sex workers more generally are mentioned sparingly in comedies from the fifth century BCE, with real women named but never depicted,[57] plays from the fourth century and particularly from the mid-fourth century onward began to feature them as characters and at the same time began to caricature real-life sex workers, as part of a move away from the mythic content in comedy that had prevailed previously. Plays such as Timocles' two separate *Neairas* and Epicrates' *Anti-Lais* seem to have been produced in response to the court cases featuring the eponymous women, and around forty titles of plays from the mid-fourth century onward use the names of historical women identified as *hetairai*.[58] In addition to such references to real women, the *hetaira* figure became a stock character during this period, so that when Menander was producing his plays at the end of the fourth century, she had become a standard generic inclusion. The *hetaira* characters in Menander's plays became, for the most part, much more sympathetic figures than the women who were used to symbolize excess in Aristophanes' plays and in those from the mid-fourth century. Due to the fragmentary nature of our evidence for comedy from the mid-fourth century, it is challenging to assess just how important the *hetaira* characters were to individual plots,[59] but the many titles that feature them and the many references to real-life women suggest a significant stage presence.

Hetairai are named quite a few times in fourth-century comedy, just as they are in oratory, so it is worth considering why this happens. Even in the plays of Aristophanes where it seems as though anything goes, free men generally do not name free, respectable women (that is, women who are not enslaved or sex workers).[60] The women who are addressed by name in comic plays are therefore either enslaved or sex workers, or both, and therefore not directly related to a household guardian, by whose name they could be addressed (e.g., as the wife of, mother of, or daughter of "X"). When women are referred to by their own names in oratory (as in the cases of Neaira and Alke), the opposite effect is achieved, whereby their independence from a man is emphasized alongside their disruptive presence in society; the same is true on the comic stage. In this way, being named in a play functions in much the same way as being named in a court case, marking out those women as being not respectable. At times, those names could be piled upon one another for comic affect, as in Timocles' mythical parody *Orestautocleides*, when he lists a group of *hetairai*; here he turns historical women into Furies alongside the infamous pederast Autocleides who takes on the role of Orestes:

περὶ δὲ τὸν πανάθλιον
εὕδουσι γρᾶες, Νάννιον, Πλαγγών, Λύκα,

Γνάθαινα, Φρύνη, Πυθιονίκη, Μυρρίνη,
Χρυσίς, † Κοναλίς †, Ἱερόκλεια, Λοπάδιον

Around the wretch sleep old hags, Nannion, Plangon, Lyca, Gnathaina, Phryne, Myrrhine, Chrysis, Konalis (?), Hieroclea, Lopadion

Timocles, *Orestautokleides* fr. 27 K-A

This play must have been performed once Phryne and the other named women were past the prime of their careers, but still sufficiently notorious to have name recognition for the Athenian audience, therefore likely some time in the 330s.[61] Thus the humour of this scenario rests on the recognizability of the women listed. If this play was truly mimicking its Aeschylean predecessor, *Eumenides*, one can even imagine a group of actors dressed as each of these women onstage as a burlesque of the chorus from the tragic play, perhaps with some recognizable detail for each *hetaira*/Fury.

Comparing sex workers to monstrous figures was not unusual on the comic stage. In Timocles' play, the *hetairai*-as-Furies may have been chosen because Autocleides was notorious for his sexual interest in boys and men and so their pursuit may have been attributed to their monstrous desire for money.[62] In his play *Neottis*, likely staged in Athens in the 340s, Anaxilas offers a lengthy list of *hetairai* who are paired with mythological monstrosities, with an emphasis on their greed:

ὅστις ἀνθρώπων ἑταίραν ἠγάπησε πώποτε,
οὐ γένος τίς ἂν δύναιτο παρανομώτατον φράσαι·
τίς γὰρ ἢ δράκαιν' ἄμεικτος, ἢ Χίμαιρα πυρπνόος
ἢ Χάρυβδις, ἢ τρίκρανος Σκύλλα, ποντία κύων,
Σφίγξ, Ὕδρα, λέαιν', ἔχιδνα, πτηνά θ' Ἁρπυιῶν γένη,
εἰς ὑπερβολὴν ἀφῖκται τοῦ καταπτύστου γένους;
οὐκ ἔνεσθ'· αὗται δ' ἁπάντων ὑπερέχουσι τῶν κακῶν.
ἔστι δὲ σκοπεῖν ἀπ' ἀρχῆς πρῶτα μὲν τὴν Πλαγγόνα,
ἥτις ὥσπερ ἡ Χίμαιρα πυρπολεῖ τοὺς βαρβάρους.
εἷς μόνος δ' ἱππεύς τις αὐτῆς τὸν βίον παρείλετο·
πάντα τὰ σκεύη γὰρ ἕλκων ᾤχετ' ἐκ τῆς οἰκίας.
οἱ Σινώπῃ δ' αὖ συνόντες οὐχ Ὕδρᾳ σύνεισι νῦν;
γραῦς μὲν αὐτή, παραπέφυκε δ' ἡ Γνάθαινα πλησίον,
ὥστ' ἀπαλλαγεῖσι ταύτης ἔστι διπλάσιον κακόν.
ἡ δὲ Νάννιον τί νυνὶ διαφέρειν Σκύλλης δοκεῖ;

οὐ δύ᾽ ἀποπνίξασ᾽ ἑταίρους τὸν τρίτον θηρεύεται
ἔτι λαβεῖν; ἀλλ᾽ † ἐξέπεσε † πορθμὶς ἐλατίνῳ πλάτῃ.
ἡ δὲ Φρύνη τὴν Χάρυβδιν οὐχὶ πόρρω που ποιεῖ
τόν τε ναύκληρον λαβοῦσα καταπέπωκ᾽ αὐτῷ σκάφει;
ἡ Θεανὼ δ᾽ οὐχὶ Σειρήν ἐστιν ἀποτετιλμένη;
βλέμμα καὶ φωνὴ γυναικός, τὰ σκέλη δὲ κοψίχου.
Σφίγγα Θηβαίαν δὲ πάσας ἔστι τὰς πόρνας καλεῖν,
αἳ λαλοῦσ᾽ ἁπλῶς μὲν οὐδέν, ἀλλ᾽ ἐν αἰνιγμοῖς τισιν,
ὡς ἐρῶσι καὶ φιλοῦσι καὶ σύνεισιν ἡδέως.
εἶτα "τετράπους μοι γένοιτο," φησὶ † "τήνπρος ἢ θρόνος,"
εἶτα δὴ "τρίπους τισ᾽, εἶτα," φησί, "παιδίσκη δίπους."
εἶθ᾽ ὃ μὲν γνοὺς ταῦτ᾽ ἀπῆλθεν εὐθὺς ὥσπερ <Οἰδίπους>,
οὐδ᾽ ἰδεῖν δόξας ἐκείνην, σῴζεται δ᾽ ἄκων μόνος.
οἱ δ᾽ ἐρᾶσθαι προσδοκῶντες εὐθύς εἰσιν ἠρμένοι
καὶ φέρονθ᾽ ὑψοῦ πρὸς αἴθραν. συντεμόντι δ᾽ οὐδὲ ἓν
ἔσθ᾽ ἑταίρας ὅσα περ ἔστιν θηρί᾽ ἐξωλέστερον

What man ever was content with a *hetaira*
who could say that there isn't a more lawless race?
for what savage serpent or fire-breathing Chimaera
or Charybdis or three-headed Scylla, hound of the sea,
Sphinx, Hydra, lioness, echidna, winged race of Harpies,
exceeds their abominable kind?
There isn't one; they outdo all evils.
We shall examine them from the beginning, Plangon first,
who like the Chimaera, scorches barbarians:
a single horseman destroyed her:
grabbing all her things, he disappeared from her house.
Now, those who are with Sinope, aren't they sleeping with a Hydra?
She's a crone, and Gnathaina is there along with her,
so those who switch this one for that get a double evil.
Now why does Nannion seem any different from Scylla?
Didn't she choke down two pals and still sets out
to catch another? But the ship with the fir oars got away;
and is Phryne no more Charybdis than when she grabs
a ship-captain and swallows him down, ship and all?
Isn't Theano a plucked siren?
The looks and voice of a woman, but the legs of a blackbird.
We can call all the whores Theban Sphinxes,

who say nothing straightforward, but in riddles,
how they desire and kiss and do the deed gladly.
Then "I'd like a four-legged couch or a chair" they say,
then again "I'd like a tripod" then they say "a two-legged slave girl."
Then the one who catches on to these demands, gets out of there right away, like Oedipus,
pretending not to see her, he alone is saved, but unwillingly.
And those thinking that it's love are uplifted
And she takes them to cloud nine. In short,
of all the beasts, nothing is more abominable than a *hetaira*.

fr. 22 K-A

In this list we also see Plangon and Nannion, who were among the Furies mentioned by Timocles, and from such lists we can determine which women had enough notoriety in Athens that their names could serve as punchlines; each monster was likely carefully selected by Anaxilas to correspond to each woman's reputation. Phryne may be the worst of all according to this monstrous calculus: she drains the wealth of a man completely, which in turn accords with other anecdotes focused on her own great wealth.

Outside of such collections of *hetairai*, listed one after the other to compound their comic potential, there are other mentions of Phryne specifically from comedies of the mid-fourth century. A reference to Phryne in her youth also appears in Timocles' *Neaira*. (*Orestautocleides* was not Timocles' only engagement with the law courts or with sex workers, as this comic playwright was one of the most political of his era.)[63] Although what remains is focused on Phryne, *Neaira* must have been a response to what was a scandalous trial and the play may have dealt with sex work more broadly, making Phryne an expected reference in such a context. In the longer of the two remaining fragments of *Neaira*, Phryne is depicted as a once-humble woman, who has become so rich that she can reject suitors:

ἀλλ' ἔγωγ' ὁ δυστυχὴς
Φρύνης ἐρασθεὶς ἡνίκ' ἔτι τὴν κάππαριν
συνέλεγεν οὔπω τ' εἶχεν ὅσαπερ νῦν ἔχει,
πάμπολλ' ἀναλίσκων ἐφ' ἑκάστῳ τῆς θύρας
ἀπεκλειόμην

But I, the unlucky one,
fell in love with Phryne when was still
picking capers, and did not yet have what she has now,
despite spending absolutely everything, each time at her door,
I was shut out.

fr. 25 K-A

Much like the legal speeches featuring sex workers that I have discussed in this chapter, this passage highlights the possible social and economic mobility of sex workers, with a touch of disappointed entitlement on the part of a former client. Although a comical scenario in which the former lover now finds himself shut out,[64] we might also presume that such a passage indicates that Phryne had reached a point where she was able to exercise power over precisely whom she would take on as a client. She may only have been invoked here, rather than actually portrayed onstage, perhaps as an example of the typical sex worker with ever-shifting loyalties determined by their economic fortunes, but even her name becoming shorthand for a wealthy sex worker tells us a great deal about her notoriety and position in Athens when this play was produced.

Other fourth-century comic poets seem to have been gentler on Phryne than Timocles and Anaxilas were, and there may have been some interest in her possible connections to Apelles and Praxiteles. Antiphanes wrote a play, possibly produced in the 350s, titled either *The Birth of Aphrodite* or *Aphrodite's Offspring* (αἱ Ἀφροδίτης Γοναί), that could be a reference to Phryne's famous emergence from the sea at Eleusis that inspired Apelles' painting, or perhaps the work itself. Another play that may connect to Phryne and Praxiteles is Alexis' *The Woman from Knidos/The Knidian Goddess* (ἡ Κνιδία), which could be a reference to the famous statue of Aphrodite that he created with Phryne as model.[65]

One play produced after Phryne's death, likely sometime in the early third century BCE, also gives us insight into Phryne's legacy in the generations immediately after her lifetime, while further highlighting the relationship between the courts and the comic stage. Posidippus, the son of a Macedonian who began producing plays in Athens shortly after the death of Menander (the playwright died in 289 BCE), wrote a play called *The Ephesian Girl* (ἡ Ἐφεσία), that features the following lines of dialogue:

Φρύνη πρό <γ'> ἡμῶν γέγονεν ἐπιφανεστάτη
πολὺ τῶν ἑταιρῶν· καὶ γὰρ εἰ νεωτέρα
τῶν τότε χρόνων εἶ, τόν γ' ἀγῶν' ἀκήκοας.
βλάπτειν δοκοῦσα τοὺς βίους μείζους βλάβας
τὴν ἡλιαίαν εἷλε περὶ τοῦ σώματος
καὶ τῶν δικαστῶν καθ' ἕνα δεξιουμένη
μετὰ δακρύων διέσωσε τὴν ψυχὴν μόλις.

Phryne was the most famous by far
of the *hetairai* before our day; and even if you are
from a younger generation, you've heard of her trial.
They thought she was harming the citizens and
brought her to court on a capital charge;
going to the judges one by one
in tears she barely saved her life.

fr. 13 K-A

Although there is no mention of her being stripped naked in front of the jury as in the later versions of the story of her trial,[66] three aspects of this short speech stand out: the charges Phryne faced, her superlative fame, and its connection to her trial, which I will argue in Chapter 3 likely did occur, if not in the exact way the anecdotes portray it. The charges are important, if vaguely described here: she is accused of "doing greater harms" (βλάπτειν δοκοῦσα τοὺς βίους μείζους βλάβας), presumably to those in her circle, with the implication being that these are elite Athenian citizens. As with Neaira and Aristagora, the concern seems to have been that her connection to Athenians was in some way degrading their status, with this concern likely related to her ability to move easily through various circles in Athenian society. This play demonstrates how Phryne's name and the stories about her were still well-known enough in the generations immediately after her lifetime to be an easy comic reference.

The connection between the trial and her position as the most well-known of the *hetairai* of her generation is in fact key to Phryne's fame and it is likely because of her presence in the courtroom that she merited inclusion on the comic stage. I would argue that this is true of many of the historical *hetairai* who are mentioned in comedies. The courtroom brought these women to mainstream attention and that attention then became comic currency that playwrights could take advantage of as in Posidippus' play. In the case of Phryne, her trial gave her added notoriety during her own lifetime that then sustained her high profile in subsequent generations in Athens. As the Alexandrians developed a taste for Athenian comedy, collections of anecdotes based on these plays were beginning to circulate and Phryne began to shift from historical sex worker to legendary woman.

Comedy, Oratory, and Phryne's Cultural Footprint

The sources from Phryne's own lifetime do little to help us identify the specific historical details of her life but do give us a sense of her profile in Athens and what discourses shaped it. They also allow us to explore various options for how she may have gained such a high profile and how she may have moved through Athenian society, while confirming that taking part in the sex trade in fourth-century Athens allowed women a kind of mobility not available to their "respectable" counterparts. That mobility and the potential for independence that it offered, however, created vulnerabilities for women like Phryne and taking part in the sex trade also made sex workers more likely to be involved in vindictive court cases. As court cases like Neaira's brought sex workers into mainstream discourse, they also positioned those women as a threat to mainstream Athenian values, leaving them exposed to the kind of accusations that Phryne eventually faced.

Yet facing charges as Phryne did only augmented her fame as demonstrated by Posidippus' play. In this sense, notoriety became its own form of social and cultural currency, with infamy leading to fame. For Phryne to be used as a cultural touchstone, as she was on the comic stage during her own lifetime and after it, she needed a large enough cultural footprint that not only would her name be easily recognized, but her reputation and the jokes about it would be legible to most of the audience. In Phryne's case, she seems to have become shorthand for the greed of the *hetairai*, which in turn can be attributed to the large fortune she managed to amass through her work. In the fourth-century sources that remain, we see a Phryne who found her way to good economic fortune, in several different stages of her life that involved some significant changes in status, but at the same time a woman who was perceived as a peril to the social structure of Athens and so was made vulnerable to the whims of elite Athenian men. She embodied the threat of the *hetairai*, whose labile status exposed the ultimate fragility of social structures, with her fame bringing her wealth and notoriety in equal measure.

2

Phryne the Artist's Model

Alone among the *hetairai* of the fourth century BCE, Phryne left a visual legacy in the famous artworks that used her as a model and they in turn spurred creative literary engagements with her image that centered Phryne's visual appeal. While the comedies that mention Phryne emphasize her great wealth and notoriety, they speak less to precisely what it was that made her appealing enough to her clientele to acquire such wealth. The sources from the Hellenistic period and beyond that discuss images of her, however, make great claims about her beauty as well as about the power of the images that were created of her. Some of the sources mention the paradox that despite her great beauty, Phryne was typically quite cautious in allowing her body to be seen, and such a choice must be understood to be a result of her identity as a *hetaira* and the need to make the beauty of her body exclusive to a select few. As I have discussed in the previous chapter, being a sex worker allowed Phryne to move through Athens in ways that were not available to many women at that time and so a woman like Phryne, especially once she had achieved a significant amount of notoriety, would have to be quite calculating about her public presence, but especially her physical appearance when in public. Other sources connect her beauty to the love she inspired in Praxiteles the sculptor and insist on the erotic connection between the *hetaira* and the artist. All of these sources invite the reader to envision Phryne herself, turning her beauty and her body into a focal point for the nostalgia that is an essential part of much of the literature featuring *hetairai*.

The most famous image with which Phryne was associated, and of which many ancient copies survive to this day, is the Aphrodite of Knidos, renowned as the first monumental statue of a female nude in the ancient Greek world. Phryne's relationship with Praxiteles, the sculptor of that statue, forms the core of this chapter, beginning with an examination of the epigrams that describe the statue of Eros he created and was said to have gifted to Phryne. Copies of Praxiteles' statues proliferated around the Mediterranean once the Romans had conquered the Greek world,[1] and they also appeared on coinage from the cities in which they were set up, granting a wide-reaching visual imprint on Roman culture to her lover and through him, possibly to Phryne. A sculptor whose position in the canon of Greek art was well-established by the Hellenistic period and who was greatly admired by the Romans for his naturalism, Praxiteles was known for his images of the gods, but especially of goddesses. He flourished in the middle of the fourth century BCE.[2] I will also briefly examine the stories about the painter Apelles' "Aphrodite Rising from the Sea," now lost and also said to be inspired by Phryne.[3]

Like Praxiteles, Apelles' place in the canon was widely accepted and although his works do not survive, we know a great deal about his famous paintings such as his portraits of Alexander the Great and his father, Philip. I will consider Phryne in relation to both artists and to the artistic canon as I explore later sources' emphasis on Phryne as a model and indeed co-creator of these images. Phryne's beauty, her association with nudity, and her role as a *hetaira* will further inform these discussions.

Phryne's body is central to discussions of her beauty, yet beyond the mention of her pale complexion in Plutarch (*Mor.* 401a), none of the sources describe any specifics of her appearance at all (e.g., her hair or eye colour, the shape of her features or body). If anything, there is an insistence on Phryne's natural beauty, as exemplified by Galen's anecdote, in which Phryne, during a game at a dinner party, has all the women present wet their fingers, touch their faces, and then wipe them with napkins. As the cosmetics they are all wearing come off, only Phryne's innate beauty shines through, illustrating Galen's point that true beauty is separate from ornamentation (*Protr.* 1.26).[4] As a result, the reader is always told that Phryne is beautiful through the responses of others to seeing her or to seeing her image and thus is invited to envision her beauty without specific guidance from the text. This technique is very powerful in that it allows for the subjectivity of beauty (each reader can envision Phryne to their own taste), while also imbuing a text with *enargeia*, summoning Phryne's presence as the reader recreates her appearance through their own imagination.[5]

The most fulsome example of this process comes from Athenaeus, as part of Myrtilus' defence of the *hetairai* against Cynculus' invective in a lengthy string

Figure 1 Bronze statuette of Aphrodite Anadyomene, 1st–2nd century CE, Metropolitan Museum of Art (2021.40.56).

of anecdotes about Phryne and her peers like Lais. (It is worth noting here that many of the passages Cynculus quotes come directly from fourth-century comedy which is less likely to be favorable to the *hetairai*, while many of Myrtilus' come from texts assembled or written in the Hellenistic period.) After telling the story of her nudity at the conclusion of her trial, he connects her beauty and public nudity to her role as a model and muse:

ἦν δὲ ὄντως μᾶλλον ἡ Φρύνη καλὴ ἐν τοῖς μὴ βλεπομένοις. διόπερ οὐδὲ ῥᾳδίως ἦν αὐτὴν ἰδεῖν γυμνήν· ἐχέσαρκον γὰρ χιτώνιον ἠμπείχετο καὶ τοῖς δημοσίοις οὐκ ἐχρῆτο βαλανείοις. τῇ δὲ τῶν Ἐλευσινίων πανηγύρει καὶ τῇ τῶν Ποσειδωνίων ἐν ὄψει τῶν Πανελλήνων πάντων ἀποθεμένη θοἰμάτιον καὶ λύσασα τὰς κόμας ἐνέβαινε τῇ θαλάττῃ· καὶ ἀπ' αὐτῆς Ἀπελλῆς τὴν Ἀναδυομένην Ἀφροδίτην ἀπεγράψατο. καὶ Πραξιτέλης δὲ ὁ ἀγαλματοποιὸς ἐρῶν αὐτῆς τὴν Κνιδίαν Ἀφροδίτην ἀπ' αὐτῆς ἐπλάσατο

But Phryne was really quite beautiful in the areas not seen. On account of this it was not easy to see her in the nude, for she was in the habit of covering herself up with a clingy shift and she didn't use the public baths. But when it was the Eleusinian festival or the Poseidonia, in sight of all the Greeks she set aside her dress, let down her hair, and went into the sea. And based on her, Apelles painted his Aphrodite Emerging from the Sea. Praxiteles the sculptor, her lover, also created the Knidian Aphrodite from her.

13.590f-591a

Here Phryne not only carefully protects her body from public view, but also selects specific events at which her nudity will have maximum impact on those who see her. The religious setting of the two festivals makes her public nudity somehow divine, while potentially offering a legitimate reason for her to bathe publicly,[6] and Apelles and Praxiteles turn her into a goddess in response, creating a triangulation between woman, goddess, and artwork. As readers, we are left on the shore gazing at her as she bathes, while we simultaneously imagine the famous works based on her image.

Helen Morales sees the connection between these works of art and Phryne's stories as ekphrastic, yet she points out that rarely does the model get included in such descriptions; her article on Phryne and the psychology of the ekphrastic process explores what it means when "the model is put back into the picture."[7] One impact of including Phryne in discussions of those famous artworks that we might consider is how that link affects the reader's vision of her: with no significant physical descriptions of Phryne available other than "beautiful" or "pale,"[8] Apelles' painting and Praxiteles' sculpture provide a visual touchstone. Yet these touchstones are hardly more specific than the basic descriptions of her appearance. As Morales points out, the connection between image and woman provokes "ontological anxiety" since one cannot reach the woman herself in looking at the statue and vice versa,[9] and I would suggest this could also be true of the versions of Phryne envisioned by readers of Athenaeus. But the process by which the reader is invited to picture Phryne when her beauty is connected to famous artworks can also avoid that anxiety because it is a product of nostalgia. The reader can only access a fleeting impression of beauty through these anecdotes that is in turn impossible to pin down in the kind of detail one would expect from a lengthy ekphrasis, yet the mentions of Phryne are imbued with the *enargeia* that is characteristic of that literary technique. Were her visual image to be enduringly available to us, her beauty would find comparanda and therefore could be found unsuitable to many tastes, and so Phryne would descend from her pedestal.

Many of the literary passages in which Phryne's beauty is discussed seek to animate the statue through its model and so the genres in which this particular strand of Phryne's biographical tradition is found are also important to a consideration of image, woman, and nostalgia. In the introduction to this book, I discussed the anecdote as its own genre, which uses concision and pithiness, but it is also necessary to consider how the anecdotes are conveyed to us through quotations and references in sources like Athenaeus' *Deipnosophistae* or Plutarch's varied *Moralia*. These contexts cannot be ignored, with both the catch-all approach to accumulating knowledge and the dialogic nature of such sources shaping the information they present. Athenaeus has his speaker Myrtilus choose a story (the one quoted above) to align Phryne with elevated culture while defending her public nudity. Other sources like epigrams and fictional letters want to bring both the woman and the image to life by offering their voices "directly." These more transparently fictionalized depictions nevertheless operate on a similar basis to anecdotes, in their concision, call to visualize, and inclusion of clever punchlines. In some sense, these generic standards for anecdote, fictional letter, and epigram operate as aides-mémoire, helping readers sift through the vast amounts of text and information available in the Hellenistic and Imperial periods. If we consider the epigram within a collection or the anecdote within a dialogue, their mnemonic qualities become essential to the Hellenistic and Imperial trends toward collection and curation of information; both require *energeia* for this purpose. The anecdote as a means of sharing information was designed to be part of a larger collection, while the epigram, equally pithy and memorable, was, in the words of Alan Cameron, "destined by its very nature to be anthologized,"[10] and comes to us in collections that are carefully assembled by later editors, typically by theme, in much the same way that Athenaeus and Plutarch collect the anecdotes.

Praxiteles and His Muse

Connecting artists and their models with specific works of art was not unusual in the context of Hellenistic and later Roman literature in Greek and in Latin, especially when those connections were erotic. Famous artists were commonly used as the subjects of anecdotes that were created and collected through a similar process to that of the anecdotes about *hetairai* as the canon of visual art was established during the Hellenistic period. In the case of noted artists, there was the additional sense that through assessing anecdotes about their lives, greater insight into their art might be gained;[11] their relationships to models were common themes in these anecdotes that helped to animate the artists' lives and work. For example, Plutarch tells us that the painter Polygnotus depicted his likeness of Laodice in the Painted Stoa with Elpinice's features out of love for her (*Cimon* 4.5), while Pliny says that Pausias painted several versions of Glykera, his lover, with garlands (*NH* 35.125).[12] Praxiteles' anecdotes follow a similar literary historical pattern to those of Phryne, appearing first in the third century BCE, then becoming embellished in subsequent periods.[13] The stories about Phryne modeling for Praxiteles largely insist on their erotic connection; as I mentioned earlier in my discussion of the passage from Athenaeus connecting Phryne to Apelles and Praxiteles, a triangulation is created in these stories that connects the woman to the goddess to the artwork. In the sources that focus on Phryne and Praxiteles' relationship, we see a further association that brings the woman, the artwork, and the sculptor into creative alliance and emphasizes the importance of her connection to Praxiteles in her lasting fame.[14] These stories established a pattern that would be followed for centuries and revived in the modern world, as stories about models and artists continued to center on the connection between inspiration and erotic relationships, typically in the form of anecdotes.[15]

The sources that deal with Phryne and her relationship to Praxiteles do not have as much detailed focus on the Aphrodite of Knidos as one might expect,[16] but rather on the statue of Eros that Praxiteles is said to have gifted her out of his desire. Having already created an image of Eros (known as the "Archer Eros"), Praxiteles is said to have sculpted this second image of Eros in the middle of the fourth century BCE, inspired by his love for Phryne. The *hetaira* then selected it as a gift from among several of his sculptures. In Pausanias' version of the story, she asked Praxiteles for the most beautiful of his creations, which he, as her lover (*erastes*), agreed to, but he would not tell her which he thought was the most beautiful. Ever the clever *hetaira*, even in Pausanias' straightforwardly descriptive work, Phryne had a slave dash in to say that his workshop was on fire and many of his sculptures had been destroyed. Praxiteles lamented the loss of his Satyr and his Eros, thereby inadvertently confessing which of his works he found most beautiful and leading Phryne to make her choice (1.20.1-2).[17] No matter how she acquired the Eros, the sources agree that Phryne then had it installed in the sanctuary of that god in her hometown of Thespiai (Ath. 13.591a-b).[18] Indeed, it is only appropriate that a woman who became known as the embodiment of beauty and desire hailed from a town known for its ancient cult and panhellenic festival of Eros, the Erotidia.[19]

With so many visual remnants of Praxiteles' work remaining in the centuries after his lifetime, the stories of Phryne and Praxiteles and their relationship were ripe for further literary exploration, especially in genres that had an interest in visualization and material culture. To that end, I have chosen several epigrams indicative of this interest that blur the line between word and image while underscoring Phryne's erotic subjectivity. These poems, from the collection of epigrams written during the Hellenistic period and later known as the *Greek Anthology*, mention the Eros of Thespiai and feature Phryne, emphasizing the connection between desire and power, thereby binding the sculptor and his model together in the act of creation. There is also the potential that poems such as these were inscribed on the bases of copies of the statue,[20] thus combining reading, imagining, and viewing into a single act. As seen in the following poem attributed to Julianus, these short and pithy poems insist on the desire of Praxiteles for Phryne and therefore the power of a muse over an artist:

Κλίνας αὐχένα γαῦρον ὑφ' ἡμετέροισι πεδίλοις,
   χερσί με ληϊδίαις ἔπλασε Πραξιτέλης.
αὐτὸν γὰρ τὸν ἔρωτα τὸν ἔνδοθι
   κευθόμενον με
χαλκεύσας, Φρύνη δῶκε γέρας
   φιλίης·
ἡ δέ μιν αὖθις Ἔρωτι προσήγαγε·
   καὶ γὰρ ἐρῶντας

δῶρον Ἔρωτι φέρειν αὐτὸν Ἔρωτα
θέμις.

Bending his proud neck below my sandals,
Praxiteles molded me with captive hands.
For creating me in bronze,
his very love stashed within,
he gave me to Phryne as a present of love;
And she brought it in turn to Love,
For it is right that lovers bring the gift of Love itself to Love.

16. 203

Here Praxiteles is described as subservient to his desire for Phryne (with bent neck and hands captive to love), but Phryne's actions are also important beyond simply being the inspiration for the statue. Phryne is the one who enshrines the statue at Thespiai and brings Praxiteles' work to the god.

In Leonidas' epigram on the Eros at Thespiai, the theme of Praxiteles' captivity to Phryne's erotic sway continues, with an elision between the *hetaira* and Aphrodite, the mortal woman the origin of the sculptor's eros and the goddess mother of the god:

Θεσπιέες τὸν Ἔρωτα μόνον θεὸν ἐκ Κυθερείης
  ἄζοντ', οὐχ ἑτέρου γραπτὸν ἀπ' ἀρχετύπου,
ἀλλ' ὃν Πραξιτέλης ἔγνω θεόν· ὃν περὶ Φρύνῃ
  δερκόμενος, σφετέρων λύτρον ἔδωκε πόθων.

The Thespians revere only the god Eros, born of Cytherea,
  not carved from another model,
but from the god Praxiteles knew;
  recognizing that one in Phryne, he gave him as a ransom for their desire.

16. 206

The use of the term *lutron* ("ransom") is striking here, reiterating the concept of Praxiteles the prisoner of love, as well as the gifts of desire to a god who embodies that emotion. The use of *spheterōn* ("both of theirs"), implies a mutual desire between Phryne and Praxiteles.

Two more epigrams explore the statue as a gift between the two lovers as well as to the god himself. Tullius Geminus' epigram plays with the idea of gift as payment in the relationship between *hetaira* and artist, recalling some of the definitions of the term for that category of sex worker, both ancient and modern, that have focused on gift exchange. Rather than being concerned with a specific economic arrangement, however, this poem emphasizes the reciprocity that defines the relationship between a model and artist who are also lovers, tying them together in an erotic and artistic act, with Love the price of love:

Ἀντί μ' ἔρωτος Ἔρωτα βροτῷ θεὸν ὤπασε Φρυνη
  Πραξιτέλης, μισθὸν καὶ θεὸν εὑρόμενος.
ἡ δ' οὐκ ἠρνήθη τὸν τέκτονα· δεῖσε γάρ οἱ φρήν,
  μὴ θεὸς ἀντὶ τέχνης σύμμαχα τόξα λάβῃ.
ταρβεῖ δ' οὐκέτι που τὸν Κύπριδος, ἀλλὰ τὸν ἐκ σοῦ,
  Πραξίτελες, τέχνην μητέρ' ἐπισταμένη.

In return for love, Praxiteles granted me, Love the god,
to mortal Phryne, devising compensation as well as a god.
And she did not deny the sculptor; for she was deeply afraid
that the god would take up his bow to fight for the creation.
She is no longer concerned over the son of Cypris, but the one from you,
Praxiteles, recognizing skill as his mother.

16. 205

The web of reciprocity here is so tangled that the emotion, the god, and the statue are commingled while Phryne, overwhelmed by her own desire, cannot deny Praxiteles, who has created the statue to reciprocate for her love for him. In this context, there is no origin for their feelings, but instead an ongoing circuit of desire and creation between the woman, the sculptor, and the god. A similar dynamic is present in Geminus' epigram, which also brings Aphrodite into the mix as yet another co-creator:

Φρύνη τὸν πτερόεντα, τὸν εὐτέχνητον Ἔρωτα,
  μισθὸν ὑπὲρ λέκτρων, ἄνθετο Θεσπιέσιν.
Κύπριδος ἡ τέχνη ζηλούμενον, οὐκ ἐπιμεμφὲς
  δῶρον· ἐς ἀμφοτέρους δ' ἔπρεπε μισθὸς Ἔρως.
δοιῆς ἐκ τέχνης αἰνέω βροτόν, ὅς γε καὶ ἄλλοις
  δοὺς θεὸν ἐν σπλάγχνοις εἶχε τελειότερον.

Phryne dedicated the winged, beautifully-made Eros,
compensation for her lovemaking, to the Thespians.
The art of Cypris a jealous, blameless gift;

> Eros fittingly compensation for both.
> I praise the mortal for his double gift,
> who gave a god to others while he had the more perfect one inside.
>
> 6. 260

Here Phryne's relationship to Praxiteles, the reason he is giving her the gift, is explicitly sexual; Geminus says that it is a *misthos huper lektrōn* ("compensation for lovemaking"), with the term *lektra* ("couches/beds") a common euphemism for intercourse. The duality of Eros the god and *eros* as desire is also present here, once again tying the emotion inspired by Phryne to Praxiteles' act of creation.

Athenaeus, as always our most comprehensive collection of sources on Phryne, quotes an epigram that Praxiteles apparently selected for the pedestal of his Eros, which stood by the scene building in the Theater of Dionysus:

> Πραξιτέλης ὃν ἔπασχε διηκρίβωσεν Ἔρωτα
>   ἐξ ἰδίης ἕλκων ἀρχέτυπον κραδίης,
> Φρύνῃ μισθὸν ἐμεῖο διδοὺς ἐμέ. φίλτρα δὲ τίκτω
>   οὐκέτι τοξεύων, ἀλλ' ἀτενιζόμενος.

> Praxiteles portrayed precisely the Love he felt,
> pulling his model from his own heart,
> he gave me to Phryne as compensation for me. I no longer
> cast spells by shooting arrows, but by being gazed upon.
>
> Ath. 13. 591a=16. 204

This version of the epigram picks apart the tangled directionality of the poem I have just discussed: Praxiteles feels or even "suffers" (*epasche*) desire, which he then returns to Phryne in the form of the statue as compensation (*misthos*). This poem, however, introduces a further element to the equation of love and creation, vision, which is an essential aspect of understanding Phryne and her relationship to desire which I shall address shortly.

Although these epigrams focus solely on the statue of Eros, we can further conceive of it in its Thespian context, alongside one of Phryne (in the middle of the trio) and one of Aphrodite (on the viewer's right-hand side), all attributed to Praxiteles.[21] Plutarch, referring to the statue group, even suggests that Phryne was regarded as equal to Eros in sacredness (the term he uses is *sunieros*) by the Thespians (*Mor.* 753f).[22] A fictional letter by the second-century CE nostalgic miniaturist Alciphron who devotes an entire book to letters to and from *hetairai* in fourth-century Athens, addressed from Phryne to Praxiteles, further explores the connections between desire, vision, and creation that are tied up in Phryne's role as muse to the sculptor:

> …μὴ δείσῃς· ἐξείργασαι γὰρ πάγκαλόν τι χρῆμα, οἷον δή τι οὐδεὶς εἶδε πώποτε πάντων τῶν διὰ χειρῶν πονηθέντων, τὴν σεαυτοῦ ἑταίραν ἱδρύσας ἐν τεμένει. μέση γὰρ ἕστηκα ἐπὶ τῆς Ἀφροδίτης καὶ τοῦ Ἔρωτος ἅμα τοῦ σοῦ. μὴ φθονήσῃς δέ μοι τῆς τιμῆς· οἱ γὰρ ἡμᾶς θεασάμενοι ἐπαινοῦσι Πραξιτέλη, καὶ ὅτι τῆς σῆς τέχνης γέγονα οὐκ ἀδοξοῦσί με Θεσπιεῖς μέσην κεῖσθαι θεῶν. ἐν ἔτι τῇ δωρεᾷ λείπει, ἐλθεῖν σε πρὸς ἡμᾶς, ἵνα ἐν τῷ τεμένει μετ' ἀλλήλων κατακλινῶμεν. οὐ μιανοῦμεν γὰρ τοὺς θεοὺς οὓς αὐτοὶ πεποιήκαμεν. ἔρρωσο.

> …don't be afraid; for you have brought to fruition an absolutely beautiful thing, such a thing as no one ever saw of all the things made by hand, you have dedicated your very own *hetaira* in the sacred precinct. For I stand in the middle, by Aphrodite together with your Eros. But don't refuse me the honour; for those who gaze at us praise Praxiteles, and because of your art, the Thespians don't think me unworthy to be placed among the gods. One thing still remains for your gift, that you come to us, so that we may lie with each other in the sacred precinct. For we will not stain[23] the gods whom we ourselves have created. Farewell.

> 4.1[24]

In format alone, this letter toys with the idea of recreating a physical object, encouraging the reader to imagine Phryne penning the letter to Praxiteles or the recipient holding it in his hand, but at "Phryne's" invitation we also envision the statue group at Thespiai, with her image in the center. The letter itself highlights the position of Phryne's image between the statues of Aphrodite and Eros and so I have opted to translate the instances where Alciphron uses *hēmas* ("us," the first-person plural pronoun) in the plural, as opposed to the singular form ("me) that most translators have chosen,[25] in order to call attention to how Phryne envisions herself among the gods in the sacred precinct.

Even more so than the epigrams I have discussed here, Alciphron's letter creates a triangulation between sculpture, sculptor, and model:[26] she refers to the sculpture first (*ti chrēma*), then calls the image *hē seautou hetaira* ("your own *hetaira*"), before shifting into the first person when she writes "I stand in the middle (of the precinct)" (*mesē gar hestēka*).[27] Playing with person and pronouns in this way reflects the pattern observed in the epigrams discussed above; both Alciphron and the epigrammatists have an interest in confusing the authorial persona with the object (in the case of the epigrams, the statue Eros, and in the letter, Phryne),[28] but the letter takes that phenomenon to the extreme, expanding the dyad of Phryne and Praxiteles to include not just the image of Phryne, but also those of Eros and Aphrodite, to "dizzying" effect.[29] In doing so, Alciphron has Phryne seem to reassure the sculptor that praise of the statue is praise of his work rather than praise of her beauty ("for those who gaze at us praise Praxiteles"), but taking into consideration Alciphron's inconsistent application of person and pronouns, we see that Phryne collapses the distinction between herself and the statue when she tells Praxiteles that the one thing lacking in his gift is their sexual union. Here she emphasizes the primacy of her actual self over the statue and confirms it when she goes on to say that they will not defile the gods that they made, crediting her own role of erotic muse in the creation of Praxiteles' group of statuary.

As the "author" of this letter, Phryne controls the reader's gaze. When the reader of the letter/Praxiteles sees the sculpture/Phryne, they are directed to see her creation as much as his. In the words of Rosenmeyer, with her as the Muse, he is "merely the obedient assistant,"[30] and so her control of vision in this letter grants her erotic agency in addition to her artistic agency. Here I would like to pause to consider the role of visual erotics and agency in these sources on Phryne. I base this conversation largely on the work of Laura Mulvey on the cinematic gaze and how it can turn women in particular into objects of control and on the work of John Berger on women in art as both "surveyor and surveyed."[31] Mulvey's most influential assertion, one that has been applied to literature despite originally being devised as a commentary on film, is that pleasure in looking is divided between "active/male and passive/female", a concept which is built on the idea that subjectivity, the recognition and articulation of the self, originates in looking at one's own image.[32] Thus when watching a film, the spectator is encouraged to identify with the men onscreen, seeing them as more perfect, complete, and powerful versions of themselves;[33] when watching women, the spectator aligns with other characters in the film to see her as an erotic object.[34] Berger's understanding of vision in art and women is a simpler version of Mulvey's formulation: "men act and women appear. Men look at women. Women watch themselves being looked at."[35] In Berger's formulation, women's subjectivity is fundamentally reflexive and tied to their position as visual objects.

Yet when we turn back to Alciphron's letter, we see that Phryne, as "author" of the letter, controls the looking and troubles the paradigms laid out above. The agency displayed by Phryne here is shaped by two main factors: epistolarity, wherein a letter writer has ultimate control over the narrative they present in that letter,[36] and Phryne's fame, just as prevalent as that of her lover if not more.[37] As a woman whose fame only adds to the notoriety of the statue and so to the reputation of the sculptor, her claim to be its cocreator has merit. In the final portion of the letter, Phryne also guides the reader to envision the entire group, the three statues and the two humans alongside them, together in the sacred precinct, so it is no longer just Praxiteles who has been invited to look upon Phryne. In this invitation to lovemaking, with very little coyness employed, Phryne is an object that acts, drawing power over those who see her by being seen by them, just as the Eros from the epigram on the statue base from the Theater of Dionysus does.

We can develop this concept even further by adding in Kathryn Gutzwiller's argument that the epigrams discussed above have some basis in Aristotelian and Stoic theories that connect perception and artistic creativity: the sight of Phryne arouses a *phantasia* ("impression upon the soul") in Praxiteles which is *eros*, which he then expresses in sculpture.[38] If Phryne is the one directing Praxiteles' gaze, which causes his desire, as she does in Alciphron's letter, then by this logic she is the ultimate source of the sculpture.

Anna Peterson offers another helpful way of considering Phryne's self-presentation in this letter as she considers the ways that Alciphron's *Letters of Courtesans* look beyond the geographic boundaries of Athens. The visual nature of this letter is rooted in place, with the sanctuary of Eros at Thespiai the specific location where we are invited to imagine Phryne and Praxiteles being together. In Peterson's configuration, Alciphron uses the reader's desire to see Phryne's body as a means of leaving Attica behind.[39] This may also be a sly nod to Phryne's origins that reflects the *hetaira*'s renewed relationship to her hometown after she had achieved success and fame, with the Thespians happy to accept the gifts of her largesse. In this letter at least, Phryne the statue and Phryne the author find their way back to her hometown.

Phryne and the Aphrodite of Knidos

Although it is not explicitly mentioned in Alciphron's letter, Praxiteles' most famous and enduring connection to Phryne, the Aphrodite of Knidos, lingers in the background of that missive. As with many of Praxiteles' other works, including the Eros of Thespiai, the statue was famous throughout the Mediterranean, having been copied many times,[40] but more importantly, the original had become a tourist attraction in the sanctuary of Aphrodite at the city of Knidos in southwestern Asia Minor. (It remained there until being transported to Constantinople, where it was destroyed in a fire in the late fifth century CE.) It may have been produced during the period which Pliny identified as Praxiteles' floruit (the late 360s BCE) or perhaps around 350,[41] and so if an image of Phryne, she was likely relatively young (maybe in her early twenties) when it was produced.[42] Another option is that it was created in the 330s, shortly after Praxiteles had worked on the Mausoleum at Halicarnassus, not far from Knidos, meaning that Phryne would likely have been at least middle-aged at that point, if indeed she was the model for that statue. The image is typically understood as the first monumental female nude in ancient Greek art.[43] Pliny also offers an account of how the statue of Aphrodite, which he claims was the greatest marble statue in the whole world (*ante omnia est . . . in toto orbe terrarum*), ended up at Knidos. According to Pliny, Praxiteles had sculpted two images of Aphrodite, one clothed and the other nude. The people of the island of Kos (close enough to Knidos to be seen from that city on a clear day) had first choice and opted for the clothed version out of propriety. The people of Knidos bought the nude version, which drew a great deal of attention (the Bithynian king Nicomedes later offered to buy it) and turned the shrine into a tourist attraction (*NH* 36.20-21).

As with the Eros of Thespiai, Roman-era coinage from its home city gives us insight into the appearance of the original statue:[44] Aphrodite stands nude with her weight supported on one leg (in contrapposto), her head turned partially to the side, with her right hand gently resting over her vulva and the left holding some clothing that drapes down toward a hydria, with the vessel for water suggesting bathing. Her hair is bound up and she wears an armlet on her upper left arm.[45] The pose suggests a narrative to the viewer, but an incomplete one: is she about to bathe or just coming from a bath?[46] Does the hand covering her

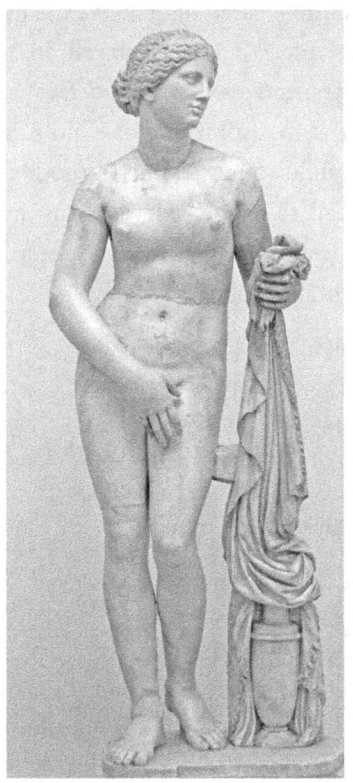

Figure 2 Aphrodite of Knidos, Copy of Praxiteles; restorer: Ippolito Buzzi (Italian, 1562–1634), Musei nazionale romano di palazzo Altemps (8619). Photographer Marie-Lan Nguyen.

genitals suggest that she has been surprised, or is it a recognition that she is being viewed in public? Does her sidelong look suggest shyness from the viewer's gaze or does she turn toward someone else? Because of her complex pose, each new perspective on the statue offers a shift in narrative.[47] The statue would also have been painted, if not the entire surface of the marble then at least its details such as facial features, hair, and jewelry, adding to its complex appearance. The effect of her attire and appearance (the hairstyle, the depilated vulva, etc.) may have suggested a woman preparing herself to seduce someone.[48] It was often referred to as the "Knidia" and worshipped on site at Knidos as Aphrodite *Euploia* ("Aphrodite of the Fair Voyage").[49] The statue most likely stood in the round structure located high above the port where visitors to the sanctuary would disembark:[50] being displayed in the round would have allowed viewers many perspectives on its multi-faceted image.

As with Praxiteles' Eros, the Aphrodite of Knidos inspired many epigrams marvelling at the artist's ability and melding the goddess with her image.[51] The following poem attributed to a poet named Plato imagines Aphrodite as a tourist, visiting her own image in its shrine, and reckoning with several of the aspects of its display mentioned above:

Ἡ Παφίη Κυθέρεια δὶ οἴδματος ἐς Κνίδον ἦλθε,
   βουλομένη κατιδεῖν εἰκόνα τὴν ἰδίην·
πάντη δ' ἀθρήσασα περισκέπτῳ ἐνὶ χώρῳ,
   φθέγξατο· "Ποῦ γυμνὴν εἶδέ με Πραξιτέλης;"
Πραξιτέλης οὐκ εἶδεν ἃ μὴ θέμις· ἀλλ' ὁ σίδηρος
   ἔξεσεν οἷ' ἂν Ἄρης ἤθελε τὴν Παφίην.

Paphian Cythera came through the sea to Knidos,
wishing to look at her own image;
gazing at it in its spot open on every side,
she uttered: "Where did Praxiteles see me nude?"
Praxiteles did not look upon that which was not allowed,
but the iron carved the Paphian as Ares would wish her.

16. 160

Praxiteles' Aphrodite seems not to have made an immediate splash upon its installment at Knidos, despite being a great work by a widely renowned artist, unless we accept that the Athenian play (Alexis' *The Woman from Knidos/The Knidian Goddess*) mentioned in Chapter 1 was in some way connected to the statue. Coins featuring the statue did not appear until the Romans had taken over that area, and the poetry that comments on it did not appear until well into the Hellenistic period, around the second century BCE. As exemplified in the epigram mentioned above, the nudity of the statue was commonly remarked upon in literature from that time onward, although this may not have been the sole reason for its fame.[52] The late Hellenistic period is also the point at which copies of the Aphrodite of Knidos began to appear. Although there is no sudden appearance of new material on Phryne and Praxiteles' relationship at this point, we can contemplate a scenario in which the increasing fascination with all things Classical, the formation of an artistic canon for

Greek art, and the continued circulation of anecdotes about the *hetairai* came together to contribute to a surge in its notoriety.

Indeed the relationship of Phryne and Praxiteles offers an instructive example of how the smallest details of her biography are seized upon in wider discourse and circulated on end, especially in modern scholarship. One of the only remaining sources that directly links Phryne to the Aphrodite of Knidos (as opposed to other works of Praxiteles) is the passage from Athenaeus that I included at the beginning of this chapter and yet it is one of the most often-repeated details of Phryne's biography in modern scholarship.[53] Any scholar who wishes to discuss the Aphrodite of Knidos needs to wrangle with Phryne in some way. I repeat the relevant portion of Athenaeus here: "Praxiteles the sculptor, her lover, also created the Knidian Aphrodite from her" (καὶ Πραξιτέλης δὲ ὁ ἀγαλματοποιὸς ἐρῶν αὐτῆς τὴν Κνιδίαν Ἀφροδίτην ἀπ' αὐτῆς ἐπλάσατο, 13.591a). Other sources, including Pliny, who otherwise discusses the Knidia in great detail and mentions Phryne modeling for other statues by Praxiteles, do not mention Phryne as the model for this statue. The second-century CE Christian theologian Clement of Alexandria, in his discussion of images of the pagan gods depicted as the artists' lovers, does mention that Praxiteles had carved the Aphrodite of Knidos in the image of his "beloved" (the term he uses is *erōmenē*, rather than *hetaira*), but he calls this woman "Cratina." Quizzically, Clement then says the following about Phryne, identifying her with the term *hetaira*: "And at the time when the Thespian *hetaira* Phryne was flourishing, all the painters made their images of Aphrodite depictions of the beauty of Phryne," (Φρύνη δὲ ὁπηνίκα ἤνθει ἡ ἑταίρα ἡ Θεσπιακή, οἱ ζωγράφοι πάντες <τὰς > τῆς Ἀφροδίτης εἰκόνας πρὸς τὸ κάλλος ἀπεμιμοῦντο Φρύνης, *Protr.* 4.4.35-6). This passage, in combination with Athenaeus' anecdote about Phryne's nude appearance at the festival, suggests that there were well-established connections between Phryne and images of Aphrodite by this point in the Imperial period. Add this to the anecdotes related to Phryne's public nudity and the often-commented upon relationship between Phryne and Praxiteles, and it is no surprise for an author like Athenaeus to associate her with the sculptor's most famous work, famous in part for its beguiling and highly visible nudity. We see here an example of Elias' coercive fragment at work, with a single sentence leading to centuries of scholarship and art reckoning with the connection between Phryne and the Aphrodite of Knidos.

As I alluded to in my earlier discussion of Alciphron's fictional letter from Phryne to Praxiteles, the epistolographer included a sly nod to this connection in the *hetaira*'s invitation to her lover. Like many other statues that feature in epigrams and as exemplified in several of the epigrams on the Eros of Thespiai, the Knidia as she appears in literature is often construed as being alive or conscious in some sense, particularly through the use of first-person.[54] The slippage between object and real woman is often commented upon in stories about the statue, such as in Pseudo-Lucian's account of travelers coming to see the statue. First, one visitor calls out and tries to kiss the statue when he first sees it, while another begins shouting uncontrollably about its great beauty when he sees it from behind (*Am.* 13-14).[55] But it is the following event in Pseudo-Lucian's story that allows us to understand the final punchline in Alciphron's letter: the statue has a stain on one of its thighs, which the temple attendant reveals to the visitors was left behind by a young man who had fallen in love with the statue of the goddess, contrived to be locked into the temple with it, and left the mark of his semen behind, in the words of Pseudo-Lucian, a "new Anchises" (*ho kainos Anchises, Am.* 16).[56] Thus when Alciphron's Phryne tells Praxiteles not to worry because they will not "stain" the gods they have created, she gestures to this other famous story of desire inside a sacred precinct, with the word *miainō* carrying the sense of both a literal and metaphorical pollution.[57]

Another joke on the connection between the *hetaira* and the sculptor that likely refers to the Aphrodite of Knidos also comes from Athenaeus, at the end of a string of anecdotes illustrating her great wit. When a particularly money-hungry client attempts to endear himself to her by calling her "Praxiteles' little Aphrodite" (*Aphrodision . . . Praxitelous*),[58] she retorts with "and you're Pheidias' Eros" (Ath. 13.585f), suggesting not that he resembles any statue by that famous sculptor, but alluding to the scandal in which Pheidias was accused of embezzling gold intended for the statue of Athena in the Parthenon and playing on the meaning of the god's name.[59]

The way that this joking anecdote and Alciphron's wry letter conflate Phryne, the statue, and Aphrodite suggest something more about the specific goddess with whom Phryne is so often associated. If we return to Athenaeus' story of Phryne inspiring Apelles to paint his "Aphrodite Rising from the Sea" after her nude appearance at the festival, we see the ways in which Phryne's nudity is depicted as inspiring a near-religious awe in those who saw her. If Phryne did emerge from the sea in this way, she was most likely knowingly engaging with a long-standing set of stories and images depicting the goddess' birth. The carving from the late fifth-century BCE Ludovisi throne is an example of such imagery that pre-dates Phryne's lifetime: in the carvings on the throne Aphrodite rises from the water, her wet clothing clinging to her torso. If indeed she was as cautious about sharing the sight of her body as Athenaeus suggests, then this visual association was a calculated way of suggesting that Phryne too was desire embodied. Yet statues like the Aphrodite of Knidos are not always a straightforward depiction of desire, available to any viewer for their immediate consumption and Phryne was not available to anyone who wished to be with her either. Pseudo-Lucian's story of the young man who stains the statue ends with him taking his own life in despair. When viewing the Aphrodite of Knidos and considering the stories that connect Phryne to various depictions of that goddess we see potential for the real woman to exercise as much control of the gaze toward her as the fictionalized version from Alciphron.

We can also consider the influence of the story of Pygmalion on the connection between Phryne and the Aphrodite of Knidos. As preserved in Ovid's *Metamorphoses*, the sculptor creates an image of his ideal woman, prays to Aphrodite, and discovers that his sculpture has come to life (10.243-97). With earlier versions of the Pygmalion myth in circulation around the time that the statue came to even greater prominence (*c*. late third century BCE),[60] the idea of a man in love with a statue also resonates in the story of the origin of the semen stain on the statue.[61] In Ovid's version, the statue comes to life just as she sees her lover, Pygmalion, for the first time (10. 294), and in this coming to life and looking back there is a kind of wish fulfillment on the part of the one viewing the statue, a validation of their fantasy that the statue can reciprocate their desire.[62] Making Phryne the living, breathing Aphrodite of Knidos, a statue already subject to such fantasies, is in one sense an extension of the crude fantasies that left the statue with a stained thigh, the insistence on Phryne's reciprocal desire for Praxiteles a way to make the object of desire desiring in return.[63] A more positive reading of the connection between statue and living woman, one introduced by Patricia Rosenmeyer in her chapter on Phryne's letter in Alciphron, is that the epistolographer's assumption of Phryne's voice inverts the typical Pygmalion theme by giving the statue its own voice.[64]

A further insight that we may gain from the tenuous connection between Phryne and the Aphrodite of Knidos comes from the ways that both gained prominence in antiquity and beyond. Although many tourists would have visited Praxiteles' statue at Knidos, most people who encountered its image in the ancient world would have done so through the many recreations that made their way around the Mediterranean. The image of the Knidia would have circulated but only "a vague, mutable, perhaps only symbolic one,"[65] that in some cases would have been poorly executed and an inaccurate representation of its appearance. Nonetheless, these images would have communicated a certain sense of cultural awareness and perhaps longing for a different time on the part of their owners. The Phryne of anecdote is not unlike the many copies of the Aphrodite of Knidos, left with only a symbolic connection to the real woman yet still able to convey a great deal for those who wrote and read about her. In Hellenistic and then again in Imperial Roman culture, the idea of both the statue and the woman took precedence over the real thing again and again.

Praxiteles' Other Portraits of Phryne

Even if the connections between Phryne and the Aphrodite of Knidos are frail, she was commonly understood to have modeled for other statues by Praxiteles, and it is this connection of model and artist that has informed a great deal of the ancient and modern receptions of Phryne, especially in Italian cinema, which I will explore in detail in Chapter 4. In antiquity, Pliny, for example, mentions that Praxiteles' statue of a smiling *meretrix* (a Latin term which I presume to be Pliny's equivalent of *hetaira*) is a portrait of Phryne. In his description of that statue, we see a similar reciprocal dynamic between the two as in the epigrams on the Eros of Thespiai, with the desire of Praxiteles and her reward for him in return: "and they detect in her the love of the artist and on the face of the *hetaira* his reward" (*deprehenduntque in ea amorem artificis et mercedem in vultu meretrices*, NH 34.70).[66]

The portrait of Phryne by Praxiteles that seems to have drawn the most opprobrium, however, is the one made of bronze and then gilded before being installed in the sanctuary at Delphi.[67] Athenaeus says that it was commissioned by the people of Thespiai and mounted on a column of Pentelic marble (13.591b),[68] while Pausanias claims that it was Phryne herself who dedicated the statue (10.15.1).[69] If so, this would have been a very bold move on her part but an act in keeping with the kind of woman who had accumulated a great deal of wealth and was eager to show it off, the kind of woman who appears in anecdotes like the one in which she offers to rebuild the walls of Thebes. The inscription of her name, her father's name, and her hometown on its base also suggests a claim on Phryne's part to legitimate citizenship at Thespiai.[70] In any case, the idea of a gilded statue of a sex worker in such a prestigious and holy place proved ripe for commentary from those who thought it did not belong there.[71]

The anecdotes about the gilded statue at Delphi also provide several further examples of philosophers and *hetairai* being placed in opposition to one another. Diogenes Laertius relates that the Cynic Diogenes, a common foil for the *hetairai*, upon seeing the statue, wrote upon it "from the excess of the Greeks" (ἀπὸ τῆς τῶν Ἑλλήνων ἀκρασίας, 6.2.60). Plutarch tells of Diogenes' fellow Cynic, Crates, making a similar comment upon seeing the statue (he called it a "monument to the Greeks' excess," τῆς τῶν Ἑλλήνων ἀκρασίας τρόπαιον, *Mor.* 336d). The same author inserts a nearly identical comment into a dialogue that features a tour of Delphi. When one character, Sarapion, points out where the famous *hetaira* Rhodopis would dedicate a tithe from her earnings, another responds with indignation. Sarapion responds by pointing up to the golden statue of Phryne, with a brief disquisition on her real name, Mnesarete (*Mor.* 401a). The conversation continues as they consider how to defend Phryne from Crates' charge (i.e., erecting a monument to excess), which a man named Theon does, accusing them of excluding Phryne from a place filled with offerings that have come from murder, war, and plunder, when she is but a woman who "made use of the beauty of her body not in a way fit for a free person [i.e., for sex work]," χρησάμενον ὥρᾳ σώματος οὐκ ἐλευθερίως (*Mor.*401c). For placing the statue there, Theon says that Praxiteles ought to be commended for placing the golden *hetaira* beside golden kings, thus putting the lie to wealth being something admirable (*Mor.* 401d). The "Corinthian Discourse," attributed to Dio Chrysostom, the first-century CE orator, ironically defends the golden statue's placement (and all statues) (37.28), while Aelian, writing his miscellany in the early third century CE, repeats the claim that it is there due to excess, although he only attributes this to some, not all, of the Greeks (*VH* 9.32). Catherine Keesling argues that this statue, along with the others associated with Phryne at Thespiai and Knidos is the beginning of the trend of assimilating sex workers to Aphrodite observed in the Hellenistic period, especially with royal mistresses being depicted as the goddess,[72] and so this opprobrium is more a literary than a real-life phenomenon. Yet the placement of this statue, near images of Archidamus of Sparta and Phillip of Macedon may have also been a clever nod to her Boeotian origins, since Archidamus was traditional enemy of that part of Greece, and she was associated with Hypereides, a notoriously anti-Macedonian figure (see Chapter 3 on Hypereides' connections to Phryne).[73]

Based on the sheer number of sources linking Phryne to Praxiteles, I would suggest that we can safely associate the two historical figures. While the substance of their relationship remains unclear, the monuments to their collaborations, whether erotic or not, testify to a real and ongoing connection between the two as well as hinting at the great wealth she must have acquired by the point that the golden statue was dedicated at Delphi. Whether Phryne was the model for the Aphrodite of Knidos is another question that requires further proof for a definitive answer,[74] but in Athenaeus' connection of artwork, artist, and model, as well as in its later receptions, we see a desire to animate one of the most famous statues of the ancient Greek canon by inserting one of the most famous Greek women into the story of its creation.

Phryne's Beauty and Nudity

As I mentioned at the beginning of this chapter, very little description of Phryne's appearance remains, beyond the suggestion that her pale complexion let to the nickname Phryne ("toad," *Mor.* 401a). Mentions of her beauty are most often linked to the moments when she is seen or depicted naked and so a consideration of Phryne, nudity, and desire in light of presentations of the female body in Greek antiquity is called for here. When she is naked in public, Phryne's beauty is powerful: it inspires some of the most famous works of ancient Greek art and saves her life at trial (I will explore her nudity at trial in the following chapter as well as its cultural resonance in *fin-de-siècle* Paris in

Chapter 4). Thus when Phryne is seen without clothing, she is not naked in the sense of being vulnerable, but she is nude and her beautiful body becomes a compelling and forceful presence. The dichotomy between being naked and nude in the context of creative representation is perhaps a false one (as many dichotomies ultimately are),[75] but examining the ways that nudity operates in the sources on Phryne in light of thinking on the female nude in art may prove useful, since Phryne is a figure whom we can only consider in the context of creative representations and whose literary presence is bound up with the art historical record.

The standard work on nudity in European art is Kenneth Clark's *The Nude: A Study in Ideal Form*, first published in 1956.[76] Tracing the history of nudity in art beginning with Classical Greece, Clark's study begins with the distinction he offers between being naked, a state of vulnerability and embarrassment, and being nude, the body "re-formed" in confidence and prosperity.[77] Clark's nude is an idealized fantasy that possesses formal qualities, whereas nakedness in this understanding suggests a lack of mediation; kept out of sight by his nude is the imperfect reality of the naked human body. Although he discusses both male and female nudes, desire forms the center of Clark's discussion when it comes to female nudes;[78] for him the female nude is often an expression of the artist's personal appetites and so becomes a space in which viewers and critics can explore their own desires. (We might think back to the epigrams on Praxiteles' Eros and their emphasis on desire made tangible here.) John Berger also plays an important part in the conversation on artistic nudity, with the second episode of his 1972 four-part series *Ways of Seeing* focused on the female nude. To Berger, the female nude is intimately tied to spectacle, that is, nudity requires a spectator and entails objectification. Nudity prevents the recognition of the individual on display.[79] However, Nicholas Chare and Ersy Contogouris add further nuance to this formulation, showing how an image of a nude woman can "resist objectification through acknowledging a sitter's singularity and, by, extension, their subjectivity."[80] Lingering in the background of both Clark and Berger's configurations of nudity and nakedness is the suggestion that there is a real woman in a real body that is ultimately separate from the nude; in Nanette Solomon's discussion of this phenomenon as related to the Aphrodite of Knidos, the phenomenon of nudity aligns the viewer of the nude with the artist, seeking to understand his creation.[81] In all of this, there is an insistence on the artist as male and the one posing as female;[82] the male artist refines the "reality" presented by the female model.

In her survey of scholarship on the female nude, Lynda Nead argues against this nakedness vs. nudity discourse on the grounds that the body as formulated by society, culture, and the psyche is too dense with meaning to ever be "outside of representation,"[83] that is the "real" woman's body is just as heavily signified as that of the nude. She points out how Clark works to separate spiritual and sensual by categorizing female nudes into two types: the Celestial Venus and the Earthly Venus, with intentional shades of Plato's *Symposium*.[84] In Clark's insistence that the nude is seductive without tipping over into obscenity,[85] Nead finds a sense of limitation: the nude is restrained while obscenity is "defined in terms of excess."[86] Images of undressed women that have such an excessive quality are by Clark's understanding, not art.[87]

Although Nead and other feminist scholars rightfully question this distinction in the realm of visual depictions of the nude, concerns over excess and the vulnerability of nakedness set against the idea of the artistic nude can help us think through the implications of the literary depictions of Phryne's nudity. Since in ancient Greek art the nude woman is a category that is marked as significant (we must ask why she is not clothed),[88] and in public life this would be absolutely remarkable, it is essential to explore what it means when Phryne is nude in our literary sources. I am not trying to force Phryne into Clark's and Berger's boxes, but she demands to be read as both a literary creation and a woman exercising agency in her self-representation within that literary context. As explored in my discussion of Alciphron's ventriloquism of her voice, understanding Phryne means looking at how and why authors were so interested in her agency and why they depicted such exceptional expressions of it. It is clear from the contexts in which her nudity or nude images of her are mentioned that the contrast between sublimity and excess informs how her body and beauty are meant to be received. As I mentioned above, when Phryne appears nude at the festival in the passage from Athenaeus, she is not just observed naked by chance, but presents herself as exalted with intention, and ultimately as sacred once Apelles turns her into his "Aphrodite Rising from the Sea," then twice over as Praxiteles' Aphrodite of Knidos.[89] The epigram on the Knidia that I have quoted above considers what such divine beauty and its attendant power mean, with the clarification that Praxiteles was not sneaking an illicit peek at the goddess

("Praxiteles did not look upon that which was not allowed"). In the words of Bonfante, it is only the gods who "can afford to be naked ... without being diminished,"[90] and so Aphrodite's nudity is part of her divinity;[91] seeing the entirety of her beauty means facing the goddess in all her power.[92] Translated to Phryne in Athenaeus, the power in the *hetaira*'s beauty to inspire not just art, but *the* most canonical depictions of a goddess associated with desire and beauty, removes the vulnerability that would normally be associated with being naked, especially in public and especially as a politically powerless sex worker. Beauty in this case becomes subjectivity (per Chare and Contogouris' formulation).

However, if we return to Clark's concern with obscenity and its connection to excess in art, we can see the limitations of the power of Phryne's beauty. Although it is unclear from the sources whether the golden statue of Phryne placed at Delphi depicted her nude or not, the reactions to her image being placed within such a major sanctuary suggest that the mere presence of her image (i.e., her body) in such a space is obscene, with their near-unanimous emphasis on the excess such an inclusion signifies. The beauty of her body and what it entailed for her career is the central concern here, as Theon articulates in Plutarch's dialogue: "she made use of the beauty of her body in a way not fit for a free person [i.e., for sex work]" (χρησάμενον ὥρᾳ σώματος οὐκ ἐλευθερίως, *Mor*.401c). Phryne's use of her body and therefore the representation of it ceases to be a strength in this context and becomes a vulnerability when she is simply Phryne the sex worker and no longer associated with Aphrodite. Andrew Stewart's reading of Aphrodite is helpful here as well: the sexuality of Aphrodite was the center of her power and could not be restrained, while representing it could challenge the stability of the patriarchy.[93] When Phryne's body was disentangled from the divine aspects of desire, the destabilizing threat of her sexuality was laid bare, and the charges of excess ensued.

It is this complicated erotics of looking that Phryne and her beauty embody: like the Aphrodite of Knidos in the epigram, her example shows that "power can lie on both sides of the looking and being-looked-at divide."[94] When later authors like Alciphron turn to her visual legacy, it is precisely this complex and reciprocal dynamic of the relationship between desire and vision that they explore. Once again the Knidia and its careful arrangement of pose, always redirecting the viewer's narrative, offer us a means of thinking about Phryne's use of her beauty through nudity. I return to Andrew Stewart, via Clark, Berger and Mulvey, to think about what female subjectivity means if we assume a male gaze. For Phryne to claim subjectivity in such a context, and certainly we can assume such a male-dominated context in fourth-century Athens and in the later texts that depict it, she needed to both placate the gaze (by showing her nude body) and subvert it (by aligning herself with Aphrodite).[95] Phryne's body, and more correctly the literary versions of it, became a space to work through the tangled implications of men's desire for sex workers, and even for women more generally, in societies that did not offer much space to female sexual desire.

Nostalgia and the Body

By using Phryne to recall canonical works of art, both Alciphron and Athenaeus are indulging in what I have argued elsewhere is a kind of visual nostalgia, one that stops short of a full ekphrasis, but rather inspires a momentary sensation of nostalgia that is designed to be transitory when the images are briefly envisioned.[96] In the examples I have discussed above from these authors, Phryne's body is central to this process, as we envision her beauty alongside Apelles' painting and Praxiteles' sculpture. In this way, Phryne becomes nostalgia embodied, in the most literal sense. Both artists had reputations for creating art that was hyper-realistic (which itself may be a commentary on art-historical trends toward naturalism during the fourth century),[97] so attaching a model to the image was an extension of this discourse. The period during which Praxiteles and Apelles were working on their naturalistic crafts was also the period in which Plato's theory of forms was circulating,[98] and so we may think of Phryne the model as a means of reconciling that suspicion of mimesis with acclaimed artworks. As with the animated sculptures of epigram, the connection between Phryne and the famous depictions of Aphrodite helped navigate the sometimes discomfiting experience of viewing great beauty, whether embodied by a woman or a work of art.

Additionally, in the Greek literature of the Imperial period, of which both Alciphron and Athenaeus are prime examples, the bodies of the *hetairai* were certainly treated as metaphors for creative craft, display, and performance, since these were women who had to carefully present themselves to the public and thus were understood as talented practitioners of artifice.[99] Much of this artifice was centered on disguising the fact that as sex-workers, they used their bodies to make a living (as in Theon's comment from Plutarch discussed above). Yet when we consider the presence of a figure like Phryne in literature and the way that her body and beauty are foregrounded, especially when she is associated with famous works of art featuring nudity, that artifice becomes less obvious as her body becomes central to our vision of her. The spectacle of Phryne's body, through its association with canonical works of art then becomes a means of conjuring the wider spectacle of Classical Athens. As I have discussed here, the vision of Phryne's body in the epigrams, Athenaeus, and Alciphron is heavily mediated, first through our images of the Aphrodite of Knidos and her carefully arranged pose (itself subject to many layers of interpretation as we sort through the varied copies of that statue) as well as through Apelles' painting, which again, we must reconstruct through various pieces of art created in its image. Then we must reckon with the literary uses of Phryne's body too.

As with the idea of the nude (vs. naked) image of a woman that suggests a "real" woman lurking in the background, all of this imagining Phryne and using her and the other *hetairai* as a means of conjuring up the Classical past, suggests that the "real" version of it also lurks behind the literary versions. And as with the images of nudes that align the viewer with the creator of the image, the reader of works like Alciphron's letters or Athenaeus' dinner conversation is aligned with those authors, gazing at what they assess to be "real" and remaking it with their words. The process by which a body and its changeability can be frozen in time through its depiction in art or literature mirrors the way that a complex and ever-changing city can be made static. Both processes allow for a more comfortable consumption of the beautiful body and city by the reader/viewer. And as the nude presents something that seems unmediated at first, but that upon closer inspection, reveals the artistry in its production, the reader's appreciation of the nostalgic vision of the past unfolds into recognition of the creative work required to create that vision.

Using the bodies of Phryne and the *hetairai* as they appear in Imperial literature to understand the processes behind literary nostalgia also allows us to see how much artifice is required for it to be successful and therefore how fragile that nostalgia is. I return to the discourse on the bodies of sex workers in Cynculus and Myrtilus' conversation from Athenaeus to illustrate that fragility. Cynculus' invective against *hetairai* concentrates on sex workers' bodies. In quotations from comedies describing brothels, the girls and women working there are described as naked and lined up for easy inspection by potential clients (13.568e and 13.569b), while other selections take aim at the ways that sex workers manipulate their appearances (13.557f and 13.568a-d).[100] When executed clumsily or transparently, unsuccessful deception ceases to be artifice; when considering nostalgia through this lens, we can see how easily the illusory world it creates can fall apart. Even within Athenaeus' text, the same *hetairai* can be unappealing, old, or ugly as in Cynculus' view, or figures of great beauty and charm, as in Myrtilus', with those depictions aligning with the two speakers' variant appreciation for Classical culture itself.

In this nexus of beauty, body, and nostalgia, Phryne's body is never just a body and her beauty is never just the sum of her physical features. When we strip her down, so to speak, and look closely at what little remains in the literary record, we are able to see just how much of her we are called to envision on our own and how much of the artistic record we have projected onto her. When we "see" Phryne in the sources, what we see is our own understanding of beauty, according to each viewer's expectations of what that means. In the following chapter, I will consider just how the broader reputation of Phryne as a great, even sacred, beauty contributed to narratives of her trial and how they were shared. For now, we may think about how understanding Phryne's reputation for beauty and her connections to famous artworks grew alongside one another and became a fundamental part of her story.

3

Phryne on Trial

Phryne's courtroom tangle with Euthias, perhaps the most famous story in her biographical tradition, also has the most fulsome set of literary sources to support it out of the most famous stories about the *hetaira*. The sources that relate the story of her trial and desperate appearance before the jury come from the usual Imperial Greek sources (Athenaeus and Alciphron), Hellenistic treatises, studies of rhetoric, and the fragments of a single comic play; these sources tell a story that encapsulates many of the themes I have discussed so far: the power of Phryne's nudity (especially in public), the use of that imagery to invoke the world of fourth-century Athens, the vulnerability of foreign-born sex workers in that political and legal context, and the labile status of such women. In the evidence for this trial, which may have happened but very likely did not conclude with Phryne being stripped in the middle of the courtroom, we find a woman, who, like Neaira and Alke, was understood to subvert Athenian ideals, yet Phryne was ultimately acquitted.[1] We also find a woman whose reputation had become so prominent that it likely shifted the narrative of the trial to accommodate prevailing ideas about her. The trial and its fabled conclusion then became fodder for some of the most famous receptions of Phryne, especially in the nineteenth century, which I will explore in the next chapter, and so it provides an excellent case study for how the process of fictionalizing augments the cultural impact of individuals and events.

The key details of the trial, as gleaned from the sources mentioned above, are as follows: Phryne was brought up on charges of *asebeia* (translated as "impiety," but flexible enough to include "any act that could be construed as violating a rule ... affecting sacred matters"),[2] seemingly because of her negative influence on the youth of Athens via introducing a new god, bringing together groups of men and women to worship, and improper behavior at the

Lyceum, a sanctuary of Apollo located on the outskirts of the city (the charges are listed in Anon. Seg. *Ars Rhet.* 215).[3] These charges, brought by a man named Euthias who is linked to Phryne romantically by some of our sources,[4] necessitated a public indictment, known as a *graphē*, meaning that any citizen could indict her rather than just the aggrieved party,[5] and she was brought to trial before a jury of Athenian citizens. There was also no limit on the potential punishment, meaning that prosecutors could propose any penalty up to capital punishment.[6] A comment by the legal scholar Harpocration on the speech given by Hypereides in her defence claims that the deity she introduced was called "Isodaites," which the scholar calls "a foreign deity, worshipped by common and trifling ladies" (ξενικός τις δαίμων, ᾧ τὰ δημώδη γύναια καὶ μὴ πάνυ σπουδαῖα ἐτέλει, Fr. 177 Jensen).

The most infamous detail of the trial was its conclusion, a detail likely added later in order to reflect more closely the stories told about Phryne's beauty and her association with Apelles' and Praxiteles' Aphrodites as well as longstanding literary traditions about female supplication: when it seemed as though Phryne would lose the case, Hypereides stepped forward, removed her clothing, and the sight of her beautiful breasts (or entire body according to Quintilian, 2.15.9) caused the jurors to acquit her. According to Athenaeus, Euthias never prosecuted another case and a decree was passed preventing the display of the accused while the jury made their decision. Hypereides' histrionics while pleading on behalf of Phryne also led to another decree banning lament for another person in the courtroom (Ath. 13.590e-f). Taken together, the ways that Phryne's nudity and Hypereides' dramatic use of rhetoric captured Imperial imaginations show that such theatrics were not thought to be out of the question in the courtroom.[7]

The three most fulsome sources on the trial come from Athenaeus, in which Myrtilus relates the story of it shortly before he tells of Phryne's emergence from the sea, Plutarch's biography of Hypereides, and three of Alciphron's letters, which fictionalize the reactions of *hetairai* to the trial. Athenaeus' full account of the trial is as follows:

ἦν δ' ἡ Φρύνη ἐκ Θεσπιῶν. κρινομένη δὲ ὑπὸ Εὐθίου τὴν ἐπὶ θανάτῳ ἀπέφυγεν· διόπερ ὀργισθεὶς ὁ Εὐθίας οὐκ ἔτι εἶπεν ἄλλην δίκην, ὥς φησιν Ἕρμιππος. ὁ δὲ Ὑπερείδης συναγορεύων τῇ Φρύνῃ, ὡς οὐδὲν ἤνυε λέγων ἐπίδοξοί τε ἦσαν οἱ δικασταὶ καταψηφιούμενοι, παραγαγὼν αὐτὴν εἰς τοὐμφανὲς καὶ περιρρήξας τοὺς χιτωνίσκους γυμνά τε τὰ στέρνα ποιήσας τοὺς ἐπιλογικοὺς οἴκτους ἐκ τῆς ὄψεως αὐτῆς ἐπερρητόρευσεν δεισιδαιμονῆσαί τε ἐποίησεν τοὺς δικαστὰς καὶ τὴν ὑποφῆτιν καὶ ζάκορον Ἀφροδίτης ἐλέῳ χαρισαμένους μὴ ἀποκτεῖναι. καὶ ἀφεθείσης ἐγράφη μετὰ ταῦτα ψήφισμα μηδένα οἰκτίζεσθαι τῶν λεγόντων ὑπέρ τινος μηδὲ βλεπόμενον τὸν κατηγορούμενον ἢ τὴν κατηγορουμένην κρίνεσθαι.

Phryne was from Thespiae. When she was indicted by Euthias on a capital charge, she was acquitted; in his anger over this, Euthias never brought another charge, as Hermippus says. Hypereides argued on behalf of Phryne, and when he accomplished nothing with his speech and the jurors seemed likely to vote against her, bringing her before them he ripped her robes and bared her breasts and while he was giving his final words he lamented at the sight of her and caused the jurors to feel religious awe at the agent and servant of Aphrodite and to not put her to death as they indulged in pity. And when she was acquitted, after this a decree was passed that no speaker lament on behalf of anyone nor an accused man or woman be judged while on display.

Ath. 13.590d-f

Athenaeus' version is notable for its addition of religious awe to the jurors' response to Phryne, which may have come from Hypereides' speech itself.[8] Plutarch's account, while not as lengthy as Athenaeus', shares the same key details: the charge (*asebeia*), Phryne's disrobing by Hypereides, and the acquittal. Like Athenaeus, he also links Phryne and Hypereides romantically (*Mor.* 849e), but unlike Athenaeus Plutarch does not refer to any sense of religious awe among the onlookers. Craig Cooper has shown that Athenaeus' version of the story and Plutarch's were adapted from the work of a biographer named Hermippus (*c.* 200 BCE), who had adapted it in turn from Idomeneus of Lampsacus (*c.* 300 BCE). Both works mentioned it as part of a retelling of Hypereides' various erotic entanglements.[9]

The fictional letters from Alciphron emphasize the unsuccessful relationship between Euthias and Phryne, as well as Phryne's connection to Hypereides and the resulting dynamics between all three. Letter 4.3, from a *hetaira* named Bacchis to Hypereides, is a thank you letter which suggests that the conflict between Phryne and Euthias was over payment (4.3.1). Praxiteles' statue of

Phryne from Delphi is also alluded to when Bacchis, expressing gratitude on behalf of all the *hetairai*, offers to set up a gold statue of Hypereides anywhere in Greece (4.3.3). The following letter in the collection, also from Bacchis but addressed this time to Phryne, further explores the relationships between Phryne, Euthias, and Hypereides, and credits the trial with making Phryne famous all over Greece (4.4.1).[10] It shifts one key detail, however, in making Phryne the one who revealed herself, rather than Hypereides: "And don't believe those saying that if you hadn't torn off your dress and shown off your breasts to the jurors, your advocate wouldn't have been any help" (μηδὲ τοῖς λέγουσί σοι ὅτι, εἰ μὴ τὸν χιτωνίσκον περιρρηξαμένη τὰ μαστάρια τοῖς δικασταῖς ἐπέδειξας, οὐδὲν ὁ ῥήτωρ ὠφέλει, πείθου, 4.4.4). The shift to emphasize Phryne's agency in the courtroom revelation changes the narrative to make Phryne seem far less vulnerable at the trial, a fitting inclusion in a genre which purports to represent women's voices directly. The final letter in this trio, again from Bacchis and addressed to another *hetaira* named Myrrhine, whom Athenaeus links to Hypereides (13.590c), scolds its addressee on behalf of all the *hetairai* for entering a relationship with their collective enemy Euthias.[11]

Alciphron's letters referring to this case may reflect the earliest source that mentions Phryne's trail and her resulting fame, Posidippus' third-century comedy *Ephesian Women*, also preserved in Athenaeus. In what is likely a discussion of famous women or even sex workers from the previous century, Phryne's fame is linked directly to the trial:

Φρύνη ποθ' ἡμῶν γέγονεν ἐπιφανεστάτη
πολὺ τῶν ἑταιρῶν. καὶ γὰρ εἰ νεωτέρα
τῶν τότε χρόνων εἶ, τόν γ' ἀγῶν' ἀκήκοας.
βλάπτειν δοκοῦσα τοὺς βίους μείζους βλάβας
τὴν ἡλιαίαν εἷλε περὶ τοῦ σώματος
καὶ τῶν δικαστῶν καθ' ἕνα δεξιουμένη
μετὰ δακρύων διέσωσε τὴν ψυχὴν μόλις.

Phryne was by a great deal most famous
of the *hetairai* from before our time.
Even if you are more recent than that time, you've heard of the trial.
Accused of doing harm to the citizens,
she went before the *heliaia* on a capital charge,

and going to the jurors one by one
she barely saved her life with tears.

fr. 13 K-A

Like Alciphron, and perhaps even the inspiration for the epistolographer's attribution of Phryne's agency, Posidippus focuses on Phryne's actions rather than Hypereides' in bringing the trial to a successful close. Here, rather than reveal her famously beautiful body to them, Phryne beseeches the jurors individually, her tears perhaps connected to Hypereides' infamous lament on her behalf. Rather than a moment when her beauty overpowers the jury, it is one in which Phryne becomes an object of pure pity, barely escaping with her life. One might expect a comedy to make light of Phryne's nudity in the courtroom, so this fragment can also be used to argue for the later inclusion of that detail in the tradition.

The legacy of this case in antiquity was significant, not only due to Phryne's participation, but largely because of Hypereides' apparent eloquence in her defence. Although no substantial fragments of the speech remain,[12] several later authors sing its praises. Quintilian, the first-century CE Roman rhetorician, mentions that Messala Corvinus, an earlier Roman statesman, had included this speech among his translations from Greek, deftly dealing with the fine detail of the speech (10.5.2). Composed around the same time that Quintilian was writing his treatise, Longinus' *On the Sublime* mentions the speech as something the likes of which Demosthenes himself would not have been capable (34.3-4).

Despite its notable reputation in antiquity, scholars have long debated over the details of the trial, and sometimes even the historicity of the event itself. Many of the details that we find in Athenaeus, Pseudo-Plutarch, and Alciphron seem to have come from a polemic on Athenian demagogues written by Idomeneus of Lampsacus, an early third-century BCE figure associated with Epicurus.[13] Esther Eidinow places the trial in the decade between 350 and 340 BCE,[14] meaning that if it did happen, it took place in the same period as the trial of Neaira (dated to sometime between 343 and 340 BCE by Konstantinos Kapparis),[15] which offers a helpful comparandum for thinking about the implications of bringing a foreign-born sex worker to trial in Classical Athens. This trial may not even have been Phryne's only tangle with the legal system, since Athenaeus mentions a speech by the notorious political figure Aristogeiton titled *Against Phryne* (13.591e).

The Dramatis Personae

In addition to Phryne's infamous nudity, the fame of the trail was also enhanced by the reputations of the men involved. As mentioned above in my discussion of Alciphron's letters on the case, the prosecutor, Euthias, may have been involved with Phryne prior to bringing charges and is depicted as a spurned lover, while Hypereides is her gallant rescuer. Beyond the fragments of Hypereides' speech, Athenaeus' account of the trial and Alciphron's letters, however, there is little record of Euthias. In what remains from the speech itself Hypereides accuses him of being a sycophant (fr. 176) while a fragment of Hermippus' account of the trial claims that he had hired Anaximenes of Lampsacus to write his speech (fr. 67). Eleonora Cavallini suggests that, not unlike the ways that the case *Against Neaira* used a vulnerable woman to litigate what was ultimately a dispute between men, Euthias' prosecution may have been a means of drawing Hypereides into court for the pro-Macedonian side.[16]

Athenaeus, however, is forceful in his depiction of Hypereides as an unrepentant libertine, who upends the traditional organization of his household by kicking his son out of the house (Athenaeus calls it "the ancestral home," *hē patrōē oikia*), and then taking up with the *hetaira* Myrrhine (noted as being "very costly," *polutelestatē*). Myrrhine was apparently not enough for Hypereides, so while he kept her in the city proper, he also had Aristagora in the Piraeus, and a third woman, Phila, who had once been enslaved, but then set free and put in charge of his home in Eleusis (13.590c-d).[17] And yet according to Athenaeus, in the speech he gave in the courtroom, Hypereides also confessed to his love for Phryne, even as he was establishing Myrrhine in one of his homes (13.590d). Craig Cooper has demonstrated that this is not an unusual characterization for the famous orators depicted in Idomeneus' work that formed that basis of Athenaeus' account, referring to the biographer's portrait of Demosthenes as a man driven to violence by his desire for Aristarchus.[18] Since this detail was largely derived from a speech by Demosthenes' rival Aeschines, we might approach Idomeneus' insistence on Hypereides' sexual profligacy with equal caution while noting his historical connection to several sex workers (six of seventy-seven speeches attributed to Hypereides in antiquity involve *hetairai*).[19]

But who was this man, whose speech from the trial was lauded for its eloquence? Like Phryne, he was also mentioned in comedies produced during his own lifetime. Timocles, the same playwright who referred to Phryne the youthful caper-gatherer and then put her onstage as an elderly Fury, calls him "vehement in his speeches" (ὁ τ' ἐν λόγωσι δεινός, fr. 4, l. 7).[20] A similar reference from an earlier play by the same playwright to the "River Hypereides" describes it as having gentle tones and rational arguments (fr. 17). As with the comic fragments that feature Phryne and her avarice, such references suggest that Hypereides' reputation for persuasive speech in his own lifetime was sufficiently pervasive to be used as a punchline.[21]

Such a characterization should not be surprising for a student of the noted rhetorician Isocrates, who established the first formal school of rhetoric at Athens, and of Plato, the famous philosopher. Plutarch tells us that Hypereides became a public figure around the time that Alexander the Great was turning his attention to mainland Greece and so spoke against Macedonian involvement in Athens. Apparently his wealth, possibly due to the speeches he wrote and cases he argued, was sufficient to make him liable to pay a liturgy (*Mor.* 848e). Like many of his logographer colleagues, he was not immune to scandal and prosecution and so faced his own trial for illegally proposing a decree to grant citizenship to metics and free slaves after the Battle of Chaeronea in 338 BCE in order to bolster Athens' fighting forces.[22] (He mounted a successful defense against those charges by linking them to the threat of the Macedonians (*Mor.* 849a). Seventy-seven speeches credited to Hypereides were known to Plutarch, of which the biographer claims that fifty-two were genuine, and so we can envision Hypereides as a very prominent Athenian who was a peer of other orators like Demosthenes and whose legacy was already well-established in antiquity.

In many ways, Phryne and Hypereides are an apt pairing in this story: two figures who were prominent in their own lifetimes and whose later biographies feature gossipy details, coming together in one of the most sensational trials of Classical Athens. Despite the orator's prowess in the courtroom and political activities, Idomeneus' interest in Hypereides' sexual appetites did not escape Plutarch's notice. Like Athenaeus, Plutarch mentions his patronage of the very costly Myrrhine at the expense of keeping his own son in the household.

Aristagora and the recently freed Phila also appear in this account, and Plutarch proposes that these connections are evidence that he was likely involved with Phryne too (*Mor.* 849e). But their pairing in the trial also contrasts how an Athenian man and a foreign woman were treated in public sentiment, both in their own time and in later accounts.

Although Hypereides was brought to court by his own political opponents on a separate occasion, at that time he was able to speak in his own defense, and while he may have employed some dramatic rhetoric in that case, there is no reference to any individual beseeching of the jury or actions as dramatic as Phryne's disrobing. Although those are likely great exaggerations of what happened at the conclusion of Phryne's trial, both Athenaeus' and Plutarch's accounts speak to Phryne's vulnerability in the courtroom in a city where she had no meaningful rights, as well as to the desperation a woman like her might have felt in such a situation. Where Hypereides could marshall his wealth and prominence in his own defense, Phryne was ultimately reliant on a man to speak on her behalf, with the added assumption that she must have been romantically involved with him because they were associated publicly. Certainly her wealth would have helped her acquire the services of an orator like Hypereides, but Phryne would have had to sit passively while her case was heard and so the mentions of her either beseeching the jury or disrobing herself are intended to offer shocking displays of female agency in a male-dominated space.

After the case passed into the historical record, the legacy of the two main characters also diverged. We have many remnants of Hypereides' own words from his speeches and a fulsome biographical narrative from Plutarch, in addition to the Roman sources praising his rhetorical prowess. In Plutarch's biography, one can see the importance of the anecdote in shaping Hypereides' life story, but in the case of Phryne, anecdote is all that remains. As far as I have been able to ascertain, even in antiquity, despite the magnitude of interest in the *hetairai* from the Hellenistic period onward, no single text was devoted to Phryne alone or to tracing a fulsome narrative of her life, as is the case for nearly all prominent women in antiquity.[23] The cultural space devoted to narratives about prominent men and how prominent women's stories must be assembled from scattered bits and pieces is no clearer than in the nexus of connections to Phryne's trial.

The Charges

One of the longest-standing debates around her trial is what Phryne could have done to draw such charges (*asebeia*) from Euthias and precisely what the fragment of Euthias' speech refers to when it mentions the introduction of a new god, formation of *thiasoi* with both men and women, and finally Phryne's improper behavior at the Lyceum (see above).[24] A helpful means of reviewing such charges (corrupting the youth and introducing new gods) is to compare Phryne's trial to another of the most famous trials in Classical Athenian history, that of Socrates from 399 BCE. In Socrates' case, the charges were the same and the penalty proposed was also death (Socrates seems to have been the first individual charged with introducing new gods).[25]

Yet later Athenians seem to have recognized that such charges against Socrates were relatively hollow. Hypereides, Phryne's advocate, noted several decades after that trial that Socrates was punished "for his words" (*epi logois*, *Against Autocles for Treason*, fr. 1) and not the actual actions he was charged with, suggesting that the motive for the accusation was less religious than political.[26] Jan Bremmer notes that Xenophon claims certain members of the jury felt *phthonos* ("envy, ill-will") toward Socrates (*Apology* 14.3) because of his special connection to the divine, and while it is hard to assess any of the jurors' individual motivations, one can imagine Socrates drawing such negative attention simply due to the unconventional ways he moved through Athenian society and the resulting access to elite circles he gained through them. As Esther Eidinow clarifies, *phthonos* can be seen as "the dark companion of good fortune: its appearance signals the breakdown of the reciprocal relationships that ran like nerves through the ancient social body."[27]

In his biography of Pericles, Plutarch brings up the trial of his partner, Aspasia, whom he claims was also put on trial for *asebeia*,[28] with additional allegations that she had brought free-born women to Pericles for sex (*Per.* 32). Athenaeus also mentions the trial (*Epit.* 2.2.117), with both authors depicting a dramatic conclusion in which Pericles weeps in front of the jury and Aspasia is acquitted. While the historicity of such a trial is certainly in question,[29] the model it offers for taking an unconventional woman to trial accords with Phryne's courtroom stories: the charge is the same and a prominent Athenian man must go to great lengths to defend a metic woman. If it is the case that

Aspasia and Phryne were actually taken to court, then their unconventional status had proven to be a major vulnerability.

In the cases of both Aspasia and Socrates, because their relationships to elite men were unconventional, they did not have the buttressing effects of convention to support them when those ties broke down and so their movement into and through elite circles was always predicated on the interest and ongoing goodwill of the men with whom they associated. The same is true of Phryne. Once the reciprocity between a foreign sex worker like Phryne and a notable citizen like Euthias was broken, in this case possibly with the end of a romantic relationship (as suggested by Alciphron), the man in question had access to the fullest extent of Athenian law in order to pursue his grievance against the woman he had been involved with. *Asebeia*, a charge that could encompass nearly any unusual activity, had been successfully deployed in the past against other controversial individuals, and held the threat of capital punishment, would have been ideal for Euthias' purposes.

There are also two other fourth-century cases with women defendants to which Esther Eidinow has productively compared Phryne's trial, those of Theoris and Ninon. Theoris, a metic woman from Lemnos who practiced as a *pharmakis* in Athens,[30] was mentioned in other cases due to her use of *pharmaka* and *epodai* ("encantations").[31] She was also likely charged with *asebeia* in her own case dating to the late 320s BCE.[32] Ninon was also brought to trial and executed, probably in the late 360s,[33] accused, like Phryne, of forming *thiasoi*. The official charge against Ninon may also have been *asebeia*, given the specific accusation she faced.[34] If these two cases did indeed center around charges of *asebeia*, they, along with the conviction of Socrates, illustrate the convenience of using this charge against any rival, and in the case of the women mentioned here, the flexibility of the charge in its application to nearly any activity deemed unusual. As Konstantinos Kapparis points out in his discussion of Theoris, fear and anger are likely the motivating emotions behind such charges,[35] which in turn recalls the *phthonos* attributed to Socrates' enemies. With religion deeply embedded in Athenian daily life, any activity deemed novel could conveniently be tied to inappropriate religious practice.

The specific accusations in Phryne's case are a bit more difficult to pin down. The anonymous rhetorical treatise that quotes Euthias' speech says that she held a shameless *komos* in the Lyceum, introduced a new god, and held a *thiasos* with both men and women. I begin with the first of these allegations, the *komos* in the Lyceum. Given that a *komos* is the kind of raucous revel one might expect in Dionysiac worship, I am not surprised to find a *hetaira* associated with one, since these women are also often linked to the symposium (an all-male drinking party associated with elite men in Classical Athens). The Lyceum was a sanctuary to Apollo Lyceus (in his guise as the "wolf-god"), which also hosted a great deal of philosophical activity in the fourth century BCE, and eventually it became home to Aristotle's school in the 330s.[36] Thus it would not have been an unusual place to find notable Athenians in Phryne's time, especially the young men associated with both philosophers and *hetairai*, and so the suggestion that Phryne was brought to court for corrupting citizens (cf. Posidippus above) is not surprising, especially when juxtaposing Phryne's trial with that of Socrates. Given the political instability that seemed ready to erupt at any time in the mid-fourth century, concerns over those who could easily influence elite men are not surprising.

The god that the comment on Hypereides' defence speech identifies, Isodaites (see above), also seems an appropriate choice for a *komos* and the kind of celebration that would feature a famous *hetaira*. Plutarch mentions Isodaites in a discussion of the gods at Delphi, linking him with Dionysus, Zagreus, and Nyktelios, the final two being alternate names for the first (*Mor.* 389a).[37] The claim from Harpocration that this deity was worshipped by low-status women also suggests that this may not have been isolated worship,[38] and therefore this accusation may have been one of convenience rather than an ongoing cause for concern to most Athenians. Without significant evidence of malfeasance available to Euthias, the charge faced by Socrates may have offered a useful precedent, and he could have seized on its ambiguity to punish Phryne.

The accusation of organizing *thiasoi* ("religious groups") with men and women may have been a response to concerns over political subversion from the groups that gathered at places like the Lyceum that were prevalent in that period.[39] By the fourth century, the *thiasos* was established as a semi-political association in Athens, a sub-grouping within the *phratry*.[40] On the other hand, it also seems that mixed-gender *thiasoi* were a feature of ecstatic and mystery cults in this period, with a membership that could be drawn from a variety of social classes (cf. Dem. 18.260). Consequently the term could encompass a group foundational to the organization of Athenian government and so also foundational to status within its society or it could refer to a group that disregarded those categories. Even if Phryne had been doing nothing disruptive to society as part of the *thiasos*, its very existence as a group that destabilized Athenian identity categories would have added to her vulnerability as a foreign sex worker.

Phryne as Suppliant before the Jury

Given the import of a *graphē* ("public indictment") and its concern over harm to the public good, Phryne's trial for *asebeia* would have been preceded by a hearing with a magistrate (the *archon basileus*, who was responsible for hearing cases related to religious matters), before going to the courtroom. In the courtroom, Phryne would have been faced with a jury of at least 500 Athenian men and one can imagine the prurient interest many of them would have had in a trial featuring a notorious and beautiful sex worker. With the *agon timetos* (a secondary debate between the prosecutor and defense over punishment after a guilty verdict had been established) that was part of an *asebeia* trial, the stakes were high (anything up to capital punishment was possible). Phryne's vulnerability in this scenario cannot be emphasized enough and so one can also consider that she may have felt a great deal of desperation. As I have already mentioned in this chapter, it is highly unlikely that Phryne or Hypereides would have removed her clothing in the courtroom, or even that Phryne would have been allowed to beseech the jurors individually, but in such anecdotes we get a sense of the extreme imbalance of power between a metic sex worker and the official mechanisms of the Athenian state. It is perhaps the case that the later authors wanted to express this through the idea of supplication and were considering how one woman might supplicate a crowd of men who held life and death power over her. Accordingly, I now intend to place Phryne's supplication, especially the dramatic revelation of her breasts, in the context of similar scenes of supplication to show how later writers may have used common literary and visual tropes to explore the high stakes of Phryne's trial.

Supplication was a common theme in ancient Greek literature going back to the poetry of Homer. Book 22 of the *Odyssey* contains a famous scene featuring this act, in which Odysseus is supplicated by the suitors he is in the process of massacring. In his analysis of this scene, Fred Naiden identifies four common steps in supplication: first, the suppliant approaches an individual or place, then they make a distinctive gesture, followed by a definite request, with the supplication concluded by the one being approached, who may or may not grant the suppliant's request.[41] In many literary scenes of supplication, the suppliant demands pity through a personal appeal as they ask for mercy.

If the disrobing was also an extrapolation from the text of Hypereides' speech, as with some of the other details that Idomeneus extracted from it that found their way into Athenaeus' and Plutarch's accounts, then it may have come from an image of Phryne as suppliant that Hypereides drew from that common literary trope.[42] Although many of the suppliants from Greek literature are men, for the purposes of comparison to Phryne, I would now like to look at three famous women suppliants from literature: Hecuba, Clytemnestra, and Helen. As in the most prevalent version of the story of Phryne's trial, each of these women reveal their breasts to trigger pity in the person they are supplicating, but each hopes for a different outcome. In Hecuba's example, the revelation is to identify the suppliant as a potentially bereaved mother, while in Helen's it is intended to be erotic. In all cases, it involves using the most vulnerable part of the body to gain power over a situation. The earliest version of a supplication scene in which a woman bares her breasts is Hecuba's interaction with her son Hector in Book 22 of Homer's *Iliad*, when she and her husband, Priam, are begging him not to go into battle. After the warrior is not convinced by his father's desperate pleas, Hecuba reaches into her robes and pulls out her breast, reminding her son of the comfort he found there as an infant (22.79-83). This invocation of Hector's infancy and Hecuba's maternal care reveals a key aspect of such supplications and the use of the breast to bring about pity: its revelation ties past memory to future mourning, in this case the bereavement of a mother. Hecuba's breast is then a means for her to force Hector to identify with her through shared memory.[43] In a perversion of the scene from the *Iliad* and its use of memory,[44] Clytemnestra in Aeschylus' *Libation Bearers* also reveals her breast to her son, Orestes, reminding him that she nursed him as an infant in order to prevent him (unsuccessfully) from killing her in vengeance for his father's murder (896-98).[45]

Two anonymous rhetorical works recount the revelation at Phryne's trial, with one mentioning how Hypereides managed to save Phryne with "a plenitude of pity and the rending of a garment" (ἐλεεινογίας τε πλήθει καὶ τῇ περιρρήξει τῆς ἐσθῆτος, Walz 4.414). The second offers much more detail on this scene and turns the *hetaira* into a tragic victim on par with Hecuba. In this version, she beats her naked chest as she tears her garment, suggesting a moment of total despair to which the jurors respond with unadulterated pity (Walz 7.335). Both of these accounts feature similar vocabulary to that found in Athenaeus, Plutarch, and Alciphron (a form of either *perirrēgnumi* or *katarrēgnumi*, both of which mean "to tear/rend completely"), which Craig Cooper uses to argue that the disrobing must have originated from a single source (Idomeneus' discussion of Hypereides).[46] While I agree with Cooper, I further contend that the images of famous female suppliants like Hecuba and Clytemnestra shaped such depictions, especially the version in the second anonymous treatise.

Another scene of supplication from tragedy that features the legendary beauty Helen and her husband, Menelaus, in the aftermath of the Trojan War adds further nuance to our understanding of Phryne, her nudity, and the ways that the power of beauty can be depicted. Euripides' *Trojan Women* contains a reunion between Helen and Menelaus, in which he resolves to take her back to Greece to be put to death (1052-59). But this scene is not the only reference to Helen as suppliant and lurking in the background is a version of Helen's supplication found in another of Euripides' earlier plays, *Andromache*. Peleus, the elderly father of Achilles, reveals in his anger at Menelaus that when the Greek king was taking part in the sack of Troy, he came upon Helen but did not kill her. Peleus accuses him of being powerless at the sight of Helen's breasts:

οὐκ ἔκτανες γυναῖκα χειρίαν λαβών,
ἀλλ', ὡς ἐσεῖδες μαστόν, ἐκβαλὼν ξίφος
φίλημ' ἐδέξω, προδότιν αἰκάλλων κύνα,
ἥσσων πεφυκὼς Κύπριδος, ὦ κάκιστε σύ.

You did not kill your wife when you had her in hand,
But when you saw her breast, you tossed aside your sword,
accepted her kiss as you fawned over the cheating bitch,
your character found wanting by Cypris, you absolute wretch.

628-31[47]

The reference to Aphrodite (Cypris) differentiates Helen's supplication from those of Hecuba and Clytemnestra by adding erotic overtones to the baring of the famous beauty's breasts. While meant to recall the other two women's bared maternal breasts and therefore to link Helen to a more generalized sense of female desperation, this scene also tied into a long visual history concerned with the power of Helen's beauty.[48]

For roughly a century prior to the inclusion of the moment above in Euripides' play, vase painters had been depicting the moment of Menelaus and Helen's reunion among the ruins of Troy, either showing Menelaus preparing to kill her or the moment afterward, when Helen's beauty had doused the flames of his anger, causing him to drop his sword. In the first version on a sixth-century BCE Attic black-figure amphora, Helen is typically looking directly at Menelaus, fixing him with her gaze and lifting her veil to allow her beauty to stop him.[49] A painting on an Attic red-figure krater from roughly 450 BCE depicting the moment when Menelaus drops his sword makes the connection between his mercy to Helen's beauty and its powerful sway more explicit by showing her running toward the protective embrace of Aphrodite as a tiny figure of Eros flies above the couple.[50]

The power of Helen's beauty as she begs Menelaus for her life, but especially others' reactions to seeing her bared breasts, informs the courtroom scene that Athenaeus and the anonymous treatises relate.[51] While it is quite common in Greek art and literature to see women bare their breasts in moments of distress (as I have just discussed),[52] I argue that when the jurors are reported as being struck by religious awe at the sight of Phryne's nudity in Athenaeus, this is a deliberate engagement with the specific imagery of Helen as suppliant, and through her to figures like Hecuba and Clytemnestra: "While (Hypereides) was giving his final words he lamented at the sight of her and caused the jurors to feel religious awe at the agent and servant of Aphrodite and to not put her to death as they indulged in pity (ποιήσας τοὺς ἐπιλογικοὺς οἴκτους ἐκ τῆς ὄψεως αὐτῆς ἐπερρητόρευσεν δεισιδαιμονῆσαί τε ἐποίησεν τοὺς δικαστὰς τὴν ὑποφῆτιν καὶ ζάκορον Ἀφροδίτης ἐλέῳ χαρισαμένους μὴ ἀποκτεῖναι, 13.590e). The reference to Aphrodite is key here: it not only brings to mind the works of Apelles and Praxiteles that supposedly depicted Phryne as the goddess, but it ties this scene to the version of Helen's supplication from

Andromache and in the vase paintings, in which eroticism (the beauty of Helen and the power of Aphrodite) and pity (the plight of the female suppliant) are combined.[53] In Helen's case it is the beauty of a demigoddess that inspires this pity, while for Phryne it is the mere association with the divine that accomplishes this effect. The baring of Phryne's breasts then further ties her into the tradition of female supplication going all the way back to Homer's Hecuba.

The reference to Phryne as Aphrodite's "agent and servant" in Athenaeus most likely only identifies her as a sex worker and not a literal religious attendant, but in affiliating her with the goddess through her divine beauty, it also links this moment to the religious aspects of supplication that were still part of active Athenian practice in the fourth century. There were codified ways to become a suppliant at that time that linked legal, political, and religious practices. The Aristotelian *Consitution of the Athenians* describes a meeting of the assembly in which anyone wishing to may place the suppliant's olive branch with wool wrapped around it on the central altar in order to be allowed to address the assembly on any matter he wished (43.6). The same work also mentions this process being open to metics and enslaved people. Andocides' "On the Mysteries" also mentions the suppliant's bough as being in use by the late fifth century BCE, and a law preventing its being placed on the altar during the Eleusinian Mysteries (1.110). These references and the restrictions on the practice of supplication they describe suggest concerns over how and when supplication was enacted, who was eligible to be a suppliant, and who could be supplicated (often the Athenian *demos* as represented by the assembly, but it does seem that some magistrates, especially those concerned with religious affairs, could be supplicated too).[54] To be executed properly, the suppliant's request was expected to be *ennomos* ("within the law/tradition," but more broadly meaning from the right person at the right time).[55] While Phryne's supplication of the jury does not reach such official status, it most certainly connects the right woman to exactly the right moment, maximizing the chances of her success. Even if her chest was not revealed and her supplication was more along the lines of the version from Posidippus' play, her actions may have tapped into powerful traditions that could be used to protect someone as legally vulnerable as she was.

The Power of Phryne's Nudity

As I have already stated, despite it becoming a key element in the stories of the trial by the Imperial period, Phryne's courtroom nudity is likely a fictionalized detail of a trial that did occur. The popularity of this detail, however, demonstrates just how powerful Phryne's beauty was understood to be in those later sources. Laura McClure argues that Hypereides' disrobing of Phryne in these versions of the story allowed the orator to use her body in place of his words; his action turns her body into a "rhetorical *schema*" through associations with supplication (as I have just discussed) and therefore to religious practice too.[56] Several sources from after the Classical period hint at the possibility that the display of a body (whether a defendant's or not) in court was a powerful rhetorical technique. The third-century Sicilian mime author Herodas depicts a scene in which a sex worker's battered body is displayed to a jury to prove that she was assaulted, while her genitals are also pointed out to the onlookers (2.69-70).[57] In his discussion of Phryne's trial, the Roman rhetorician Quintilian mentions an example from the Roman courtroom in which Antonius revealed a client's scarred body (2.15.8). Even without the actual display of her body in the courtroom, Apollodorus' descriptions of Neaira's open sexual activities invites the jury to envision her naked (59.33).[58] In considering the ramifications of McClure's argument about display of Phryne's body as rhetorical technique and in light of these examples, I find echoes of the many ways that Phryne's body is used in Imperial literature. In the previous chapter, I considered how Phryne's body was invoked by authors like Alciphron as a metaphor for craft and performance; Athenaeus' courtroom scene literalizes such metaphors by having the display of Phryne's body effect her acquittal when Hypereides is unable to do so by more conventional means. And so while I have already explored Phryne's nudity in the context of her possibly inspiring and then being depicted in canonical artworks, I would now like to turn to the overwhelming power of her beautiful nude body and the results it was able to effect.

As explored above, female nudity (particularly the baring of breasts) and supplication have a long literary history, but now I would like to consider the power of nudity outside of the context of supplication and the ways that beauty is understood to cause those who view it to react in ways beyond their own control. In doing so, I will return to some of the discussion about visual erotics from the previous chapter and Squire's point that "power can lie on both sides of the looking and being-looked-at divide."[59] Although I have already indicated the vulnerability of a woman like Phryne in the Athenian courtroom, I now want to think through the ways that authors such as Alciphron reimagined the moment of her revelation as a display of agency. In my earlier discussion of the passage from Athenaeus on Phryne's nude appearance at the seaside, which that author connects to Apelles' and Praxiteles' versions of Aphrodite, I argued that the setting of a religious festival allowed Phryne's nudity to be associated with the divine, thereby legitimizing a potentially scandalous public appearance but also maximizing its impact on those who would see it. Praxiteles' statue of Aphrodite and the stories about its effects on viewers also offer insight into the connection between nudity and power over those who view it that can help us further understand the account of Phryne in the courtroom.

The unavoidable effects of beauty on those who gaze upon it has a long history in Greek thought, with sources like Plato's *Phaedrus* exploring the connections between vision and desire. Female beauty and its power has its own specific presence in literature, going back to poetic depictions of Aphrodite and her mortal avatar, Helen. The metaphors used in such scenarios typically have the onlooker captured by desire and no longer able to think clearly. In the Homeric Hymn devoted to her, Aphrodite is herself love-struck at the sight of the Trojan Anchises and then immediately goes to Paphos, where she bathes, anoints herself, then dresses and accessorizes herself elaborately (52-66).[60] She then comes to Anchises, who takes in her dazzling appearance ("a wonder to see," *thauma idesthai*, 90) and is immediately seized by *eros* (93). A similar scenario unfolds when Helen goes before Paris in their bedchamber in Book 3 of the *Iliad* and Paris is so struck by his desire for her that he says that never before has *eros* enfolded his heart in such a way (3.442).[61]

In the poetic realm, fragment 31 by Sappho details the physical effects of looking at her female object of desire in a poem almost entirely focused on the viewer's reaction:

ὡς γὰρ ἔς σ' ἴδω βρόχε', ὥς με φώναι-
σ' οὐδ' ἓν ἔτ' εἴκει,
ἀλλὰ κὰμ μὲν γλῶσσά' <μ'> ἔαγε, λέπτον
δ' αὔτικα χρῷ πῦρ ὐπαδεδρόμηκεν,

ὀππάτεσσι δ' οὐδ' ἒν ὄρημμ', ἐπιρρόμ-
βεισι δ' ἄκουαι,
κὰδ δέ μ' ἴδρως κακχέεται, τρόμος δὲ
παῖσαν ἄγρει, χλωροτέρα δὲ ποίας
ἔμμι, τεθνάκην δ' ὀλίγω 'πιδεύης
φαίνομ' ἔμ' αὔτ'[ᾳ.

For when I look at you, even briefly, then I can
speak no longer,
but my tongue is broken, suddenly
a thin fire runs beneath my skin,
my eyes see nothing,
I hear a roar,
and sweat pours down, while a tremble
seizes me all over, and I am greener than grass,
and I feel nearly dead.

7-16

In this poem, we are given no detail of what the object of Sappho's desire actually looks like and the audience's impression of her attractiveness is shaped only by the various physical responses to her presence that the poet describes. As I argued in the previous chapter, the reactions of others are an effective means of depicting great desirability, and this poem makes that technique the center of the poem,[62] with desirability conveyed only through the viewer's uncontrollable physical symptoms and the experience of the powerless one centered.

The viewer of female beauty rendered powerless before it is also a theme in the stories connected to the Aphrodite of Knidos. Pseudo-Lucian's account of a group visiting the shrine to see the famous statue features at least three instances of unchecked desire in response to the visual stimulus of its beauty. One of the tourists, Charicles, cries out upon laying eyes on the statue and immediately attempts to kiss the statue (*Am.* 13). Then, upon seeing the statue from behind, Callicratidas, who had been impassive prior to this moment, also cries out at the perfection of its backside and is described as being "inspired" (*entheastikos,* with divine associations in that term), while Charicles, in tears at viewing this new angle, stands astonished (*Am.* 14). At this moment, the men viewing the statue discover the semen stain on its backside (discussed in the previous chapter) and the temple attendant tells the story of the young man who fell in love with the statue and spent his days in the temple with it, staring at it uninterrupted from dawn to sunset (*Am.* 15). She tells the men how his desire turned to despair, he finally contrived to spend the night with the statue, and subsequently ended his life by throwing himself off a cliff (*Am.* 16).

In all of the examples I have provided here, the reaction to female beauty is an immediate loss of control. Anchises and Paris are seized by *eros*, with desire ascendant over rational thought. In Sappho 31, the poet's physical response is all-consuming and no thought can find its way in, while in Pseudo-Lucian, the men who view the Aphrodite of Knidos all behave inappropriately, even sacrilegiously, with the young man driven to suicide over its beauty. In Phryne's trial, this pattern continues as her nudity, the great source of her beauty in all accounts that mention it, disarms the jury and causes them to vote for her acquittal, when moments before they seem to have been ready to condemn her to death. I would like to return to Helen again as the best comparanda for Phryne, since a fragmentary reference to the effect of her beauty during the sack of Troy in Stesichorus' poetry reveals a dynamic between Helen and the Greeks that is similar to the one between Phryne and the jury. Unlike the scenes from drama in which Helen supplicates Menelaus, Stesichorus' version seems to have featured her before the Greeks, who were prepared to stone her to death. Yet according to the scholion that preserves this scene, the Greeks dropped their stones immediately upon seeing her (fr. 106 F). Patrick Finglass suggests that this scene may even have been "quasi-judicial," with a lone woman facing down punishment at hands of an entire army,[63] and so we can see how Phryne in the courtroom with only her beauty to protect her mirrors such a scene. Although it is not clear whether Helen disrobes in Stesichorus' poem, the impact of her beauty remains the same. As in Helen's case, it is Phryne's beauty and its attendant notoriety that placed her in danger in the first place.

The scene from Stesichorus also parallels Phryne in the courtroom in having a group react en masse to Helen's beauty. Another text that works with Helen's story, Gorgias' *Encomium of Helen*, shows how the power of rhetoric and vision can be enhanced when a large crowd of spectators (such as the jury) is involved.[64] At the moment when Athenaeus says that the jury felt religious awe in looking upon the beautiful body of the "agent and servant of Aphrodite" (*tēn hupophētin kai zakoron*, 13.590e), the collective response to Phryne is emphasized, which in turn maximizes the power of her beauty, just like the Greek army collectively dropping their stones at the sight of Helen. Semenov has argued that in this moment, the jury felt they were actually seeing Aphrodite before them and this is what led them to acquit her,[65] yet the stories of Helen and the well-established tradition of other descriptions of uncontrollable reactions to seeing a beautiful woman indicate that no such religious epiphany would be required for the jury to respond as they did, especially in the context of a heavily fictionalized account as loaded with literary allusions as this one.

The Vulnerability of Phryne in Court

Phryne's supplication in the courtroom is also bound up in the vulnerability of her position, a theme which Alciphron's fictionalized accounts of the trial emphasize. As I have already mentioned in this chapter, someone like Phryne would have been uniquely unsafe in such a context, as a woman entirely reliant on Hypereides to speak on her behalf and as a metic unprotected by durable ties to the Athenian community.[66] Letter 4.3, addressed from Phryne's colleague Bacchis to Hypereides, opens with the gratitude of all of the *hetairai* as Bacchis considers the risk they all face should a relationship with a client go sour:

Πᾶσαί σοι ἴσμεν αἱ ἑταῖραι χάριν καὶ ἑκάστη γε ἡμῶν οὐχ ἧττον ἢ Φρύνη. ὁ μὲν γὰρ ἀγὼν μόνης Φρύνης, ὃν ὁ παμπόνηρος Εὐθίας ἐπανείλετο, ὁ δὲ κίνδυνος ἁπασῶν. εἰ γὰρ αἰτοῦσαι παρὰ τῶν ἐραστῶν ἀργύριον οὐ τυγχάνομεν ἢ τοῖς διδοῦσιν ἐντυγχάνουσαι ἀσεβείας κριθησόμεθα, πεπαῦσθαι κρεῖττον ἡμῖν τοῦ βίου τούτου καὶ μηκέτι ἔχειν πράγματα μήτε τοῖς ὁμιλοῦσι παρέχειν.

We *hetairai* are all grateful to you and certainly each of us no less than Phryne. For although the trial was Phryne's alone, which that absolute wretch Euthias brought forward, the danger was all of ours. For if we insist on getting money from our lovers and don't happen to get it or if we come across those who do give it we will be prosecuted for impiety, the better choice for us is to stop this lifestyle, no longer do business and don't offer ourselves to those who spend time with us.

4.3.1-2

Bacchis' connection of the life of the *hetaira* to their susceptibility to vengeful prosecution highlights how a citizen could leverage his legal privilege (the ability to bring a public suit) to gain revenge over what was ultimately a personal matter. She also identifies their clientele, presumably elite men, as the particular danger to the *hetairai* in such a context.

One possible means of understanding the recourse to law courts as a means of gaining revenge on a female sex worker, or at least the status-based anxiety expressed in Bacchis' letter, is to think of the ways in which the courts and their relationship to Athenian citizenship codify status, in contrast to the ways an affair with a *hetaira*, especially as depicted in Imperial sources like Alciphron's *Letters*, obscures the social position of both partners. Since payment to a *hetaira* can take many forms, the performance of ongoing desire for her client or at least friendship with him is required, and because she is not typically brought into a household in a formal fashion, the relationship between *hetaira* and client is not well delineated.[67] This also allows the *hetaira* control over the end of the relationship; one of the defining aspects of the *hetaira* is her supposed ability to consent to relationships, largely based on whether she has received sufficient payment from her client (e.g., Alciphron 4.15 on lack of payment). Yet as Bacchis points out in her letter, this is a delicate arrangement. Demanding money may not be successful and even a previously happy client may leave behind the blurred lines of their relationship, dissolve the agency of the *hetaira*, and assert his own legally established power by turning to the courtroom should he choose.

This anxiety is not just rooted in later literary constructions of sex workers and their relationships, but also in the real political sphere of Athens in the fourth century. Public suits, which could be brought by any citizen who wished (*ho boulomenos*, "the willing"), could even be used vindictively against other citizens; of thirty-one speeches preserved from public prosecutions in Classical Athens, at least eleven address the prosecutor's personal motivation for bringing the charges, while others, without mentioning interpersonal conflict, are clearly connected to ongoing hostilities.[68] The case *Against Neaira* is a familiar example of such retaliatory use of the courts, in which Apollodorus identifies Stephanus as a previous courtroom opponent. While a conflict like the one between Apollodorus and Stephanus may have ultimately been rooted in politics and focused on the disagreement of two citizens,[69] the personal nature of the prosecution of Neaira shows how convenient a target a woman perceived to have been a sex worker was, not just despite, but because of that close association with a citizen. Her association with Stephanus is what brought her to Apollodorus' attention in the first place.

The individual foreign female sex worker, unaffiliated with any household, would be in even more danger as the target of personal animosity from a male citizen, which is the dynamic that Bacchis acknowledges in Alciphron's letter. In this configuration, there is something to be said for the assimilating force of sitting on the jury as a spectator in this kind of trial. As in the trial of Neaira, the jurors would be encouraged to consider the foreign origins of the woman on trial as well as the threat she posed to the most deeply held values that structured Athenian society and therefore the jurors would also be encouraged to determine their judgment as Athenian citizens first and foremost. Simon Goldhill has argued that in the context of the Athenian dramatic festivals, being a "judging, viewing spectator" is an ideal form of citizenship.[70] I argue that this applies to the courtroom as well (see my comments in Chapter 1 on the similarities between the courtroom and the stage), most certainly in a context such as Phryne's case when the person on trial held a low social status. We should also account for the theatrical impact of Phryne's gestures (whether stripping herself or beseeching the jury members) and their tragic allusions.[71] The men on the jury, who were there because of the practical implications of the configuration of Athenian citizenship, can be imagined looking on as a homogenous group facing Phryne alone, taking pleasure from the surprise spectacle of her nude body.[72]

The versions of the trial that end with Phryne nude and the jury gawking at her in awe are a literalization of this dynamic. No one else could be on display in quite the way that Phryne was: a great beauty, an object of intrigue and scandal finally brought before the men of Athens for their assessment. If she had been a respectable Athenian woman, she would not have been brought to trial on such charges in the first place and certainly could not have been stripped (either by herself or by Hypereides). Her nudity further marks her as outside, even beyond, the institutions of Athenian men as a female sex worker.[73] In that moment, she suddenly stands apart from their laws.

Despite it being highly unlikely that such an event could have happened in a fourth-century courtroom, the ongoing fascination with the revelation of

Phryne's nude body in combination with the literary tropes to which it responds shows that the dynamic of Phryne against a jury full of citizens heightened the prurience of such a scene. As I shall explore in the following chapter, this is the story about Phryne that acquired the most cultural currency in antiquity and went on to inspire many influential paintings, stage performances, and films. The combination of beauty, lasciviousness, and the reversal of an overwhelmingly unbalanced power dynamic proved as irresistible to later audiences as it did to those in antiquity as Phryne's nudity became a blueprint for later generations to navigate the divide between eroticism and public morality.

4

Phryne's Afterlife

Just as it had in antiquity, Phryne's cultural footprint grew in times and places when prurient fascination in her life also carried the weight of public debate around shifting moral values. In antiquity and from the nineteenth century onward, the primary allure of Phryne's stories was the public display of a beautiful female body and so accordingly the anecdotes about her that were retold and adapted were her trial and her modeling for Praxiteles. In antiquity, such stories about Phryne's body had offered their audiences means of thinking about a woman who was in many ways out of place, moving into and through Classical Athens with a freedom not accorded to many other women at that time. For later Hellenistic and Roman Imperial readers, these stories also inspired a visual connection to Classical Athens; in imagining Phryne's nude body, the reader re-envisioned Athens itself. When she resurfaced centuries later, Phryne and the stories about her once again became a means of conjuring up the world of Classical Greece and she was once again the focal point of larger cultural conversations about eroticism and the place of women in public. Once more, the female body and its presence in public was the center of these conversations as art, live performance, and film turned the literary construction of Phryne back into flesh once more.

The poem "Phryne," written by British poet Robert Conquest and published in 2000, captures the dynamic of longing that characterizes all of these attempts to revivify Phryne:

"It's such a pity that we don't have
Anything like a photograph
Of her about whom the ancients rave..."

He'd been talking about the well-known tale
Of her lawyer at her blasphemy trial
Baring her breasts to gain an acquittal.

Now, it wasn't the 'beauty' of what they saw
That made the judges loosen the law,
But what's been described as 'sacred awe.'

Would visual be better than verbal, though,
Projected into the long-ago
Till we think we know what we'll never know?

Fragments, copies, our museums still hold
Of statues she modelled, or so we're told
(Though not the Delphi one in gold).

Well, at Thespiae, how did they feel as
Praxiteles, daring celestial malice,
Set up together, on equal pillars

Statues of her and of Aphrodite.
A girl and a Goddess damn-near Almighty
With a temper not to be taken lightly?

He could only pre-empt their sacred fear
With what could unarguably appear
As spillover from another sphere

On to physique made partly free
From the pressures of externality
Which is all that the subtlest lens can see.

(And Marilyns, Sophias, the very cream
Of our time, aren't sewn without a seam
Directly into the fabric of dream.)

But she's gone! Long gone! Gone to the grave
And left us, instead of a photograph,
The residual glow of an ancient grief.

The Phryne left to us in the fragments I have discussed thus far is inarguably an object of desire. The fragmentary nature of the sources on her life tantalize and those who read about her are inevitably left longing for the whole. In this chapter, I focus on receptions of Phryne that attempt to capture the woman by addressing Conquest's "ancient grief." In each case that I will discuss here, that process involved the negotiation of real women's roles in public; here I am most interested in how the reputations of the women who were associated with her as artists, models, and performers were elided with the ancient stories of Phryne herself. I begin with a discussion of Phryne as featured in European oil paintings, from the late eighteenth century onward, with a particular focus on the explosion of images of Phryne after the incendiary debut of Jean-Léon Gérôme's painting *Phryné devant l'Aréopage* at the Salon de Paris in 1861. Gérôme's painting epitomized a moment in French painting in which the relationship between models and painters was becoming ever more collaborative and the female nude was taking a more prominent, if controversial, place in painting. At the same time in France, the nude spectacle was also becoming a hotly contested phenomenon and Phryne's story, especially that of her trial, was depicted so many times on burlesque stages that her name became shorthand to reference the infamous *femmes nues* of Paris who, like their ancient predecessor, were also running afoul of the law. By the turn of the twentieth century, Phryne had become a genuine cultural sensation spreading across Europe, with comic operas, advertisements, and political cartoons all featuring her image.

Because this new set of visuals and performances had re-established Phryne's reputation for beauty and eroticism in mainstream culture in the first half of the twentieth century, her story became fodder for 1950s Italian filmmakers who wanted to put beautiful women onscreen, especially in the so-called "peplum" films so popular on Italian screens at that time. I begin my discussion of this aspect of Phryne's reception with an examination of "Il processo di Frine," the final episode in Alessandro Blasetti's 1952 film anthology, *Altri Tempi* ("Times Gone By"). Here, the trial of Phryne has been transposed to late nineteenth-century Naples and the stunning Gina Lollobrigida plays the woman on trial and so my discussion will consider how aligning a cinematic sex symbol with a figure like Phryne configures desire as connected to female beauty, ancient and modern. Phryne and her trial also proved irresistible to Mario Bonnard, the prolific actor/director who had already tested the waters of "sword and sandal" films with his 1945 *Romulus and the Sabines*. *Frine, cortigiana d'Oriente* ("Phryne, Courtesan of the Orient," 1953) tells the story of the trial in a relatively straightforward manner, and my exploration of this film will focus on how Phryne's story is shaped by the expectations of its genre. Another entry in the sword and sandal genre, this time an Italian–French collaboration, *La Venere di*

Cheronea (also known as *Aphrodite, déesse de l'amour* and *Goddess of Love*, 1957), draws on the connection between Phryne and Praxiteles in its tale of Iride, a young woman in fourth-century Greece, torn between a Macedonian soldier, Luciano, and the sculptor for whom she has been a model. In this discussion I return to the issues explored in Chapter 2, particularly the ways that art and divinity are fused in the person of Phryne. Although I make no claims to comprehensiveness in this chapter, I hope to demonstrate that when it comes to the reception of Phryne, many of the same conversations from antiquity that her stories brought to light continue to resonate as we seek to understand beauty, desire, and the place of women in the public eye.

Phryne on Canvas: Angelica Kauffman

As with so many other Classical subjects in art, visuals of Phryne emerged in the modern world as part of the larger Neoclassical movement in the eighteenth century,[1] when a variety of creative media turned to the cultures of ancient Greece and Rome for inspiration.[2] As the remains of Pompeii and Herculaneum came to light once more and increasing numbers of well-off Western Europeans returned home from the Grand Tour, painters like Jacques-Louis David recreated the ancient Greek and Roman worlds as they turned away from the Baroque style. Johann Joachim Winckelmann, a German art historian and archaeologist active in the middle of the eighteenth century, set the terms for artistic Neoclassicism when he published *Geschichte der Kunst des Alterthums* ("The History of Art in Antiquity") in 1764, a massively influential work which set out a detailed chronology of ancient Greek art while establishing a set of artistic ideals that often corresponded more closely to his own tastes than to those from the ancient world.[3]

One of the few female Neoclassical painters to achieve notability was Angelica Kauffman, who was born in Switzerland in 1741 but became drawn to the Neoclassical style when she moved to Florence as a young woman in 1762. There she earned membership in the Accademia di Belle Arti di Firenze, where the style was beginning to flourish, and then lived in Rome and Naples in the following years, where she encountered many of the ancient sculptures that would influence her later paintings. In Rome in 1764, Kauffman even crossed paths with Winckelmann, who remarked on her popularity and charm in a letter to a friend after she had painted his portrait.[4] A painter of portraits as well as historical narratives, Kauffman made her way to London in 1766, where she became a member of the Royal Academy of Arts after its foundation in 1768. There she exhibited several Neoclassical works based on literary models, including *Interview of Hector and Andromache* (1769) and *Ariadne Abandoned by Theseus* (1774). In many of these paintings, which impose a Renaissance sensibility on antiquity, Kauffman depicts very fair-skinned and light-haired female figures, wearing diaphanous gowns and elaborate braided hairstyles meant to suggest antiquity.

As a woman who herself was a celebrity, unusually socially mobile for her time, and associated with several notable men including Johann Wolfgang von Goethe and Sir Joshua Reynolds,[5] Kauffman may have been drawn to the ancient stories about Phryne. Kauffman, like Phryne, featured in a series of gossipy anecdotes, such as the one that claimed that she had privately engaged a man to model nude in her studio, and like the ancient *hetaira*, after her death, many of the details about her life were heavily fictionalized.[6] Despite her personal similarities with Phryne, Kauffman was herself the artist rather than the muse and so her exploration of Phryne allowed one unconventional woman to set the terms for the depiction of another; she depicted the *hetaira* twice in her paintings with a great deal of tenderness.

In her Neoclassical work, Kauffman had already begun to explore the relationship between artists, models, and Classical sculpture, beginning with her 1764 *Zeuxis Selecting Models for His Painting of Helen of Troy*, which centers on a woman posing like the famous Hellenistic Aphrodite *Kallipygos* ("Aphrodite of the Beautiful Behind") as the painter Zeuxis positions and inspects her body. In a small tondo painted on copper from 1782, she returned to the theme of artist and model, depicting Alexander the Great bequeathing Campaspe as mistress/model to the painter Apelles, an episode which appears in Pliny's *Natural History* (35.86-87).[7] Here she had moved away from representing the actual creation of art, but instead had begun to consider the dynamic of the relationship between artist and model.

Just over a decade later in 1794, Kauffman chose the moment Praxiteles presented his Eros to Phryne to further explore the love shared between artist and model.

Figure 3 *Praxiteles Giving Phryne his Statue of Cupid*, Angelica Kauffman, 1794, oil on canvas, courtesy of RISD Museum (59.008).

Here the artist gestures to his Eros (depicted as a small child clutching an arrow) while he and Phryne sustain a mutual loving gaze, likely responding to the dynamic described in the ancient epigrams on Praxiteles' Eros, with the statue embodying their desire for each other. Phryne is depicted in this painting as many of Kauffman's other Classical heroines are, with light curly hair done up in an elaborate style, pale skin, and a draped gown, yet here Kauffman has turned away from the obvious choice of depicting her nude. Rather, she is more fully dressed than many of Kauffman's other Classical female subjects are and the fabric of her dress is not even particularly diaphanous, with the effect that Phryne is not depicted here as a sexualized, ideal beauty (or perhaps any more ideal than any other of Kauffman's female subjects), but instead as the object of Praxiteles' love.[8] Given the way that she had the central figure in *Zeuxis Selecting Models for His Painting of Helen of Troy* mimic the Aphrodite

Kallipygos, it is surprising that this image makes no reference to the Aphrodite of Knidos, which strengthens the case that the painting's main engagement with antiquity is through the epigrams on the Eros of Thespiae.

In the same year, Kauffman created a second image of Phryne based in ancient anecdote, this time a somewhat more eroticized version of the *hetaira*, as she attempts to seduce a perturbed-looking Xenocrates.

In this image, Phryne's robe is just beginning to slip from her famous breasts and the floral wreath atop her braided hairstyle is askew as she moves closer to the disinterested philosopher. Wendy Wassyng Roworth connects this image to an earlier painting by Salvator Rosa, whose 1662 painting *Xenocrates and the Shameless Phryne* was well known to English audiences due to a widely circulated engraving by Ravenet and Grignion.

Figure 4 *Phryne seduces the philosopher Xenocrates*, Angelica Kauffman, 1794, oil on canvas, private collection. Photographer Andres Salvador.

Figure 5 *Phryne Tempting Xenocrates*, Simon François Ravenet, the Elder, after Salvator Rosa, 1770, engraving, courtesy of Harvard Art Museums (R9422).

In this version, Phryne is elaborately dressed, coiffed, and jeweled, sitting with her legs suggestively open (but not revealed) as a counterpoint to the austere, standoffish philosopher, who is Rosa's focal point.[9] In Rosa's image both gesture with their hands: Phryne points at Xenocrates and Xenocrates points back to himself in a reverse image of Kauffman's Praxiteles and Phryne.[10]

Although the fact of Phryne's frustrated seduction is clear in Kauffman's painting, unlike Rosa's version in which the fortitude of the philosopher is the primary focus, her version of the scene is paradoxically tender, with the two central figures again looking each other straight in the eye. Finished in Rome, both paintings were part of a group of four Neoclassical images created for one of Kauffman's patrons, George Bowles, who also owned the images featuring the ancient artists Zeuxis and Apelles discussed above. Roworth has argued that the pair of images of Phryne are "ironic complementary subjects" since both connect to stories of Phryne's trickery (her successful ruse with Praxiteles, when she tells him that his studio is on fire, Pausanias 1.20.1-2, and her unsuccessful one with Xenocrates, when she claims that she must shelter with him, D.L. 4. 2.7), meant to illustrate love returned and love spurned.[11] In identifying the theme of these images as reciprocity (whether successful or not), Roworth shows how Kauffman has struck at the heart of the *hetaira*'s stories with her tender depictions of Phryne. Phryne's relationship with Praxiteles, as depicted in the epigrams and Alciphron's letter specifically, is framed around the mutual desire that Kauffman places at the center of her image of the two, while the sympathetic depiction of Xenocrates rebuffing the *hetaira* recenters Phryne in the story and captures something of the playfulness of the ancient philosopher and *hetaira* anecdotes.

The Néo-Grec Movement, Gérôme's Phryne, and the Nude

By the middle of the nineteenth century, the Neoclassical movement had fostered a sub-trend in Second Empire French painting known as the Néo-Grec movement, which featured vibrant mixtures of colors and borrowed elements of Greek, Roman, and Egyptian art. Beginning with the exhibition of Jean-Léon Gérôme's *The Cock Fight* (featuring a young man and woman, both nearly nude, looking on at a cock fight with Mount Vesuvius and the Bay of

Naples in the background) at the Paris Salon in 1847, a small group of painters connected to the studio of Charles Gleyre sought to capture the everyday world of ancient Greece in painstaking detail.[12] A fascination with realism combined with sensuality and anecdote, plus the growing interest among French painters in depicting the female nude, meant that a subject like Phryne was ripe for interpretation by this group. At the same time artists were becoming subjects of ever-increasing amounts of biographical literary work (as seen in the case of Angelica Kauffman) along with the women who were modeling for them.[13]

In 1848, having returned to France after several years dealing with family business interests in Algeria, Gustave Boulanger moved in with and began to work alongside Gérôme and the other Néo-Grec painters. He began to create immensely detailed paintings on ancient themes with orientalising details, one of which, *Ulysse reconnu par Euryclée*, won the Grand Prix of the Académie de France à Rome, bringing him to Rome and from there, to visit Greece and the excavations at Pompeii. During his time in Rome, Boulanger was expected to send a painting back to the Academy in Paris each year to show his artistic progress. The first one he sent, in 1850, was a heavily orientalizing image of Phryne, reclining nude on a pile of bedding and cushions, one of which is embroidered with her name in Greek letters.

She wears golden earrings and bracelet, a beaded necklace and anklet, as well as a diadem and embroidered scarf on her head and holds a mirror in her right hand. With long, wavy auburn hair and full features, she looks straight out of the canvas at the viewer.

This Phryne was not well received: her facial features were decried as being ill-proportioned and the image was thought to be too cluttered. Boulanger's professors at the Academy thought that the image was too contrived,[14] and one critic called her "fat."[15] Since the most notable image of Phryne in the nude circulating at this time was James Pradier's 1845 Winckelmann-esque sculpture of the *hetaira* in white marble with golden accents, Boulanger's painting would have been shocking for its rich colors and layering of textures, but I suspect that most of the objections to this image came down to individual ideas of what makes a woman attractive and this Phryne's unerring gaze at the viewer.[16] Without reference to any of the famous anecdotes about her or a viewer depicted within the painting to guide our response to her, Boulanger's Phryne

Figure 6 *Phryné*, Gustave Boulanger, 1850, oil on canvas, courtesy of Van Gogh Museum (s0456S1996).

challenges the viewer rather than inviting the sentiment of Kauffman's versions. Although her jeweled accoutrements suggest desirability just as Helen's and Aphrodite's did in Greek poetry,[17] the spectacle of Phryne's nudity, punctuated by her outward gaze, combine to unsettling effect for an audience whose expectations for Classical female nudity had been largely shaped by statues like the Aphrodite of Knidos and its various successors. Unlike that image with its cautiously revealing pose and suggestion that the goddess has been interrupted at her bath, this Phryne makes no pretense at covering her nudity at all, but I argue that she seems in keeping with the self-possessed, independent woman of ancient anecdote. This is a Phryne confident in her seductive powers, who understands the power of her own nudity. Boulanger's colleague and center of the Néo-Grec circle, Jean-Léon Gérôme, took up the subject of Phryne a decade later, when he exhibited his history painting *Phryné devant l'Aréopage* at the Salon de Paris in 1861.

In this image, depicting the moment that Hypereides reveals Phryne's body to the courtroom, Phryne's pose is distinctly different from Boulanger's version, or even that of the Aphrodite of Knidos. Instead of coyly shielding her breasts and genitals from the viewer, Gérôme's Phryne has raised her hands to cover her face, revealing the totality of her nude body to the men around her. Her face is barely visible as she hides it in shame, a clever ploy on Gérôme's part to avoid the kinds of criticism that met Boulanger's Phryne as well as a reflection of the ancient sources' dearth of information on her appearance (no need to represent facial details that are not even mentioned in the ancient sources). This pose also mimics the stance that Apelles most likely used for the Aphrodite

Figure 7 *Phryné devant l'Aréopage*, Jean-Léon Gérôme, 1861, oil on canvas, Hamburger Kunsthalle (HK-1910). Photographer Popszes.

Anadyomene, who is thought to have been depicted in the nude, standing in contrapposto wringing out her wet hair with both hands extended on either side of her head (see Figure 1). Gérôme's Phryne has skin so pale and smooth that it resembles marble as it glows against the backdrop of the jurors' red robes. In his lengthy description of the painting, the critic Théophile Gautier insists on the statue-like perfection of Phryne's nude body, offering an account of the judges' reactions that is not too different from Athenaeus' version, while tying in the other most famous anecdote about the *hetaira*: "These judges, whose decisions the gods themselves accept, recoiling at the thought of destroying this perfect body, a living statue which inspired Praxiteles," ("Ces juges, dont les dieux mêmes acceptaient les décisions, reculant à la pensée de détruire ce corps parfait, statue vivant qui inspirait Praxitèle").[18] In a singular image, arguably through the body of Phryne alone, Gérôme managed to incorporate much of what had fueled her ancient fame.

In the painting, Gérôme's engagement with Athenaeus' and Plutarch's version of the anecdote is clear: each of the jurors' reactions reveals their shock at the spectacle of Phryne's body, jaws are dropped and hands thrown in the air, with several members of the jury, who are seated in a semi-circle around the *hetaira*, seeming to cry out, as they look on at Phryne from a variety of angles. Critics found the juror's lascivious expressions focused too much on male desire, concerned that beauty could have that much power over those who gazed upon it, even amongst the "refined" Athenians.[19] Gérôme's use of the jury as the center swath of the painting aligns the viewer of the painting with its internal spectators, with the individualized expressions on each juror's face reminiscent of the ways that the Aphrodite of Knidos could be viewed in the round to suggest a new narrative from each perspective. In keeping with the Néo-Grec style, Gérôme has left no ancient detail unattended, from the central altar with a tiny Athena Promachos on top,[20] to the tripod beside it and the architectural detail throughout. All of this detail however only draws attention to Phryne's nude body and its statuesque presence, standing atop a stone platform that suggests the plinth of a statue, with two unoccupied platforms on either side.[21] (Could these be an allusion to the statues of Eros and Aphrodite that would have accompanied her image at Thespiai?)

The image was widely circulated in photogravure and in 1868 small sculptures of this version of Phryne by Alexandre Falguière were produced to mark the re-exhibition of Gérôme's painting,[22] leaving a lasting impression on the French public. Fittingly for a painting that does so much to remind educated viewers that they are looking at a woman who herself was understood to have been an artist's model, Gérôme's model, Marie-Christine Leroux (also known as Roux), played an important role in the creation of these images that proliferated so thoroughly in French society and had a lasting impact on French painting. One of the first women to pose nude for a photographer (in this case Nadar), in the mid-1850s she sat for photos that were commissioned by Jean-Auguste-Dominique Ingres to be used in the creation of his painting *La Source*, depicting a female nude pouring water from a jar held upon her left shoulder. The photos of Leroux, standing alone against a plain backdrop, were then requested by Gérôme, who mirrored the images of Leroux in Phryne's pose.[23] Gérôme went on to have an enduring fascination with both photography and sculpture, which he integrated into his artistic process.[24]

Leroux the model, in addition to her collaborations with photographers and artists and not unlike her ancient counterpart, inspired her own fictionalized narrative as part of *Scènes de la vie de bohème* ("Scenes from Bohemian Life"), published by Henri Murger in 1851. A collection of vignettes depicting life in the Latin Quarter that was later adapted into the opera *La Bohème* by Puccini, Murger's narrative featured a character based on Leroux called Musette, described as intelligent, rebellious, but elegant. Because of her involvement in artistic circles, association with characters like Musette, and her modeling work, Leroux was also assumed to have been a sex worker, as were many of her model colleagues. The association with Phryne must only have fueled that particular fire. Leroux was tragically killed in 1863 when the ferry she was taking from Marseilles to Algiers sank, but like Phryne, her reputation grew and shifted as her image continued to circulate after her death.

Another acquaintance of Murger who inspired a character in *Scènes de la vie de bohème*, Jules François Felix Fleury-Husson (nom de plume Champfleury), wrote a recollection of Leroux in his book of anecdotes recording the artistic world of mid-nineteenth-century Paris, *Souvenirs et portraits de jeunesse: Autobiographie et mémoires* ("Memories and Portraits of Youth: Autobiography and Memoirs"). Here he discusses Leroux (whom he refers to as "Mademoiselle M.") as a link between poetry and painting,[25] while

Figure 8 "Standing Female Nude," featuring model Marie-Christine Leroux, Gaspard-Félix Tournachon (Nadar), 1860, salted paper print from glass negative, Metropolitan Museum of Art (1991.1174).

claiming that she had made her fortune from men.[26] Leroux could not be better cast as the model who was turned into Phryne and whose image, divorced from the woman Leroux really was, circulated endlessly after her death. Champfleury describes her legacy in words which could be applied to Phryne herself:

> Nothing remains but a fleeting memory. Some men from her generation, when they review their poems, their novels, their paintings, their statues, will

recall that for a moment they captured the best of the coquette: the flower of her youth, a smile, a witticism, the way she carried herself, a chorus sung in a clear voice. The rest was worth little and could be sold for a high price to those who seek nothing but tainted love.

Il ne reste rien qu'un souvenir fugitif. Quelques hommes de sa génération, en revoyant leurs poèmes, leurs romans, leurs tableaux, leurs statues, se rapelleront qu'à un moment ils fixèrent le meilleur de la coquette: la fleur de sa jeunesse, un sourire, une saillie, un air de tête, un refrain chanté d'une voix claire. Le reste valait peu de chose et peut être vendu fort cher aux gens qui ne recherchent que l'amour frelaté.[27]

Champfleury's words also capture the fascination with women of the demimonde during that period, particularly the women who posed nude for famous artists. The female nude as an artistic trope was considered by many to be an innovation which allowed artists to express both purity of form and an interpretation of nature (cf. Gérôme's comments in his preface to Émile Bayard's *Le Nu Esthétique*), yet the women who modeled for these images were often treated as scandalous necessities of the artistic process. Their stories were circulated widely as the art they were associated with drove the prurient interest in their erotic lives: as Marie Lathers articulates, "the nineteenth century invented the female model as an individual who could be classified and whose history could be written."[28] Marie-Christine Leroux exemplifies this phenomenon, of which the ongoing interest in Gérôme's painting and then in Phryne herself were a manifestation, an echo of the ancient process by which the *hetairai* of the fourth century became an evergreen preoccupation for later generations.

The embrace of Phryne in France of the 1860s as an image that conjured up ancient beauty and the allure of a sex worker meant that her name alone could signify prurient desire in that decade. As part of a move to depict more women of that era in academic painting, Charles-François Marchal submitted a pair of images of women in contemporary clothing to the Salon of 1868. The first, titled *Pénélope*, shows a young woman in a domestic setting, wearing a demure gray dress and engrossed in her needlework, meant to recall the faithful wife of Homer's Odysseus, who famously employed handicraft (weaving) to preserve the integrity of her marriage while her husband was away at war.[29] The second one, titled *Phryné*, features another young woman in a more revealing (sleeveless and with a low-cut back) gown, turning to look the viewer in the eye in a manner reminiscent of Boulanger's version of the *hetaira*.[30] Together, the two women in these paintings and their Classical namesakes offer a commentary on the morals of women in the France of that time, offering either "the bourgeois wife" or "the high-priced whore" for the viewer's consumption.[31] Penelope is deeply ensconced within the household, while Phryne is at her toilette, seemingly about to set out for the evening, echoing the mobility of the ancient sex worker in comparison to the citizen wife. Marchal's painting marked the first time that Phryne was transposed into a contemporary setting,[32] an acknowledgment by the artist of the many resonances between the romanticized visions of nineteenth-century Parisian courtesans and the *hetairai* of ancient literature.

Thus by the final decades of the nineteenth century and into the early twentieth century there was a blossoming of works spreading outward from France that referred to Phryne, her legendary beauty, and often her nudity, in all kinds of media. These ranged from a waltz for the piano by Antonin d'Argenton ("Phryné," 1887), to political cartoons lampooning Gérôme's painting ("Phryne before the Chicago Tribunal").[33]

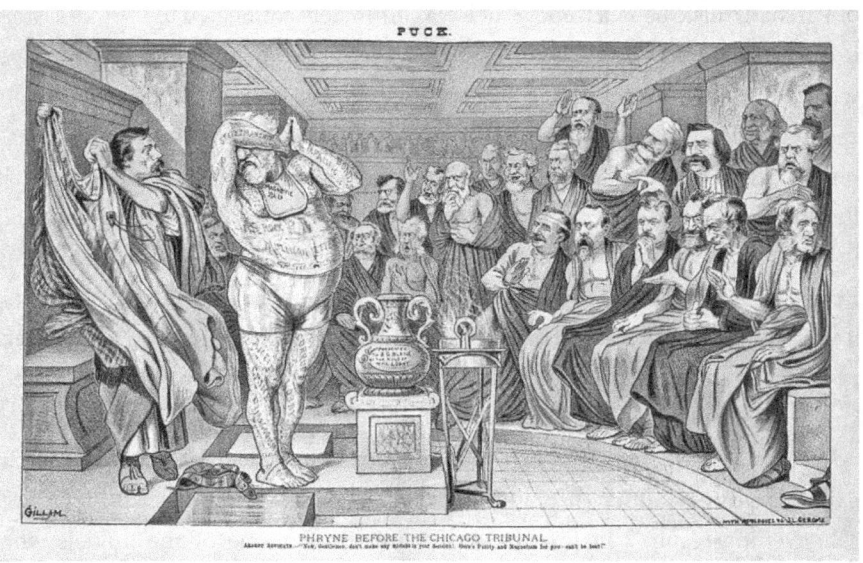

Figure 9 "Phryne before the Chicago Tribunal," Bernhard Gillam, 1884 June 4, political cartoon from *Puck* 15 (378), restored by Adam Cuerden, Library of Congress (AP101.P7).

As Lela F. Kerley argues with regard to this cultural flourishing of Phryne, "[she] reflected a male desire to visually apprehend and consume female nudity across a range of media and experiences,"[34] an argument which applies equally to her appearances in ancient literature and art. At the same time, more attention was focused on female models than ever before as the Salon de Paris was flooded with paintings featuring female nudes, following the trend set by Gérôme. Like Phryne the ancient metic, many of these women had migrated to Paris and found work outside of conventionally respectable channels and so the literature that depicted them and fictionalized their lives functioned in much the same way as the ancient literature on the *hetairai* did, offering compelling portraits of unconventional women with sensationalizing distortions of their erotic lives, as in the examples I discussed earlier that took up the biography of Marie-Christine Leroux. Because of Phryne's cultural saturation, her name even became shorthand to reference Paris' own *femmes nues* of that time, women who had come to Paris in hopes of earning a living with their own beautiful bodies and found themselves in trouble with the law, often charged with indecency after the public display of their bodies.[35]

From the 1870s onward, women had also begun to appear nude on the stages of Parisian music halls, a trend which was intimately connected to the increasing use of nude models by artists. In fact, many of the women performing on stage were the same ones modeling and so in order to explore Phryne's impact on cabaret performances, I would now like to offer some context for the sensational phenomenon of the *femmes nues* in *fin-de-siècle* Paris. A major turning point for the connection between painting, sculpture, and live performance and its place in broader culture was the second annual Bal des Quat'z'Arts held at the Moulin Rouge in 1893. Organized by faculty and students of the École des Beaux Arts, it was subject to a great deal of fanfare prior to the event, as students circulated poems and articles meant to create intrigue among the wider public. A mixed crowd was invited (remarkable since the École des Beaux Arts was still only open to male students), but the evening featured nude women meant to act as living paintings walking through the crowd, all part of a night of wild revelry.[36] The evening resulted in the arrest of Sarah Brown, one of the models who appeared nude, along with others.[37] The arrests and prosecution of the nude models by anti-vice protestors in turn led to a week of riots by students in the Latin Quarter, who were angry at the leaders of the Third Republic and their attempts to regulate morality. On the other side was the Ligue contre la License des Rues ("League for the Prevention of Public Licentiousness") and its campaigns against pornography, pitted against increasingly salacious public performances and the women who starred in these experimental cabaret shows. Class was also an important dynamic in this debate, as the establishment supporters of art and patrons of the theater faced off against the bourgeoisie who were concerned over public morality. This debate over public morality crescendoed with a series of lawsuits at the end of the nineteenth and beginning of the twentieth century about appropriate costumes in the theater and the appearances of nude women onstage. This was a moment of extreme division in French society, as the two sides sought to define popular morality and the appropriate place for women in the public sphere, all of which came to a head in the legal and moral battles over the *femme nue*.

Phryne on Stage

As the two sides in the debate over public morality continued to wrangle with each other in the late nineteenth century, Phryne made her way to Parisian stages in a variety of genres of performance. While some were understood to be more respectable than others, in all cases the intriguing *hetaira*'s story was deployed to harness the French public's seemingly endless appetite for female beauty, but especially for nudity. Phryne's particular narratives, connected as closely as they were to nudity, allowed the producers of these shows to put on a titillating spectacle with the sheen of antiquity offering legitimacy that helped to deflect the concerns of those who would censure such performances. Phryne, made famous again through Gérôme's painting and the images associated with it, became the ideal vehicle for shows about and performed by women who were admired privately but condemned publicly and so now I intend to explore a series of *fin-de-siècle* performances that told her story.

Since the cabaret was the most cutting-edge space for performance in Paris in the late nineteenth century, it is only fitting that the *femme nue* found a comfortable home on its stage. One of the most avant-garde venues at this time was Le Chat Noir in the bohemian district Montmartre, which was home to a shadow theater, with a screen 44 inches by 55 inches, illuminated from behind with electric lights. The shadows of zinc cut-outs used as puppets were projected onto the screen; their movement would be accompanied by music and a script read out loud. Introduced to Le Chat Noir in 1885, the shadow theater was immensely popular and an ideal means of presenting a *femme nue* without exposing the nude body of a real woman.

In 1891, Maurice Donnay wrote and performed his shadow theater version of Phryne's story, standing beside the piano that accompanied such performances while he recited its satirical verses tonelessly.

This was Donnay's debut, revealing his interest in the relations between men and women in Greek antiquity (he produced his own version of Aristophanes' *Lysistrata* the following year). Donnay's *Phryné* is a series of tableaux set in Classical Athens, opening with the lament of a poor elderly

Figure 10 "Phryné suppliante," zinc cut-out, courtesy of Musée de Châtellerault (2007.0.8).

poet in the year 300 BCE, who sings a song about his ruin that is all due to Phryne, "delicieuse et cupide" ("delicious and greedy"), "la courtisane adorable et terrible" ("the adorable and terrible courtesan," *Phryné* 3). The scene is set as the narrator brings the audience back twenty-one centuries "before Monsieur Gérôme's painting was completed" ("afin que ... le tableau de Monsieur Gérôme fut accompli," *Phryné* 5).

The second tableau brings us to the famous ancient Athenian cabaret the Ailouros Melas ("Black Cat" in Greek), where short poems about the famous *hetairai* Lais and Glykera are performed. The erotic story of Jupiter and Leda follows,[38] until it is interrupted by Phryne calling out a crude euphemism ("Vas-y, Léda, plume-le!" "Go on, Leda, pluck him!" *Phryné* 12): this is the crime for which she will face trial. The third tableau opens in the home of an elderly judge, where Phryne will arrive shortly to plead for her life, the judge having been duly warned by his wife about Phryne's wiles. Phryne arrives and pleads with the judge, claiming to have loved him from afar (quoting Sappho while she does this),[39] before she runs off. In the fourth tableau, Phryne has decided to exhibit herself one last time to the Athenians in the Kerameikos, with her fellow *hetaira* Melissa, who recommends the services of the orator Hypereides. Phryne scratches a note out saying that she loves Hypereides, he sees this, and sets off in pursuit of her (*Phryné* 22). Thus the fifth tableau opens with the orator and the *hetaira* in bed together on the morning of her trial and as they begin to make love, a curtain of vines falls, which the ever-witty narrator says has been prescribed by the management (*Phryné* 24). After their lovemaking has concluded, they discuss the trial, and she tells Hypereides that he now knows her in the nude, just as he knows the truth.[40] He reassures her that she is in no danger, since his plea will be the "glory of her body" ("la gloire de ton corps"), which he goes on to describe in detail, comparing her physique to architectural perfection (*Phryné* 26).

The brief sixth tableau, the trial itself, is meant to be a faithful reproduction of Gérôme's painting, with one exception: Phryne is dressed, only to be unveiled. Donnay's script does not linger on Hypereides' speech, which the narrator points out has not been preserved, nor does it tell us how much of Phryne the audience sees, but rather that the jury will appreciate the sight (*Phryné* 28). In the final tableau, the elderly poet returns. concluding by telling the audience that Eros leads everyone, the most Athenian thing of all (*Phryné* 31). Thus the erotic and the ancient were married in this performance and because of Phryne's well-known image (largely thanks to Gérôme), the *femme nue* hovered just offstage throughout the performance.

In 1893, Camille Saint-Saëns took advantage of Phryne's cultural capital when he wrote and premiered his only comic opera, *Phryné* (with libretto by Lucien Augé de Lassus), to great acclaim.[41] The opera ran for many months and immediately toured widely throughout Europe, including a performance at the ancient Roman theater in Orange.[42] Having already tested Classical waters in the 1870s with several symphonic poems based in myth, Saint-Saëns had an ongoing interest in the Classical world throughout his career and was particularly interested in ancient performance and music.[43] (Later in his career, Saint-Saëns was photographed in his home, with a table-top statue of Phryne in the nude beside him.)[44] In his opera he used the Classical references to Phryne in service of a satirical comedy that drew on the appeal of an erotic story to make fun of issues from the political to the musical.[45] In this version of her story, Phryne is a young Greek courtesan whose lover's uncle pursues her as she attempts to get the uncle to pay for his nephew's debts. There is a scene in which the older man confuses her for a statue of Aphrodite. She does go to trial, but instead of her nude body being presented to the jurors it is a statue, elegantly drawing together the major threads of Phryne's ancient narrative while avoiding the ire of those who were concerned about the women on Parisian stages.[46]

As with so many of the receptions of Phryne in the nineteenth century, this version was also tied to an unconventional woman, in this case the soprano Sibyl Sanderson.[47] Sanderson was an American socialite from California. Kicked out of boarding school and then nearly married to William Randolph Hearst, she found her way to the opera stage and fame in Paris (fans called her the "California Nightingale") and later died in her late thirties of alcoholism and resulting ill-health. Prior to playing Phryne, she had already developed a reputation for playing seductive beauties, including Manon, Esclarmonde, and Lakmé. After her tragic death, in his biography of Saint-Saëns, the librettist Augé de Lassus elided performer and character as he spoke of Phryne's divinity expressed through Sanderson's voice.[48] Capitalizing on the hubbub over nudity on stage and Sanderson's notoriety, the producers of the opera seem to have insinuated that audiences at the initial performances would see Sanderson

Figure 11 Sibyl Sanderson as Phryné, image from *Saint-Saëns* by Lucien Augé de Lassus, 1893.

herself unveiled in the critical moments of the trial, rather than the statue they did see.[49] Photographs of Sanderson in ancient costume and with props including a fluted column entwined with ivy were circulated as part of the opera's publicity. One of those portraits featured Sanderson posed at a three-quarter turn to the camera with her hands resting on her head and wearing a diaphanous light-colored gown, alluding to Phryné's pose in Gérôme's painting, which had become common visual vocabulary in French culture by the 1890s.

Several years later in 1896, Phryne left behind the confines of the Parisian stage, with a pantomime ballet devoted to her story performed at the casino in the seaside resort of Royan. The town had become a fashionable vacation spot for Parisian elites as well as their paid female companions,[50] and so a titillating performance like a ballet version of Phryne's story was a popular and appropriately themed money-maker. *Phryné* was a pantomime by Louis Ganne and Auguste Germain, choreographed by the well-known ballet mistress, Madame Mariquita. The spectacle involved a forty-piece orchestra, used choreography that drew on ancient imagery, mimed dramatic scenes, and closed with a dramatic tableau. The overall effect of the performance was to carefully navigate between the high culture of antiquity and the eroticism of the female performers' beautiful bodies.

As a ballet, it called for extended dance scenes, and so Phryne's crime in this version of her story was dancing nude before a statue of Venus, a more chaste version of which she reperforms in front of the court. At the end of this dance, however, her lover Praxiteles rips off her clothing so that all can see her nude body, thus creating a fixed tableau with Phryne in the center for the audience to admire. The impression of nudity was achieved with the actress playing Phryne wearing a pale bodysuit, lit so that the outline of her body would be the only thing visible to the audience, leaving any nudity to viewers' imaginations. Venus arrives and demands that Phryne be acquitted. Illustrations from newspapers at the time depict a scene not unlike the one in Gérôme's painting, with Phryne in an identical pose to the one from the painting, and several elderly jurors looking on, only this time with lecherous grins rather than shocked expressions.[51]

The woman at the center of this performance was Cléo de Mérode, a dancer whose life until that point had been marked by great scandal. The illegitimate daughter of an Austrian noblewoman, she posed for portraits by many of the noted artists of the period, including Toulouse-Lautrec, as well as many photographers, Nadar among them, so that images of her circulated widely on items like postcards. Rumours made their way around society that she was involved with King Leopold II of Belgium (who already had children with a different woman accused of sex work), which became further fodder for claims that she was a courtesan. In 1896, she allowed the sculptor Alexandre Falguière, the creator of the sculpted version of Gérôme's Phryne, to make a plaster cast of her body, which he then used to create a white marble statue of her. She later claimed that it was not her body at all, but the association with the statue allowed her to garner interest in her performance as Phryne. Mérode made further use of the elision between herself and the ancient *hetaira* when she would go down to the sea for a swim (unlike Phryne, attired in a bathing costume), bringing Athenaeus and Apelles' Aphrodite into the tangled web of referentiality that her persona and performance created.[52]

The following year, in 1897, another performance of Ganne and Germain's *Phryné* featuring a *femme nue* was mounted at the well-known Folies Bergère, a music hall that had begun mounting musical revues in the mid-1880s known for their elaborate costumes and sets, but especially for their increasingly risqué female performers. As with so many of these suggestive performances, the women were not entirely nude, but costumed to suggest as much. This production caused one critic to comment that the "pretty vision of ancient life makes you forget the vulgarity of the atmosphere" ("cette jolie vision de la vie antique fait oublier la vulgarité de l'ambiance").[53] This in fact seems to have been the point of using an ancient setting, which the producers thought was perhaps the easiest way of "exhibiting bare thighs" without attracting too much attention from the authorities.[54]

Jane Margyl, the actress playing Phryne in Paris, was making her stage debut, and one critic noted that in this role she was "beautiful, sculptural, fleshy, appetizing, incendiary" ("belle, sculpturale, charnue, appétissante, incendiaire"), so much so that he expressed concern for those who would be forced to sleep alone after seeing such provocative sights.[55] As with Marie-Christine Leroux in Nadar's photographs, Sibyl Sanderson in Saint-Saëns' opera, and Cléo de Mérode and Falguière's sculpture and the pantomime ballet, the woman behind Phryne was a sometimes controversial public figure, lauded for her beauty and talent but soon to die tragically young (in this case from appendicitis at the age of thirty-three). Margyl played Phryne in this show over 200 times and as with Sanderson, photographs of her in clothing suggestive of antiquity were circulated to publicize her performance. Although these images are not as directly connected to Gérôme's Phryne in terms of her pose or attire, they were created at the Atelier Nadar, where Leroux's photograph had been taken decades before. For all of these women life, art, and the character they played intertwined to such a degree that they were inseparable in the ways that they challenged the status quo and were received by society at large. Each of them provoked conservative elements in society though the use of their bodies, animating static ideas of what it meant to be a woman in the public eye, just as the Phryne we know through anecdote had done in the ancient world.

Phryné the musical revue and its ephemeral stars marked the height of the spectacularization of the nude female body in nineteenth-century Paris as well as the height of the conjunction between antiquity and female nudity on the Parisian stage. Phryne, who had been turned into a symbol of the argument over public morality in Classical Athens, in *fin-de-siècle* Paris became a convenient vehicle for those on the avant-garde of erotic performance to put the nude female body on display without drawing the ire of moral authorities. The imprimatur of antiquity provided an artistic veil for the titillation of these performances as Phryne's body was transformed into a rhetorical argument once more and cultural capital could be derived from the prurient interest in a beautiful woman and her body, so long as it was associated with a prestigious past culture. Gérôme's version of Phryne, which had kicked off this widespread fascination, proved a dominant influence as each creator grappled with an image that had become imprinted on French minds.

Phryne Everywhere

By the early twentieth century, Phryne's image had permeated European culture via advertisements, performances, and visual art, as creators engaged with Gérôme's legacy, each attempting to capture her beauty, whether on stage, on a canvas, in a lithograph, or in a photo. Posters from the stage performances in the 1890s circulated widely, as did commemorative scripts and scores, typically featuring an image of a beautiful woman on the cover dressed to invoke antiquity. Actresses, dancers, and models, responding to the popularity of images from these performances, vied to pose as Phryne for postcards that could be collected by their fans, or by those who were simply attracted to their erotic imagery. After the banning of nudity in photographs in France in 1908, women like the actress Nina Barkis would nevertheless pose with fabric draped around them to suggest nudity and append Phryne's name to the top of the image to capitalize on the eroticism it implied.

No longer just a French phenomenon, Phryne's image was taken up by artists from Poland to Brazil, each taking advantage of her overwhelming cultural presence to use her as shorthand in order to impose their own ideas of beauty and antiquity in a visual medium. Once again, I make no attempt at a comprehensive inventory of these images, too numerous to count, but have chosen several representative images to discuss.

The Polish painter Henryk Siemiradzki, working in Rome in the last decades of the nineteenth century, was known for detailed history paintings influenced by French Academic painters like Gérôme. Like Gérôme's, his 1889 version of Phryne depicts a scene from Athenaeus, in this case the moment when she goes into the sea at Eleusis and inspires Apelles.

Phryne at the Poseidonia in Eleusis is even more detailed than *Phryné devant l'Aréopage*, with a vista toward the sea, a religious procession, and a temple of Poseidon filling the space around Phryne,[56] the central figure, as Siemiradzki fleshes out the gaps in Athenaeus' skeletal narrative. She stands nude, with some drapery at her waist that covers very little of her body, in contrapposto, with her arms up to mimic the Aphrodite Anadyomene pose as the crowd around looks on, their expressions varying from delight to dismay.[57] An attendant holds a parasol above her, which shades only her half-turned face: as in Gérôme's painting, Phryne's body is the focal point, rather than her face. Since Siemiradzki saw this painting as his opportunity to represent Classical

Figure 12 *Phryne at the Poseidonia in Eleusis*, Henryk Siemiradzki, 1889, oil on canvas, Russian Museum (Ж5687).

beauty,[58] it seems appropriate that he appropriated these techniques that suggest beauty rather than portraying it directly.

As with Boulanger's Phryne, each critic's personal tastes influenced their response to Siemiradzki's exploration of beauty, with some calling her heavy and others not-so-young (this same critic, Fritz von Ostini, who found this Phryne insufficiently youthful, suggested that the version of Phryne in this painting would certainly not be enough to attract Praxiteles or Hypereides).[59] Some critics even suggested that this Phryne was insufficiently feminine.[60] These reactions belie the larger pattern when it comes to paintings of Phryne; as each artist turns to her and her body to explore the relationship between beauty and art, individual opinions on what makes a woman attractive come into play for both the painter and the viewer. Those tastes align so rarely that the painter must turn to the kinds of devices found in literary representations of Phryne to indicate, rather than portray her beauty. Internal viewers, such as the jurors in Athenaeus' literary and Gérôme's visual versions, tell us that Phryne is stunning; turning her face away from the viewer to avoid scrutiny of its appearance allows us to impose our own ideas of beauty on her. But even if an artist should make use of these conventions, as Siemiradzki did with the awed crowd, they would rarely please all critics, who have often been prone to confusing personal ideas of what makes a woman beautiful with thoughtful art criticism. These aspects of Gérôme's and Siemiradzki's depictions (the obscured face and the internal spectators) both appear in José Frappa's 1904 painting *Phryné*, which acts as a condensed version of Gérôme's.

A student of the École des Beaux-Arts who had likely been aware of *Phryné devant l'Aréopage* for most of his life,[61] Frappa started his career with images based in famous anecdotes that were also depictions of beautiful women. These two tendencies come together in his *Phryne*, with the *hetaira* standing with her back to the viewer, visible only from the waist up, a single breast only partially revealed, and her face in profile. Only four jurors are included in the image, crowded around her; one in the background cranes to get a look as Hypereides pulls her robe back and smirks. Phryne's pale skin glows where illuminated, notably at the one visible breast.

While Frappa's fair-skinned, blonde version did not differ significantly from Gérôme's, the widespread impact of Phryne at this point had begun to allow for

Figure 13 *Phryné*, José Frappa, 1903, oil on canvas, Musée d'Orsay (LUX 1235).

increasingly diverse depictions of her beauty; although this diversity still prized a youthful and white version of beauty, Phryne was no longer a strictly Academic creation who was required to have an incandescent glow like marble or to have strictly golden tresses.[62] Despite still making use of standard tropes like jeweled accessories to suggest attractiveness or luxurious fabrics to insinuate opulence, the Phrynes of Franz von Stuck (a German painter and sculptor who painted at least three versions of her between 1916 and 1917) and Antonio Parreiras (a Brazilian painter who created his version in 1909) were able to escape the requirement of the earlier French Academic artists to capture a perfected, idealized beauty and offer up images of women attractive on their own terms. Like Boulanger's version, these women make eye contact with the viewer, revealing their own bodies without others' intervention. They invite an erotic gaze but their poses are not meant to represent any canonical sculpture or ideal.

The Phrynes of von Stuck and Parreiras are closer in style to the Phrynes that appeared in advertisements during the same period, sometimes depicted by models in photographs or in artists' lithographs. The models in photos used

Figure 14 *Phryne*, Franz von Stuck, 1917, oil on canvas, courtesy of Portland Art Museum (62.9, gift of Dr. Anna Berliner).

for advertising, as opposed to the photos of actresses and dancers, seem to have had more freedom in the poses they could choose as Phryne, with suggestive clothing and often a label helping the viewer identify whom the image was meant to depict. Art Nouveau lithography offered similar leeway, since much of its generic standards had developed as a reaction against the expectations of academic art. These Phrynes were free of Winckelmann's dominating ideas of what the ancient world should look like and therefore able

Figure 15 *Phryne*, Antonio Parreiras, 1909, oil on canvas.

to embody an exuberant rather than an austere beauty, since the name in and of itself was now understood to epitomize desirability and had been animated so memorably on stage.

Phryne on Screen

Phryne's image had penetrated every corner of European consciousness in the first decades of the twentieth century, while widespread interest in the Classical world had not waned. At the same time, film was becoming a dominant form of mass culture; it was only a matter of time before Phryne's story, as centered on visual appeal as it was, made it to the big screen. As with the stage spectacles of *fin-de-siècle* France, female celebrity was harnessed by Italian filmmakers to draw in audiences, with stars like Gina Lollobrigida, who had won third place in the Miss Italia pageant in 1947, and Belinda Lee, a British actress who had played a series of leading roles in that country before coming to Italy, taking on the role of Phryne. From nineteenth-century picturesques (*Altri Tempi/In Olden Times*, 1951) to quasi-historic fantasy (*Frine, cortigiana d'Oriente/*

Phryne, Courtesan of the Orient, 1953 and *La Venere di Cheronea/Aphrodite, The Goddess of Love*, 1957), the prurient interest in a beautiful woman making her way through a society that did not always welcome her seemed an ideal match for the burgeoning genre of cinema.

Once the Second World War had come to an end and the Italian film industry had recovered, it was second only to Hollywood in public acclaim and profit, as Italian filmmakers sought to tell Italian stories. To do so, they often turned to beautiful, well-endowed women to sell their films to popular audiences; these women also typically had love affairs with notable men, often the producers of their movies, gossip that was eagerly exploited by movie studios to promote their films. Actresses from this category like Sophia Loren became known by the term "*maggiorata fisica*" (literally "physically increased" but perhaps best understood as "buxom beauty"), which originated in the 1951 film *Altri Tempi/In Olden Times* as part of the episode featuring Phryne's story.[63] That film, comprising a series of nine episodes on late nineteenth-century life in Italy, concluded with an installment titled "Il Processo di Frine" ("The Trial of Phryne"), set in Naples. The "Phryne" in question, a woman named Mariantonia, was played by Gina Lollobrigida, then in the early days of her celebrated cinematic career.

The episode is based on a short story by Edoardo Scarfoglio, an Italian author who was interested in reviving classicism in literature. In it Mariantonia is on trial for trying to poison her husband and mother-in-law. The actress who played her, Gina Lollobrigida, is seated in the defandant's chair at the front of the courtroom throughout, her hair done up in a braided peasant hairstyle, wearing a corseted dress with a significant amount of decolletage (the dress is designed with a revealing diamond-shaped peephole over her torso). Over this, she wears a shawl, which Gina Lollobrigida wraps and unwraps at key points in her dialogue to emphasize her prominent chest. The scene in the courtroom is raucous, with the audience, judge, and jury calling out throughout until Mariantonia's defense lawyer, played by Vittorio De Sica, steps forward to deliver an impassioned speech in her defence. As his speech reaches its crescendo he reminds his audience of the story of Hypereides and Phryne before the Areopagus (perhaps influenced by Gérôme's version as well), and then, his voice straining with passion, he brings Mariantonia into the center of the courtroom and tears away her shawl. The lawyer says that he

Figure 16 Poster for *Altri Tempi*, 1952, starring Gina Lollobrigida, directed by Alessandro Blasetti, Società Italiana Cines.

cannot repeat Hypereides' gesture (i.e., tear her clothes off), but he then places Mariantonia on a pedestal in front of the judge.

The episode reaches its climax as he re-covers her with her shawl, then whips the shawl off in his re-enactment of the ancient trial; the camera lingers for a moment on Lollobrigida, her cleavage at the center of the shot. De Sica turns back to his audience and delivers the most famous line from the film, which I paraphrase here: "If we can acquit some for decreased mental capacity, then why not the *maggiorata fisica*?"[64] The crowd roars in approval, Mariantonia goes free, and the defense attorney is lauded by all for his brilliance. The film was marketed with images of Lollobrigida in her revealing costume front and center; she was clearly the sensation of the film and so Phryne made her debut on the Italian screen and created a new kind of voluptuous beauty for modern cinema at the same time.

At the same time as Lollobrigida was setting the terms for a new sort of on-screen beauty in the 1950s, the sword-and-sandal film (also known as the "peplum" film after the Classical Greek style of dress) was sweeping the world of Italian cinema. As Italy moved into the post-war era, its films looked back beyond its painful recent history with escapist adventure films set in Greco-Roman antiquity, typically starring brawny heroes and beautiful heroines, all scantily clad for maximum audience appeal. Possibly inspired by the acclaim received by Lollobrigida's version of Phryne,[65] the director and screen writer Mario Bonnard collaborated on the script for *Frine, cortigiana d'Oriente/ Phryne, Courtesan of the Orient*, which was released in 1953.[66] A sumptuous black and white vision of Classical Greece with elaborate sets and costumes, this version of Phryne's story was filmed at Cinecittà Studios, the massive Roman studio central to the sword-and-sandal genre, with Bonnard's assistant, a young Sergio Leone, taking control of most of the shoot.

Frine, cortigiana d'Oriente starred Elena Kleus, like Lollobrigida a former beauty queen (Miss Greece 1952), who had been recruited to play the role of Phryne when the producer, Marquese Manca, saw her in the Miss World pageant. Telling Kleus that she was the very image of Phryne, he brought her in for a screen test. After dying her hair blonde, Kleus secured the role, which she had to learn phonetically since she did not speak Italian.[67] Like *Altri Tempi*, the film was marketed via suggestive images of its female star, Kleus' robes nearly slipping off of her breasts, as its audience was encouraged to envision Kleus as Phryne brought back to life. Just like the stars of the French stage who played Phryne, Kleus sat for photos in costume, which were published in popular magazines like *Tempo*. Kleus' career in movies was brief, largely due to the kind of attention her role had elicited: after completing only three films, she emigrated to Venezuela, frustrated by the intrusiveness of the paparazzi and the contract system of the Italian studios.[68]

Clearly intent on incorporating as many ancient anecdotes about Phryne as possible, the team of screen writers opened their story in Thebes, where the Macedonian ruler destroys the family of a young woman named Afra by

Figure 17 Poster for *Frine, cortigiana d'Oriente*, 1953, starring Elena Kleus, directed by Mario Bonnard, Zeuss Film.

burning her mother and father alive. Afra is imprisoned, but manages to escape, before she is captured by a slave trader who brings her to Athens. There she is purchased by a man named Lamaco who had betrayed Afra's family in Thebes, given the name Frine, and turned into the high-class courtesan of ancient anecdote.[69] As a year passes by, Frine becomes the most famous courtesan in the city, while Alexander has destroyed her home city. Iperide the lawyer meets her and they fall in love, but his friend Prassitele, a sculptor, convinces the young man to leave her. Frine, now wealthy and powerful, offers to rebuild the walls of Thebes. The archons are scandalized by Frine, who is convinced by Lamaco to play the part of a goddess at the Eleusinian Mysteries.

Charged with impiety, Frine is brought before the Areopagus, but Iperide arrives to save her at the urging of Prassitele. Frine is acquitted while Lamaco is convicted and the film concludes with the walls of Thebes rebuilt with the famous caption from antiquity inscribed upon them.

Throughout the film, Kleus' costumes are both revealing and elaborate, with highly wrought jewels adorning her, suggestive of the oriental luxury she is meant to embody, and hearkening back to images like Boulanger's painting. In her scene before the archons, however, she appears without jewels in a simple, but still suggestive, white dress as she advocates for Thebes. Her costume when she appears at the Mysteries as Aphrodite is equally simple but relatively covered-up (the neckline covers her entire decolletage), perhaps to suggest the power of Phryne's beauty and to disassociate her from the depraved behavior of the courtesans. This simplicity is in contrast to another courtesan character, Ate, who wears textiles woven with gold and is coated in jewels whenever she appears on screen. During the trial itself, Frine is simply dressed in a one-shouldered robe, which Iperide easily pulls off of her as she stands on a pedestal, surrounded by the people of Athens. In keeping with on-screen practices regarding nudity at the time, her revelation is not complete, but Frine covers herself almost immediately with the fabric of her dress. The crowd cheers at this moment and the scene concludes with Frine and Iperide united; there is an extended shot of a single onlooker looking at the couple in joyful awe.

Unlike *Altri Tempi*, which adapted Phryne's story to the modern world, *Frine, cortigiana d'Oriente* was focused on bringing the ancient world to life, as it tied in every possible aspect of Phryne's anecdotes to its plot, whether comfortably incorporated, like the love story with Iperide, or uncomfortably shoehorned in, like the presence of Prassitele, whose studio allowed the filmmakers to fill their set with canonical sculptures that the educated among the audience would recognize with ease. Praxiteles did receive his due, however, in the final film I will discuss here, the 1957 Italian–French co-production *La Venere di Cheronea/Aphrodite, déesse de l'amour/Aphrodite, The Goddess of Love*, directed by Fernando Cerchio and Viktor Tourjansky and filmed at Cinecittà. Like *Frine, cortigiana d'Oriente*, it was a standard sword-and-sandal film centered on a romance between a muscular hero and a beautiful heroine, but unlike the earlier film, it recast Phryne as a model rather than a courtesan, focusing on her connection to Aphrodite through Praxiteles.

Figure 18 Poster for *La Venere di Cheronea/Aphrodite, déesse de l'amour/Aphrodite, The Goddess of Love*, 1957, starring Belinda Lee, directed by Fernando Cerchio and Viktor Tourjansky, Rialto Film.

Like the earlier film starring Elena Kleus, set during a time of conflict with the Macedonians, the plot features a love triangle between Iride, a beautiful model who has posed for Prassitele's statue of Aphrodite, the sculptor himself, and Luciano, a Macedonian soldier that she saves after he has been wounded in battle. With Luciano recovering at Prassitele's studio (again filled with recognizable statues by the filmmakers), Iride falls in love with the soldier and the two subsequently try to run away together. Prassitele, also in love with Iride, sends Athenian soldiers after the two, who shoot Luciano with an arrow.

Iride returns to the sculptor's studio where she tries to get over Luciano and turns to sex work to survive. Prassitele is eventually killed by the Macedonians and Luciano returns to find Iride at his studio, contemplating a statue of Aphrodite that she modeled for (this is the Aphrodite of Knidos). There the lovers confirm their mutual love in a romantic reunion.

Iride, this film's Phryne, was played by Belinda Lee, a British actress known for her good looks who was often cast as the dumb but sexy blonde in comedies (just before making this film, she had played opposite Benny Hill in *Who Done It?*). Lee was widely understood to be a sex symbol, an English version of Gina Lollobrigida or Sophia Loren. While in Italy filming, she began an affair with Prince Filippo Orsini, a member of the noble House of Orsini who claimed descent from the Julio-Claudians of ancient Rome. The relationship led to a separation from her British husband, Cornel Lucas, and was marred by what Italian newspapers reported as dual suicide attempts by both lovers. It seemed, however, that Lee found a new freedom in Italy from her stereotyped roles in British film as she stayed in Europe after this scandal.[70] Like so many of the women who had taken on the role of Phryne before her, Lee died young, in this instance in a car crash in California at the age of twenty-six.

Like Elena Kleus, Lee was recruited to the role because of her beauty. When the producer Nat Waschberger saw her at the Cannes Film Festival, he chose her for the role based on her figure, confident that she would be able to pull off the revealing costumes planned for Iride. In the film itself, Lee is heavily sexualized, wearing a dress with the tiniest of mini-skirts, which in one notable seaside scene with Luciano is soaked with water to enhance its clinginess. When she turns to sex work, she wears a tight, low-cut red gown. Lee also periodically appears in various states of undress in scenes when Iride models for Prassitele, as the camera lingers on her exposed flesh. As with the other films I have discussed here, images of the film's star posing in her most famous costume (in Lee's case, the tiny blue dress) were circulated in magazines to publicize the film.

Each of the films I have discussed here, but especially the publicity machines behind them, worked hard to elide their stars with the characters they played, causing each real woman to become a fictionalized goddess on screen. In each case, the legend of the star and her beauty were key to the public's reception of the film; each of the three films offered a Phryne that responded to varying ideas of beauty, whether the voluptuous embodiment of Italy in Lollobrigida, the transcendant Greek vision of Kleus, or the bouncing blonde perfection of Lee. But as with all of the receptions I have discussed here from the canvas to the stage to the screen, it is the real women behind the character that the story of Phryne seems to require in service of each new adaptation in the modern world. Just as the ancient stories of Phryne worked to obscure the real woman behind them, the glamour and scandal that accrued to each of the real women associated with Phryne in her modern adaptations obscures them too. Each time Phryne was transformed back into flesh, this process turned the women who embodied her into fodder for intrigue and scandal, making each woman a dreamgirl on the model of the ancient *hetaira*.

Phryne's reception in the modern world offers an instructive example of how the cultures that created them dealt with unconventional women. Rather than understanding each woman who portrayed her on her own terms, prevalent discourse sought to highlight the ways in which she transgressed her expected social role, typically by dwelling on her relationships with men. In the case of artists like Angelica Kauffman, gossip foregrounds her connections to men like Reynolds while casting a shadow over her art. Models like Leroux, compelling figures in and of themselves, become secondary characters in their own narratives (both biographical and fictionalized ones). All of the actresses who played Phryne onstage or on screen became fodder for publicity mills that pushed them to be goddesses consumable by the public, often with very dire consequences.

It is also clear from many of these examples that there is an ongoing fascination with sexualizing and taking ownership of female beauty, as its various expressions remain available for dissection by critics and the general public alike. The static image of Phryne from nineteenth-century painting, a golden-haired, fair-skinned, statuesque beauty, yielded to the great variety of Phrynes seen onstage and in photographs, making space for bolder, more diverse Phrynes in canvases and lithographs in the twentieth century. On screen, Phryne needed to be transcendently beautiful, as long as she was perceived as sexy. Antiquity does not seem to have been too concerned with the specifics of her appearance, but Phryne, as embodied in paintings and on screen in the twentieth century, became a vehicle to reflect individual tastes, as each creator attempted to capture the idea of alluring beauty itself.

The ancient literature that connected Phryne to canonical artworks ensures that the model is key to the story of the picture and so it is no surprise that the models and actresses who embodied her were essential to her return to cultural prominence in the nineteenth century. The fascination with each model and actress who portrayed Phryne also belied the need to negotiate with the power of a woman's beauty in societies still dominated by men. As each new woman to take on the role of Phryne was either reduced to her body parts (like Lollobrigida and her *maggiorata fisica*) or found wanting by critics who did not find her sufficiently appealing (as occurred with Siemiradzki's model), the discomfort of others with their own responses to beauty and their anxieties over its power was revealed. Just as the ancient Phryne was put on trial out of concern with her unconventional place in society, each of these women faced the trial of the public eye. As with Phryne herself, beauty and notoriety had real-life consequences for these women, some of whom suffered terribly, like Sibyl Sanderson or Belinda Lee, and at least one of whom, Elena Kleus, rejected celebrity altogether. In all cases, the women involved in these images and performances offer examples of how anecdote and fragmentation reduce complex lives to easily consumed narratives: making a dreamgirl out of a real woman requires the erasure of much of the woman herself. It is the paradox at the heart of how we understand a figure like Phryne: without the real woman, like Leroux in the photos that were essential to the creation of Gérôme's idealized version of Phryne, a compelling dreamgirl cannot exist.

Conclusion

This book has been less about who Phryne was than about what she meant and still means. Although I am firm in my belief that Phryne did exist and could have moved through fourth-century BCE Athens in many of the ways I have explored here, the Phryne that remains for us is only an idea. The most useful way to approach the anecdotes about her is to closely examine that idea: how Phryne was portrayed over centuries allows us to grasp the very real forces that have shaped women's lives and our understanding of them since the Classical period. The fictionalizing process that shaped the Phryne that we have been left with is ultimately an act of desire on the part of the authors who wrote about her as they sought to take ownership over Phryne and her stories while discarding the challenging complexities of her real life. During her own lifetime, Phryne led a lifestyle that did not fit comfortably into traditional roles available to women and it is likely that she was brought to court as a result of that discomfort, but it was also her occupation of an unconventional space that allowed her to accrue a large fortune and the fame that brings her to us today.

Despite being one of the most well-documented women in antiquity, Phryne comes to us wholly through fragments, meaning that any encounter with her forces us to participate in a similar process to those who wrote the ancient sources on her as we attempt to restore the whole that we suppose must have existed, reckoning with our own desire to know Phryne.[1] When we look to the evidence from Phryne's own lifetime, the bits and pieces of comedy that have survived that mention her, we already find a Phryne whose reputation for beauty and avarice occludes the woman herself. Better then, instead of seeking to fill out the details of those fragmentary texts, to look at the broader context that produced them, as I have attempted to do in Chapter 1. Taking more fulsome sources such as *Against Neaira* and *On the Estate of Philoctemon* as examples allows for productive speculation about the lives of women like

Phryne and the circumstances of her life as a foreign sex worker in the male citizen-dominated world of Classical Athens. Leaving behind the desire to know the historical Phryne creates space in which to explore the forces that shaped her life. Accounting for the anecdotal nature of the later sources grants insights into why the Phryne of Hellenistic and Imperial literature is known for being as brash as she was beautiful, as well as why she is associated with the famous men who show up in those stories.

Identifying the intention behind the process of fragmentation in Phryne's case was also key to how I understood her as a dreamgirl; Hellenistic authors like Machon and Aristodemus had no interest in Phryne the individual, but rather wrote of her as representative of her peers. Their Phryne is more a reflection of generic expectations than a singular woman. The Imperial authors who built on this material then attempted to reinsert agency into Phryne's stories, using the anecdotes as raw material to create an even bolder Phryne than before. With each step, from Classical Athens to Alexandria to Imperial Rome, Phryne became more and more a shared idea that could vary as much as each author required while she also embodied centuries of literary and artistic tradition.

I have also suggested here that depicting the *hetairai* can best be understood as a genre of writing unto itself. The conventions of this genre include brevity, pithiness, and the inversion of typical gender roles, always imbued with artifice. Although authors like Machon, Athenaeus, and Alciphron are working in their own literary traditions (anecdotal, sympotic, and epistolary), they adhere to similar standards as they remake the *hetairai* and pull them farther from the kinds of circumstances that I described in Chapter 1. Because this early "pornography" was rooted in the Athenian comic stage via Lynceus' early curation of humorous anecdotes and because comedy was one of the primary ways that Athenian culture spread around the Greek world in the Hellenistic period, the women and the city became inextricably linked in the Greek literary imagination. As the *hetaira par excellence*, Phryne, the Thespian sex worker who had made her fortune and name in Athens, was transformed over time into a symbol of that city, even when stories like that of her trial ultimately reinforced the fact that she would have been an outsider with few rights in Athens.

Phryne therefore offers an instructive example of how cultural capital could accrue to both people and places in the ancient world. Although her reputation was already significant in her own lifetime, the shift from woman to symbol was mostly posthumous. During her own lifetime, she defied easy categorization (as did many of her colleagues in the sex trade) and so she was not easily consumable by the kind of authors and audience who would later take up the anecdotes. The city she made her fortune in, Athens, was equally complex in the fourth century, as it struggled to maintain political and economic hegemony and then fell to the Macedonians. Only once its predominance had faded could it become a space of imagination and fodder for creative diversions. In the cases of cities and women, it seems that their power needed to dim before they could be turned into the kind of cultural currency that could be circulated on end. If the real thing were present alongside the fictional version, it would always complicate the vision that an author was creating and call their mimetic skills into question. Separating figures like Phryne and cities like Athens from their historical contexts also helped reinforce the paradoxes of their fictional worlds: here a sex worker with little status could easily best the most elite man with just her wits and a city which had been flirting with instability for years could be a literary dreamscape.

Recognizing the process that brought Phryne into cultural prominence also pushes us to assess the ways that ancient women are represented in the literary record. If we can better understand the forces that shaped one woman's narrative and the ways that generic expectations selected specific aspects of her stories while discarding others, we can look for similar patterns elsewhere. We can also learn from Phryne about how unconventional women in the ancient world often bore the burden of society's unease with the ways that traditional gender roles played out and about how once these women were turned into dreamgirls they became a means of digesting the uncomfortable dynamics that were so difficult to deal with in the real world. The fragments that remain of Phryne, the object of so much desire, whether sexual, nostalgic, or cultural (or all three), are as tantalizing as ever, their incomplete state providing space for the continued negotiation of dreams and anxieties.

Notes

Introduction

1 Cf. Anderson 1993: 181 on the paradoxical *paideia* of *hetairai* and parasites in Imperial Greek literature.
2 Athenaeus mentions that Apollodorus, the author of a treatise on the *hetairai*, says that there were two Phrynes (13.591c), however the stories I have collected here refer to the Thespian woman.
3 It was common for *hetairai* to take up nicknames, as attested by the choices of Alciphron and Lucian in naming their fictional versions of these women. Cavallini suggests that the name Mnesarete, and that of her father, Epicles, may even hint at elite status (2014: 131).
4 In the same fragment, immediately after referring to her past as a caper-gatherer, Timocles mentions how wealthy Phryne is now, and Athenaeus tells us that Amphis also poked fun at her wealth (Ath. 13.591f).
5 As with so many of the witty responses of the *hetairai*, Phryne's ripostes are designed to bring their addressees down several notches. Further examples of her humor can be found at Ath. 13. 584d and 585e-f.
6 It is challenging to determine when each set of stories connected to her nudity emerged, but they seem to be intertwined and inspired by one another.
7 In antiquity, this painting was originally housed on the island of Kos, Apelles' home at the end of his life (Cavallini 2001: 205 n. 395).
8 2017: 440. Such a moment when a witty *hetaira* bests a prominent man is characteristic of the paradoxical humor that characterized the anecdotes circulated in the Second Sophistic (Anderson 1993: 180).
9 Franchise was limited to 9,000 citizens with wealth of at least 2,000 drachmas, while pay for attendance at the *ecclesia* and courts was ended and funding for training of ephebes was brought to an end, thus hindering meaningful participation in government for many. This move toward a wealthy and likely conservative power base was clearly intended to disenfranchise many of the hoplites, but especially the citizen rowers who were key to the maintenance of Athens' fleet and its naval power (Green 2004: 4).
10 Mori 2015: 94–5.

11 Fourth-century comedy from Athens is often separated into "Middle" and "New Comedy" by scholars, with the plays of Menander being representative of New Comedy when that distinction is made. For the purposes of this discussion, the similarities between both categories, especially in their treatment of sex workers, are more important, so I will speak more broadly of fourth-century comedy here. See esp. Csapo 2000 on the genres of Greek comedy and Hartwig 2014 on developments in fourth-century comedy specifically.
12 Aristodemus is typically connected to Aristarchus of Samos (second century BCE), as his student. Ioannis M. Konstantakos has argued against the security of this association due to a lack of direct evidence, suggesting that he is perhaps a late Hellenistic author (2006: 151 and n. 5 on 151). For the purposes of this argument, his date can be flexible, as long as we understand him to postdate fourth-century Athens and pre-date the Imperial authors I will examine.
13 Whitmarsh 2002: 47.
14 The Hellenism of authors writing in Greek during the Imperial period need not be exclusive of other cultural identities and should not be confused for patriotism (cf. Jones 2004).
15 Schmitz 2004: 89.
16 cf. Whitmarsh on Hellenism in Imperial Rome, 2002: 32.
17 cf. Kermode 2000: 39.
18 Here I include women in the category of citizen, since their status was integral to determining a man's citizenship status, especially in the fourth century. See Blok 2017, esp. ch. 4 for an in-depth exploration of the issues around applying the term "citizen" to women in the Classical period.
19 See Henry 1988, ch. 3 for a full accounting of *hetairai* in fourth-century comedies.
20 e.g., Anaxilas *Neottis* fr. 21 K-A.
21 The second title, *Korinthiastes*, also draws on the long-standing association of the city of Corinth with sex work.
22 Much of the concern in the play is over the potential bastard status of the baby, since Chrysis cannot be the mother of a citizen baby (Lape 2004: 89).
23 Konstantakos 2006: 154.
24 Machon was born in either Corinth or Sicyon, but was primarily associated with Alexandria during his career (*Oxford Classical Dictionary*, 12th ed. s.v. "Machon").
25 The term *chreia* was multivalent in the ancient Greek world, and eventually was most commonly used in the Imperial period to refer to a type of rhetorical exercise. With origins in the philosophical traditions of Classical Athens (cf. Searby 2019), by the time that Machon was writing his collection, the term referred to very short and pithy anecdotes (often as short as a single sentence).

Machon may also used such a title ironically for his collection, since in his time the genre of *chreiai* seems to have had moralizing undertones or serious philosophical implications (Searby 2019: 208, Kurke 2002: 23, Davidson 1997: 93).

26 Kurke reads these instances as politically subversive, especially when the *hetairai* best figures like the Macedonian dictator Demetrius Poliorcetes, and sees this subversion as an invitation to the audience to identify with the *hetairai* (2002: 40).
27 Athenaeus lists Aristophanes of Byzantium, Apollodorus, Ammonius Antiphanes, and Gorgias of Athens as authors of treatises with the title "On Athenian *Hetairai*" (13.567a-b).
28 Nervegna argues that the dominance of Menander's plays on early Hellenistic stages led to their re-performance in Italy and Rome itself, thus turning them into symbols of Greek culture within the Roman context (2013: 17).
29 Miles 2016: 52.
30 Rösch 2019: 236.
31 Elias 2004: 47.
32 Elias 2004: 71–2.
33 This portion of Čulík-Baird's introduction employs Judith Butler's work on the propagation of culture through repetition, in which they suggest that reiteration entails a state of being incomplete (Čulík-Baird 2022: 7).
34 *Deipnosophistai* contains the titles of over 1,000 plays, with quotations of at least 10,000 lines of verse (*Oxford Classical Dictionary*, 12th ed., s.v. "Athenaeus").
35 McClure 2003b: 262–3.
36 This is the first attested use of the term (Ath. 13. 567b), which is used on analogy with *zōgraphos* ("painter," lit. "one who depicts life"), so best translated as "one who depicts sex workers."
37 2002: 36.
38 cf. Goldhill 2001: 15.
39 Bowie 1970: 36.
40 Bowie 1970: 29–30.
41 cf. Funke 2018: 139.
42 Webb 2009: 100.
43 cf. Pavel: 1986: 65.
44 It was a common comic trope to associate lower-class characters with this type of subversive humor (McClure 2003b: 269).
45 2003: 28.
46 1970: 40–1.
47 McClure 2003a: 5.
48 Morales 2011: 81. This invitation to visualize also mirrors the process by which the fragments invite readers to flesh out Phryne's narrative.

49 Rosenmeyer 2001a: 257.
50 Haynes 2017.

1 Mnesarete to Phryne

1 A recent overview of the uses of these terms, as well as other terms applied to specific types of sex workers, with reference to chronological shifts in terminology can be found in Kapparis 2017: 1–2. McClure also breaks down these terms with reference to their use in literature specifically (2003a: 11–24).
2 Witzke provides a helpful explanation of the modern origins of terms like "sex work" and "sex worker," based in the activism of Carol Leigh, a US sex worker who coined the terms to bring attention to the actual labor involved (2015: 9).
3 McClure 2003a: 13–14. In the case of the literary *hetairai*, this equality is largely derived from their wit and beauty as the authors who depict them work to elide the real circumstances of sexual labor in the fourth century.
4 *Pallakē* refers to a woman who is not a wife in an ongoing, stable relationship with a man and considered part of a household.
5 The example of the relationship between Herpyllis and Aristotle is instructive here. She is often considered a *hetaira*, but once she had moved in with Aristotle as his *pallakē* and bore him a son, it is clear that her status changed to member of the household, as reflected by the significant sum left for her dowry in the philosopher's will (cf. Kapparis 2017: 128–9).
6 2009: 29. Sex workers, whether classified as *pornai* or *hetairai*, must have been a significant population in fourth-century Athens, since so many sources insist on their ready availability to citizen men (see Lape 2003: 72–3 on this phenomenon).
7 In *Against Timarchus*, Aeschines makes the distinction between the household/home, the *oikia*, and the space in which sex workers are employed (1.124). In his play *Athamas*, Amphis also makes the distinction between a wife, who is a woman that is a permanent fixture in one's home and the *hetaira*, who has to stay on good terms with her client to maintain the relationship (fr. 1 K-A). In the cases in which a sex worker is brought into a household on a temporary basis, it is clear that she has no legal standing and that the relationship can be dissolved at the whim of the man involved.
8 Although based in sociological research conducted in the 2010s, Holly Davis' definition of the pimp, an individual who derives financial gain and controls the income and activities of the sex workers they are associated with (2013: 11), is a helpful framework for this term that allows for sufficient heterogeneity to be applicable to the ancient world. A common term for this figure in Greek is

pornoboskos, which appears in legal speeches as well as comedies from the fourth century.
9 The Liddell-Scott Jones lexicon gives "companion" as primary meaning for both the masculine and feminine forms of this term, while the section on the feminine form gives "courtesan" as a secondary meaning and opposes it to *pornē* (*A Greek-English Lexicon*, 9th ed. s.v. ἑταῖρος). Kennedy 2015 argues against the use of "courtesan" as a translation for this word and for a more cautious historical approach to its application prior to the fourth century.
10 Even being characterized like *hetairai* often were in legal speeches was enough to suggest a woman was not a properly chaste wife (e.g., Plangon from Demosthenes 39 and 40, as discussed by Glazebrook 2006: 132).
11 Kennedy 2015: 63.
12 Feldman and Gordon 2006: 7.
13 Kurke 1997: 112.
14 1997: 143.
15 A representative but not comprehensive selection of such scholars over the last several decades includes Kenneth Dover (2016: 21), James Davidson (1997: 77), Laura McClure (2003a: 18), and Konstantinos Kapparis (2017: 304), among many others.
16 cf. Cohen 2006: 99.
17 2017: 2 and Chapter 4.
18 Henry 1995: 15.
19 Davidson 1997: 126.
20 Plu. *Mor.* 401b and Ath. 13. 591e.
21 See McClure 2003a: 71–4 for a list and discussion of the nicknames of *hetairai* from Athenaeus.
22 Athenian orators from 366 onward make reference to Thespiai as being destroyed/depopulated (Tuplin 1986: 327), so Phryne is unlikely to have been born after this point.
23 cf. Loddo 2022: 208–9 on Xen. *HG* 6.3.1. Kapparis claims that she was born in Athens after the destruction of Thespiai (2021: 200), although the fact that she is consistently identified as Thespian in our sources and the resulting metic status she would have had is more important than her specific birthplace.
24 It is not clear from the speech alone whether the marriage between Neaira and Stephanus was legally recognized (the crux of the accusations) or *de facto*.
25 cf. Kapparis 1999: 28.
26 The names listed by Apollodorus are Anteia, Stratola, Aristocleia, Metaneira, Phila, and Isthmias, several of whom seem to have become quite notorious, and whose

names appear in comic plays from the mid-fourth century, suggesting that he was expecting the Athenian jury hearing the case to recognize at least some of them (Hamel 2003: 4). The fact that these women began their careers in Corinth as young girls and then made their way to Athens points to a relatively common trajectory into the Athenian sex trade as well as the mobility of enslaved sex workers between *poleis*.

27 I would like to clarify here that not all female sex workers in Athens were foreign-born, despite foreignness and sex work being distinctly associated in this speech.
28 Apollodorus mentions Xenocleides the poet and Hipparchus the actor, who "kept" her while paying ongoing fees (καὶ εἶχον αὐτὴν μεμισθωμένοι, 59.26).
29 See Loomis 1998: 166 and 232 on average wages in fourth-century Athens. For enslaved sex workers, especially those categorized as *hetairai*, such a purchase price was not unprecedented, with prices of between twenty to thirty *minai* attested in various sources (Kapparis 1999: 227). A *mina* was worth roughly 100 drachmai at the time.
30 Gilhuly calls her a "commodity among commodities" (2009: 40).
31 Apollodorus mentions that each man contributed 500 drachmae toward her freedom (59.29), presumably considering this a deduction from their original purchase price.
32 Other legal speeches mentioning men who housed sex workers include Lys. 3 and 4, Antiph. 1, and [And.] 4 (cf. Glazebrook 2022: 152).
33 The language Isaeus uses to describe Alke's activities is quite euphemistic here. He says that she "sat in a stall" (καθῆστο ἐν οἰκήματι) there and that when she left, she literally "rose up" (i.e., departed) from that stall (ἀπὸ μὲν τοῦ οἰκήματος ἀνίσταται, 6.19). The term for "stall," *oikēma*, suggests a subdivided space within a larger chamber, often associated with physical labor as well as a space within a brothel for a sex worker to be with her clients.
34 Glazebrook 2021: 49.
35 cf. Glazebrook 2021: 62.
36 The means of keeping track of metics (whether recording the arrival of foreigners in Athens or some other means) is obscure, so it seems that some would have been able to avoid registration (Whitehead 1977: 75). Due to her prominence in Athens, Phryne is sure to have been noticed by the authorities once she had become well-known and so it is very likely that she would have been registered by that point in her life.
37 It seems that foreign women who were part of a household led by a male authority figure (Athenian or otherwise) were not liable to pay the *metoikion* (Kapparis 2021: 132), meaning that women who did were independent of domestic male control.

38 Whitehead 1977: 76 and Loomis 1998: 233.
39 Kennedy 2014: 2.
40 Kennedy 2014: 86–7.
41 Kapparis proposes that the first trial was a proper case in which Aristagora was acquitted and the second an example of the *doroxenia* process in which the acquittal was attributed to bribery (2021: 34).
42 Some sources, notably later lexicographers, suggest that the *graphē aprostasiou* could also apply to those failing to find a *prostates* (Kapparis 2005: 106–7).
43 cf. Gow on Machon, 1965: 7.
44 Kapparis 2017: 111.
45 e.g., Davidson 1997: 120–1.
46 Kapparis 2017: 128–9.
47 Diogenes Laertius claims that Leontium was Epicurus' *pallakē* (10.23), but she does not seem to have entered into an exclusive relationship with him or been incorporated into a household as we would expect of more typical *pallakia*.
48 McClure 2003a: 101.
49 Hermesianax of Colophon mentions their relationship (7.95-98), but the text as quoted in Athenaeus (13.599b) is rather corrupted (cf. Kapparis 2017: 131 n. 105). Diogenes Laertius also lists one of Aristippus' dialogues as "To Lais, On the Mirror" (D.L. 2.84).
50 Tertullian the Christian apologist even links Phryne to Diogenes when he attacks the chastity of Classical philosophers, although this is very likely a choice based on the fame of both individuals (*Apol.* 46.10).
51 Kapparis 2017: 136.
52 *The Stanford Encyclopedia of Philosophy* (Summer 2021 ed.), s.v. "Xenocrates."
53 See Chapter 4 for a discussion of Angelica Kauffman's depiction of Xenocrates with Phryne.
54 It seems as though women as a group were more likely to be prosecuted in the fourth century than in the century prior, perhaps due to an increasing public presence overall (Kapparis 2021: 194–5).
55 e.g., Hall 2006: 359.
56 This fragment speaks to the flexibility of the term *hetaira* in the fourth century, with the relationship here suggesting that the sex worker has been incorporated into a household.
57 While the plays of Aristophanes have many references to female sex workers, typically using *pornē* to refer to them and often comparing them to food and drink, specific references that use the term *hetaira* are quite rare; he seems to use the term interchangeably with *pornē*. A full examination of Aristophanes' references to sex workers can be found in Henry 1988: 18–31.

58 McClure 2003a: 40. This number is approximate as some of the names, or more likely nicknames, of *hetairai* were also regular nouns, such as *Palaistra* ("The Wrestling Ground", a play by Alcaeus) or *Clepsydra* ("The Water-Clock", by Euboulus). Some names could also have been shared by free Athenian women as well.

59 Auhagen 2009: 59.

60 There are only four exceptions to this rule, three of which appear in *Lysistrata* (Sommerstein 2009: 46–7).

61 J. M. Edmonds suggests 330 BCE, based on dates for some of the *hetairai* named here and Aeschines' speech *Against Timarchus*, from 345, which lists Autocleides as a client of the accused (Edmonds 1959: 620 n. c).

62 Among comic playwrights from the middle of the fourth century BCE, Timocles was known for being particularly cruel in his plays, so one could expect such a no-holds-barred approach to the *hetairai* from him. Comic burlesques of myth that made fun of prominent individuals' behavior were common in this period (Konstantakos 2011: 164–5).

63 Nesselrath 1997: 275.

64 This is also suggestive of the paraclausithyron, the scene featuring a bereft lover alone at his beloved's doorstep and a trope of poetry and comedy often associated with *hetairai*. Cummings traces the history of the paraclausithyron, with the suggestion that its earliest versions were connected to the post-symposium *komos*, which would be depicted as ending at the doorstep of one's beloved, often a *hetaira* (2001: 45).

65 The timing for both of these plays is aligned with the works of art to which they may allude, and production in the 350s puts them at the likely height of Phryne's fame. Menander later produced a play called *Knidia*, as did the comic poet Sopater, active at Alexandria.

66 Edmonds suggests ἐν τῇ δίκῃ τὰ στηθία γὰρ γυμνουμένη ("baring her breasts in the court") as an interpolation between lines 5 and 6 (1957: 234). I discuss this anecdote in detail in Chapter 3.

2 Phryne the Artist's Model

1 Copies of the Aphrodite of Knidos have been found across Italy, in France and Spain, and in Asia Minor, in addition to the Greek mainland (Ajootian 1998: 99).

2 Pliny gives his floruit as the 104th Olympiad, c. 364–361 BCE (*NH* 34.50).

3 Pliny claims that the model for this image was Alexander the Great's mistress, Pancaspe (*NH* 35.86), highlighting the interest in later authors of associating famous artworks with real women.

4 Although Galen's concern in this piece is to explore the behavior and health of athletes, his use of such an anecdote shows the medical writer's engagement with other genres such as the *chreiai* and therefore his participation in prevailing trends in Imperial literature (Curtis 2014: 48).
5 cf. Webb 2009: 100.
6 The Eleusinian Mysteries' acceptance of all kinds of people into its cult, regardless of their status, makes it likely that this would be the festival where Phryne would be welcomed among the worshippers. It is also likely that this event occurred at or near Eleusis, with the other deity mentioned, Poseidon, also being connected to Eleusis and worshipped alongside Demeter, Kore, and Athena at a sanctuary on the border between Athens and Eleusis, as well as affiliated with a notable Eleusinian family, the Eumolpidai (Simon 1983: 24).
7 2011: 75.
8 The same is true of Homer's Helen, whose appearance is not described as being any different than many other women characters (Blondell 2013: 55) and whose hair color is not even mentioned (cf. Finglass 2018: 140).
9 2011: 96. A counter-argument for this is the "ontological independence" from the creator that results from giving a character their own voice (cf. Payne 2007: 11 on direct speech in fictional literature).
10 1993: 4.
11 Kris and Kurz 1979: 11.
12 See Corso 1997: 65–6 for a discussion of artists and their model-lovers in the ancient Greek context. Glykera was also famously linked to Menander, who featured a *hetaira* with the same name in his *Perikeiromenē* ("The Girl with Shorn Hair").
13 Ajootian 1998: 92.
14 Cavallini claims that her association with Praxiteles may have been a career "breakthrough" for Phryne, which brought her to prominence during her own lifetime (2014: 133–4).
15 This type of stories about artists and models resurfaced in the Renaissance and have continued to circulate ever since, with examples including Giorgio Vasari's account of Fra Filippo Lippi's former convent girl turned model turned wife (Borzello 1982: 128).
16 This statue type is also the most securely associated with Praxiteles by modern art historians (Ajootian 1998: 98).
17 Cavallini suggests that the original anecdote illustrates the wide-reaching fame of Praxiteles' satyr, which also had innumerable Roman copies (2001: 206 n. 398).

18 Pausanias says that this Eros was taken away from Thespiai by Caligula, then returned by Claudius, before being carted off a second time by Nero to Rome, where it was destroyed by fire after all. Another version was created and placed at Thespiai by the Athenian sculptor Menodorus, who copied Praxiteles' work (9.27.3-4).
19 Although the evidence for the Erotidia only begins in the second century BCE, the cult there, centered on worship of Eros in an aniconic form, seems to have been longstanding (Gutzwiller 2004: 386). Strabo the geographer erroneously claims that the Eros at Thespiai was a gift from Praxiteles to Glykera (another famous *hetaira* associated with fourth-century Athens), who was the one to install it in the sanctuary there. He claims this was because it was her hometown (9.25), an obvious mistake for Phryne.
20 cf. Gutzwiller 2004: 398.
21 A coin from Thespiai from the time of Domitian (i.e., after the Eros was taken to Rome) features a statue of Aphrodite with a smaller female figure beside it, likely depicting the remnants of Praxiteles' trio (Corso 1997: 69).
22 Further reinforcing the connection between Thespiai and desire, Plutarch sets his dialogue on the nature of love in that town.
23 I suspect that Alciphron has included this term as a sly nod to the stories about the Aphrodite of Knidos that offer an aetiology for the stain on the statue's backside (to be discussed later in this chapter).
24 Although no manuscript has preserved a title for this letter (which we would expect to be "Phryne to Praxiteles"), the connections between epigram and the sculptures mentioned here are sufficient to identify Alciphron's writer and recipient (Granholm 2012: 149). The missing title combined with the opening of the letter, which is abrupt, has caused editors to treat this letter as a fragment (Rosenmeyer 2001b: 275).
25 Benner and Fobes' 1949 Loeb edition, for example, treats *hēmas* as an example of what might be considered the "royal we," with the translation "they have gazed at me," while Rosenmeyer points out how the first person singular appears at several other points in the letter in her argument for retaining the plural to emphasize the elision between Phryne and the statue (2001: 252).
26 cf. Rosenmeyer 2001a: 255.
27 cf. Funke 2018: 147.
28 Onofrio Vox argues that the content of this letter suggests that Alciphron was familiar with epigrams of the type I have just discussed and may be a response to them (2019: 119).
29 Rosenmeyer 2001a: 255.
30 2001: 257.
31 1972: 46.

32 Here Mulvey builds on Lacan's work on ego formation and the "mirror phase" of infancy when a child recognizes itself in a mirror for the first time (1975: 10).
33 Mulvey 1975: 13.
34 Mulvey 1975: 17.
35 1972: 47.
36 The fictional letter in particular is well suited to granting agency to women "authors" as their voices are represented without mediation and they shape the narrative directly (cf. Funke 2022).
37 cf. Rosenmeyer 2001a: 241.
38 2004: 402.
39 2022: 192.
40 At least 192 copies from antiquity that have survived to the modern world have been documented (Corso 2007: 175).
41 Stewart 1997: 97.
42 This assumes that Phryne was born prior to the sack of Thespiai in the late 370s as discussed in the previous chapter.
43 Havelock suggests a height of just over 2 metres (slightly larger-than-life) based on the Vatican's Colonna Knidia (1995: 13).
44 The coin I describe, held by the British Museum (no. XVI. 7), was minted during the reign of Caracalla (*c.* early third century CE).
45 The specific details of these features of the statue are not consistently portrayed in copies from antiquity or on the coins that depicted the statue, but these are the features that are understood as essential to the Knidia and the narrative it presents (Seaman 2004: 535, 538).
46 In either formulation, the clothing she holds in her hand only serves to highlight her nudity more, suggestive of what Lee calls a "striptease" (2015: 189).
47 cf. Osborne 1994: 84 and Squire 2011: 106.
48 cf. Lee 2015: 118. Another alternative is that a female spectator may have been reminded of the ritual bath that preceded a marriage ceremony (Seaman 2004: 566).
49 There were apparently three separate temples to Aphrodite at this site, however Praxiteles' statue was associated with Aphrodite *Euploia* (Montel 2010: 251).
50 There is some disagreement about whether the round structure found at the site of Knidos actually housed the statue (there is evidence of worship of Athena, Asclepius, and Apollo at the site, Spivey 2013: 207, and Montel concludes that the round building housed an image of Athena, 2010: 264), but the presence of a late third-century BCE inscription using the term "Knidia" on the same terrace as the round structure suggests that it did (Corso 2007: 177). Havelock dates it to the second century BCE and points out that what remains of the structure does not quite accord with Livy's description of the building (1995: 61).

51 The concept of art so realistic it is either animated or confused for the real thing is a common theme in literary anecdotes and epigrams about famous art. See Kris and Kurz 1979: 62–3 for examples from Classical literature.
52 There are many examples of female nudity in Greek art from the decades preceding the debut of the Knidia, especially in vase paintings, and fairly revealing depictions of the female body in diaphanous drapery were popular in sculpture from as early as the late fifth century (Havelock 1995: 35).
53 The other is the late antique (sixth-century CE) rhetorician, Choricius of Gaza, who connects Praxiteles, Phryne, and the statue in his eighth declamation.
54 In the religious context, there was not always a clear differentiation between deity and statue, and many were the object of ritual bathing and dressing (Elsner 2007: 11).
55 The second viewer finds that the statue from behind resembles a beautiful boy, but his reaction is striking regardless.
56 Anchises was one of Aphrodite's human lovers, as featured in the Homeric Hymn to Aphrodite. Pliny includes a shorter version of the story of the young man at Knidos in his account of the statue (*NH* 36.20). The legacy of the Aphrodite of Knidos continued in the story of Henry George Quin who, while in Florence during the eighteenth century, claimed to have snuck into the Uffizi to be alone with the Medici Venus, a Roman copy of Praxiteles' statue, and kissed it passionately (Nead 1992: 87).
57 cf. Rosenmeyer 2001a: 258.
58 The diminutive *Aphrodision* suggests a lover's nickname, along the lines of "Aphroditikins."
59 This anecdote follows a common pattern in which a man tries to come on to a *hetaira*, only to be rebuffed with a witty quip (McClure 2003b: 276). The use of Pheidias' name is also a pun on *pheidomai*, "to be a cheapskate" (Cavallini 2001: 198 n. 312).
60 The version in Ovid seems to be a reworking of a version transmitted by Philostephanos, who was writing in the time of Callimachus (Rosenmeyer 2001a: 258), although it is possible to trace the genealogy of stories of men creating women all the way back to Hesiod's Pandora (*Theog.* 560-612).
61 As with so many of the themes connected to Phryne, the stories of a man falling in love with an image, or with a woman via an image of her, may be traced to fourth-century comedies, as suggested by Renaud (1992: 380).
62 Elsner 2007: 130.
63 As Michael Squire puts it, if the model for the statue is nothing but a sex worker and not a goddess, then desiring it no longer runs the risk of divine retribution, and the viewer can now "wank away at will" (2011: 101).
64 2001a: 258–9.

65 Seaman 2004: 533.
66 The Latin term *merces* has much the same sense as the Greek *misthos*, with both meaning "compensation" as in pay and reward, an ideal choice to hint at the sexual labor implied in Phryne and Praxiteles' relationship.
67 There may have been one additional statue of Phryne at Rome, possibly located in the Portico of Pompey (Thorsen 2012: 699), included in a list of statues of women compiled by Tatian, the second-century CE Syrian theologian.
68 Luigi Todisco uses this to locate the statue, like the gilded one of Gorgias, opposite the opisthodomos of the Temple of Apollo (2020: 210).
69 Sheila Dillon argues that the prominent location of this statue supports Athenaeus' version, with the Thespians making a public dedication (2010: 48).
70 Keesling 2006: 68. The inclusion of her nickname, rather than her birth name, Mnesarete, alongside the patronym is confusing, and perhaps points to a posthumous dedication (Todisco 2020: 213).
71 Keesling, considering the statue in its fourth-century context, sees it as an anomalous inclusion in the sanctuary on the grounds that it was a statue of a woman on her own, especially when considered against the numbers of honorific statues of men during that period. According to Keesling, Phryne's statue would have been the only portrait statue of a woman outside of a family group from that period at Delphi (2006: 66–7).
72 2006: 72.
73 Cavallini 2014: 139.
74 Ridgway, for example, argues that the forms and proportions of the surviving copies of this statue are sufficient to dispute the stories of Phryne as the model for this statue, yet she agrees that Phryne is connected to other works by Praxiteles, especially the statue at Delphi (1987: 406).
75 See Lynda Nead on the use of this distinction in art historical criticism, beginning with Kenneth Clark's *The Nude* (1956) (1992: 12–16).
76 An art historical consideration of the nude as an artistic genre had begun decades earlier in Germany with Julius Lange's 1903 *Die Menschliche Gestalt in der Geschichte der Kunst* ("The Human Form in the History of Art") and Wilhelm Hausenstein's 1913 *Der nackte Mensch* ("The Naked Men"), but both were largely forgotten and certainly did not have the influence that Clark's work did on defining the genre (Stonard 2010: 317, n. 4).
77 1956: 3.
78 The Aphrodite of Knidos is in fact the point to which Clark traces the nude in art as a concept. (1956: 81).
79 1972: 53.
80 2022: 4–5.

81 1997: 207.
82 cf. Mansfield 2007: 98.
83 1992: 16.
84 1992: 19, Clark 1956: 71.
85 This distinction is made in his discussion of Corregio's *Jupiter and Antiope* (1956: 134).
86 1992: 20. There are also shades of the ancient discussion of the golden statue of Phryne at Delphi and how it signified the excess of the Greeks here in the concern over female bodies being displayed in the "wrong" way or the "wrong" place.
87 Nead 1992: 29.
88 Stewart 1997: 41.
89 Apelles' painting of Aphrodite, like Praxiteles' statue, was also the subject of epigrams that remarked on the vividness of the depiction of the goddess (e.g., Antipater on Athena and Hera leaving behind the beauty contest upon seeing Apelles' painting, 16. 178).
90 1989: 561.
91 cf. Osborne 2011: 209.
92 cf. Squire 2007: 102.
93 1997: 101.
94 Squire 2011: 110.
95 cf. Stewart on the pose of the Knidia, 1997: 106).
96 Funke 2019: 139.
97 Pliny mentions that Apelles' talent in creating accurate images from life was so strong that physiognomists were able to assess an individual's age and future age at death from his paintings alone (*NH* 35. 88).
98 cf. Mansfield 2007: 156.
99 McClure 2003a: 108.
100 cf. McClure 2003a: 110–16 on how this display and manipulation of appearance creates a spectacle for clients and differentiates sex workers from respectable citizen women.

3 Phryne on Trial

1 With only the speeches from one side recorded, we do not know the outcome of either Neaira's or Alke's trials.
2 Phillips 2013: 408.
3 The charges also recall those from Socrates' famous trial and possibly those from the trial of Aspasia (if her trial is considered to be historical) (Kapparis 2021: 79).

4 Athenaeus cites Diodorus Periegetes as saying the legal speech against Phryne was not written by Euthias, but by Anaximenes of Lampsacus, a follower of Diogenes the Cynic (13.591e).
5 Phillips argues that the threat of the death penalty suggests that the procedure in this case was *eisangelia*, a form of state prosecution (2013: 455).
6 Phillips 2013: 408. The *agon timetos* ("debate over punishment") associated with this charge alternatively meant that the punishment could be relatively light (Bremmer 2019: 1015).
7 cf. Hall 2006: 362 and Glazebrook 2021: 13.
8 Eidinow 2016: 25.
9 Cooper 1995: 304.
10 Noting their connection to 4.1, Phryne's erotic invitation to Praxiteles, Rosenmeyer suggests that these letters be read as a "proto-epistolary novel" (2001b: 272).
11 Onofrio Vox reads the trio of letters on the trial in combination with Phryne's invitation to Praxiteles as a "cycle of Phryne" that testify to Alciphron's knowledge of the variant sources on her (2019: 119).
12 Mostly individual words remain, which are insufficient to allow us to judge Hypereides' rhetorical ability.
13 Cooper 1995: 307.
14 2016: 23.
15 1999: 28.
16 2006: 217 and 2001: 203 n. 392.
17 With manumission and incorporation into a household, Phila's story has shades of both Alke's and Neaira's. Phila is also one of the names listed as Neaira's youthful colleagues in Corinth.
18 1995: 308.
19 Alexiou 2020: 261.
20 The term *deinos* has a wide semantic range and can mean powerful or terrible. In the context of oratory, there is also the sense that a forceful orator can be dangerously persuasive (perhaps the factor behind the prohibition of lament in the courtroom). In his commentary on the fragments of Hypereides' speeches, David Whitehead argues for "glib" as a translation (2000: 10). The play in which this appears was titled *The Delians*, very likely a reference to a speech Hypereides once gave in a dispute over who should control the sanctuary at Delos.
21 One of the stories about Hypereides' death relates that once the Macedonian general Antipater captured him, he had Hypereides' tongue cut out, fully silencing the persuasive orator. An alternate version is that Hypereides bit out his own tongue rather than betray any Athenian secrets to his captors (*Mor.* 849b-c).

22 The proposed decree also called for sacred objects, women, and children to be kept in the Peiraeus for safekeeping.

23 *Against Neaira* is one of the very few exceptions to this rule, as would have been Aristogeiton's *Against Phryne* (if it did exist). We may also consider the comic plays from the fourth century, such as Timocles' *Neairas*, to have been part of this category, depending on their content.

24 e.g., Cantarelli 1885, where he sums up the state of the discussion in the late nineteenth century (467–9).

25 In Socrates' case, "corrupting the youth" did not just refer to his infamous band of young male followers, but the fact that he had been influential with young men like Critias, who later was one of the leaders of the violent Thirty Tyrants (Phillips 2013: 411).

26 cf. Bremmer 2019: 1018–20.

27 2016: 163.

28 Kapparis, based on evidence from Plutarch and Aristophanes' *Clouds*, speculates that the charge of impiety was related to conversations that happened during gatherings hosted by Aspasia, in which philosophical conversations about the natural world may have included arguments against the existence of the traditional gods (2021: 42).

29 The prosecutor named by Plutarch, Hermippus, was also a comic poet. Henry suggests that this trial may have taken place on stage, a space in which Aspasia was regularly impugned, rather than in an actual courtroom (1995: 24).

30 The term suggests someone who works with *pharmaka*, a word we can translate here as "drugs," and which can mean anything from medicine to potions to poison. From this meaning, *pharmakis* can extend to mean a woman who is understood to practice magic or witchcraft.

31 Demosthenes connects her to Aristogeiton (the same one who is credited with *Against Phryne*) in his speech accusing him of owing money to the *polis* and therefore being disenfranchised (*Against Aristogeiton* 25.79-80).

32 Eidinow 2016: 12. The charge is reported by Philochorus, an Athenian historian from the late fourth/early third century BCE, in turn preserved by Harpocration, a second-century CE lexicographer (Jacoby 382 fr. 60).

33 Eidonow 2016: 20.

34 An emendation to the historian Josephus' list of people who were charged with *asebeia* identifies Ninon as being among them (*Against Apion* 2.267, cf. Eidinow 2010: 14 n.12).

35 2021: 202.

36 The Lyceum may also provide another very tenuous connection between Phryne and Praxiteles, since it hosted a statue of Apollo Lyceus that has been typically

attributed to the sculptor. Since the date of the original statue and the identity of its sculptor are far from certain, this connection cannot be confirmed.
37 Hesychius connects him to Pluto but with little detail (Hsch. s.v. Ἰσοδαίτης).
38 Eidinow 2016: 30.
39 Kapparis 2021: 79.
40 Andrewes 1961: 9.
41 2006: 4.
42 cf. Cooper 1995: 312.
43 Crotty 1994: 74 and Gherchanoc 2012: 208.
44 K. O'Neill's 1998 article comparing the two scenes identifies a host of intertextual allusions between Homer's epic and Aeschylus' tragedy that further confirm the link between Clytemnestra and Hecuba in this scene.
45 There is also a brief mention of Jocasta revealing her breasts to Eteocles and Polynices in a vain attempt to end their fatal duel in Euripides' *Phoenissae* (1567-9). For an account of the maternal breast as a means of inspiring pity in Greek poetry and tragedy, see MacDonald 1998: 245-6. The presence of Orestes' nurse in *Libation Bearers* and Clytemnestra's earlier recollection of a dream in which she nursed a snake at her breast (527-33) cause her appeal to memory to ring hollow.
46 1995: 315.
47 Aristophanes' *Lysistrata* also makes a brief reference to the beauty of Helen's breasts in this moment (155-6).
48 There may also have been precedents for this scene in the lyric poetry of Ibycus and the epic *Little Iliad* (O'Neill 1998: 219).
49 This vase is held at the Museo Gregoriano Etrusco, part of the Vatican Museums (350, BAD 31052).
50 cf. Blondell 2013: 41. This vase is held at the Louvre (424, BAD 214486). Similarly, fragment 296 of Ibycus has Helen take refuge in a temple of Aphrodite for this exchange, with the same outcome (Menelaus dropping his sword).
51 Hall 1995: 43.
52 cf. Bonfante 1997: 175.
53 cf. Naiden on Phryne, 2006: 102. This type of erotic supplication can also have the power of a charm or binding spell (Gherchanoc 2012: 212).
54 Naiden 2006: 185.
55 Naiden 2006: 177.
56 2003a: 135.
57 See Cooper 1995: 315 and Hall 2006: 362 on this scene.
58 cf. Kapparis 2021: 173-4.
59 2011: 110.

60 Dressing and adorning oneself is a common means of depicting great beauty and desirability in early Greek poetry (cf. Blondell 2013: 55 on Hera preparing for Zeus at *Iliad* 14.170-86).
61 Like Aphrodite, Helen was not immune to the power of beauty, as in his *Encomium of Helen* Gorgias defends her partially on the grounds that she too was seduced via *opsis* ("vision") when she laid eyes on Paris (19). See Gherchanoc 2012: 213 for a discussion of power and beauty of female breasts as depicted in Greek literature specifically.
62 cf. Clark 2001: 12.
63 2018: 149.
64 cf. Haskins 2018: 256.
65 1935: 279.
66 Kapparis addresses this double exclusion of metic women in the fourth century BCE: "the concept of women as active participants in politics would be an alien concept in the ancient world, and then ... legislation of the radical democracy safeguarded the legal rights of the citizen woman" (1999: 3).
67 In the fourth century, the household was the means by which an Athenian woman was integrated into the *polis* and her rights revolved around her status in that context, as wife, mother, or daughter of a citizen, and as a representative of the household in religious matters (Kapparis 1999: 25–6). The case of Neaira, in which she had been incorporated into Stephanus' household for decades before her prosecution, suggests that both foreignness and a history of sexual labor could override the protections offered by incorporation into a household (Kapparis 2021: 177).
68 Kucharski 2012: 172. Kucharski also offers the example of Aeschines and Ctesiphon (2012: 178).
69 See Kapparis 1999: 29 on the conflict between Stephanus and Apollodorus.
70 2000: 47.
71 Gherchanoc 2012: 208.
72 cf. Hall on the connections between surprise and pleasure for the spectator, 2006: 361.
73 Gilhuly 2009: 182.

4 Phryne's Afterlife

1 The term "Neoclassical" was not used widely until well into the nineteenth century, since the artistic interest in ancient Greece and Rome from the century prior was very widespread and thus interpreted in a variety of ways, often through a

Renaissance lens. In the eighteenth century, artists who took up this style generally considered it a return to proper ancient aesthetics, from which Baroque art and architecture had departed (Barker 2012: 19).
2 Phryne seems to have been mostly ignored by Renaissance painters, and only appears in three oil paintings in the seventeenth century, which I will discuss in my section on Angelica Kauffman.
3 Bond, "Why we need to start seeing the classical world in color."
4 Sandner 2007: 35.
5 As with the connection between Phryne and Praxiteles, the exact arrangement of these relationships is unclear while subject to much speculation over possible romantic connections (cf. Maierhofer 2007: 25). See also Roworth for a list of the men identified as her suitors by the British press of her time (2007: 43).
6 Kauffman has been the subject of at least eight biographies since the nineteenth century, as well as a staged melodrama (Augustus W. Dubourg's 1892 *Angelica: A Romantic Drama in Four Acts*).
7 In Pliny's version, she is known as Pancaspe, and begins as Alexander's mistress, but is then given to Apelles after he falls in love with her while painting her portrait. Pliny also suggests here that Pancaspe, rather than Phryne, was the model of Apelles' "Aphrodite Rising from the Sea."
8 Roworth 1983: 489.
9 Rosa, an Italian baroque painter, had a particular interest in depicting philosophical subjects, especially those related to ancient Greece, having created images featuring Democritus, Diogenes, and Pythagoras.
10 Roworth 1983: 491.
11 Roworth 1983: 490–1.
12 This group was alternately known as the "Pompéistes" or "Néo-Pompéiens," names given them by the critic Théophile Gautier (Couëlle 2010: 24).
13 Lathers 2001: 23.
14 Van Gogh Museum Journal, 1996, "Catalogue of acquisitions: paintings and drawings July 1994–December 1996."
15 Du Pays 1851: 227–8.
16 Even modern scholars have derided Boulanger's painting, with Pérez-Prendes Muñoz de Arraco calling it "regrettable and tacky" (*lamentable y chabacana*), identifying Phryne with a "simple whore" (*una simple ramera*) (2005: 35). Many of the female models working at this time were Italian or Jewish, often chosen by artists for an image they wished to read as exotic (e.g., the orientalising images of harems or slave markets popular at the time, Lathers 2001: 36–7), and so there is also very likely a discriminatory note to these complaints.

17 See note 57 in Chapter 3 on this phenomenon.
18 Gautier 1861: 177.
19 Smith 1996: 110.
20 This colossal bronze statue created by Pheidias, the sculptor who also worked on the Parthenon, was said to have stood atop the Acropolis, visible from as far away as Sounion (Pausanias 1.28.2).
21 Corpataux 2009: 145–6.
22 The statues were available in marble, bronze, and gilt bronze, and sizes between 30 and 84 centimetres, intended as domestic interior décor.
23 Gérôme returned to the photos of Leroux once again in his 1884 and 1886 paintings, both with the title *Vente d'esclaves à Rome* ("The Sale of Slaves at Rome"), which similarly feature a nude woman at the center of a detailed composition. In the 1884 image, the internal spectators look up at the nude, who is displayed for sale on a raised wooden platform, and the viewer sees the scene from the audience's perspective. In the 1886 version, the nude is seen from behind, from the perspective of someone standing on the platform with her, a repetition of the view in the photo of Gérôme in his studio. A similar perspective on the nude appears in his 1890 and 1892 versions of *Pygmalion et Galatée*, featuring the statue on the plinth as it comes to life in the artist's embrace, the 1890 version showing the front and the 1892 one showing the back.
24 Corpataux 2009: 149. There are later photos, from around 1890, of Gérôme at work in his studio with a nude model standing before him, her back to the camera, mimicking the pose of Leroux and so of Phryne too. Two canvases can be seen in the background, the most visible one his own version of the Aphrodite Anadyomene (*Vénus L'Étoile*, 1890).
25 1872: 145.
26 1872: 147.
27 1872: 148.
28 2001: 22.
29 In Homer's poem, the nobles of Ithaca force their way into Penelope's household in the absence of Odysseus, depleting its resources and demanding that she marry one of them. Penelope responds by promising to remarry once she has finished weaving her father-in-law's funeral shroud. She weaves all day and unravels her work by night, extending the ruse for three years until one of the enslaved women in her household reveals it (*Od.* 2.93-5, 19.141-3, 24.131-3). In the nineteenth century, as part of the revival of interest in the Classical world, Penelope became a symbol of idealized feminine domesticity because of this trick.
30 Like Boulanger's version too, Marchal's Phryne was subject to criticism of her looks, with one critic, Pierre Colinot, describing her appearance as "insolent, sulky,

and bestial; she is a redhead, of course" (qtd. in De Young 2011: 127). This did not prevent Marchal from selling the pair of paintings for the grand sum of 28,000 francs on the first day the Salon was open to the public. The location of the original canvas of *Phryné* is now unknown, but the image is preserved in engravings and caricatures.

31 De Young 2011: 126.
32 De Young 2011: 132.
33 *Puck*, June 4, 1884.
34 2017: 154.
35 e.g., Georges Normandy's defense of the Phrynes of his time with regard to their legal troubles (1909: 232).
36 Some have even referred to this event as the first modern striptease performance in France, as some of the models stood on tables and then revealed their bodies bit by bit from the ankles up (Kerley 2010: 83).
37 Later in court it was claimed that Brown had been wearing a tiny *cache-sexe* (the equivalent of a g-string) that she had worn on stage while performing as Cleopatra and so her presence at the ball was meant to be artistic only (Kerley 2017: 54).
38 The narrator here makes reference to the ancient Greek painter Zeuxis, reinforcing the connections between art and live performance that infuse ancient imagery on Parisian stages (*Phryné* 11).
39 Phryné tells the judge that when he passed by her, she became "greener than grass" ("Je devins plus verte que l'herbe," *Phryné* 17), from Sappho 31, possibly that poet's most well-known poem in the nineteenth century.
40 Academic painting like that of Gérôme had by that point made a durable connection between the female nude and the concept of truth, as illustrated by Gérôme's four-painting series depicting Truth as a nude woman thrown into a well, at the bottom of it, or emerging from it.
41 Henri Meilhac had already written a three-act comedy titled *Phryné*, which was performed at the Gymnase in 1881 (Macdonald 2019: 231).
42 The opera may even have made it as far as Hanoi, as Saint-Saëns had a copy sent there to the résident supérieur (Pasler 2012: 251).
43 Including *Phryné*, Saint-Saëns wrote seven operas on Classical themes throughout his career. The other six are *Prosérpine* (1886), *Antigone* (1893), *Déjanire* (1898), *Les Barbares* (1901), *Paryatis* (1902), and *Hélène* (1903). He also gave a lecture at the Académie Française in 1902 on ancient lyres and published an essay titled "Note sur les décors de théâtre dans l'antiquité romaine."
44 The statue in Saint-Saëns' home is neither the Pradier nor the Falguière version.
45 Pasler 2012: 251.

46 *Phryné* is no longer regularly performed, most likely due to its short running time and inclusion of spoken dialogue (Macdonald 2019: 242).
47 This was not the only story of an ancient Greek *hetaira* written for Sanderson, as Jules Massenet also wrote his *Thaïs* (1894) for her to play the title role. That opera featured a complex striptease with a carefully designed costume that would prevent Sanderson from being fully revealed, which malfunctioned on opening night, causing a great scandal. Even more so than that of Phryne, the character of the promiscuous Thaïs became associated with Sanderson herself (Rowden 2009: 281).
48 1914: 183.
49 Macdonald 2014 and Macdonald 2019: 231.
50 Garval 2012: 77.
51 cf. the illustration from *Le Journal Amusant*, 1897.
52 Garval 2012: 79.
53 Curnonsky 1897: 361.
54 Coutelet 2014: 121.
55 Ténarg, 1897.
56 Cavallini suggests that the high level of detail in this painting is a reflection of increased archaeological research at the time that Siemiradzki was painting it (2006: 227); the artist had visited Pompeii during his time in Italy.
57 In her assessment of the painting, Maria Nitka divides the onlookers into three groups: a group to the left gathered around a column who respond to Phryne with delight, the participants in the mysteries to the right of the painting, and Phryne and her attendants in the center (2020: 139).
58 Nitka 2020: 137–8.
59 Von Ostini thought that Siemiradzki's Phryne was "an insult to Aphrodite born of sea foam" (1890: 3).
60 Nitka offers a thorough summary of critical response to Siemiradzki's painting (2020: 140).
61 Despite his use of a Spanish-sounding pseudonym, Frappa was French, with the real first name Joseph.
62 There is one very unusual painting of Phryne from this period that demonstrates just how pervasive the image of Phryne and the judges had become. In this 1912 painting by the British painter Walford Graham Robertson, Phryne is a toddler standing naked before her judges, three dolls and several stuffed animals. Her back is turned to the viewer and a print of Gérôme's painting is partially included in the frame, to "Phryne's" right. The child's skin remains as marble-white as her adult counterpart with a mop of blonde curls. The child is likely Rachel Hill, a neighbor

who appeared in a later self-portrait with Robertson. It is, to say the least, a confusing image.
63 This kind of beauty, exemplified by women like Lollobrigida and Sophia Loren who were physically striking and had personalities to match, was popularized as a response to the more slender women who had dominated Italian cinema in the 1920s and 1930s (Celli and Cottino-Jones 2007: 81).
64 The joke in Italian centers on the pairing of the two comparative forms for "decreased" and "increased."
65 cf. Cavallini 2007: 227 and interview with Elena Kleus, 2013
66 Bonnard returned to the theme of sculptor and muse with his *Afrodite, dea dell'amore* ("Aphrodite, the Goddess of Love") in 1958, which alluded to the Phryne/Praxiteles relationship through the characters of Demetrius and Lerna.
67 Eleanora Cavallini, interview with Elena Kleus, 2013. Kleus is actually brunette throughout the film but several of the posters show her as blonde.
68 Eleanora Cavallini, interview with Elena Kleus, 2013.
69 The inclusion of a character named Lamaco (Lamachus) may be due to influence from Henri Meilhac's 1881 three-act comedy *Phryné*, which features a character by that name in addition to Phryne and Praxiteles.
70 One of her final roles was the title role in *Messalina* (1960), in which she played another ancient woman whose infamy obscured the historical details of her life.

Conclusion

1 cf. Elias 2004, ch. 1 on the "coercive" fragment.

Bibliography

Ajootian, Aileen (1998), "Praxiteles", in Olga Palagia and J. J. Pollitt (eds), *Personal Styles in Greek Sculpture*, 89–129, New York: Cambridge University Press.
Alexiou, Evangelos (2020), *Greek Rhetoric of the 4th Century BC: The Elixir of Democracy and Individuality*, Berlin: De Gruyter.
Altri Tempi (1951), [film] Dir. Alessandro Blasetti, Italy: Società Italiana Cines.
Anderson, Graham (1993), *Second Sophistic: Cultural Phenomenon in the Roman Empire*, Hoboken: Taylor and Francis.
Andrewes, A. (1961), "Philochoros on Phratries", *The Journal of Hellenic Studies* 81: 1–15.
Arnott, William Geoffrey (2012), "Machon", in Simon Hornblower, Anthony Spawforth, and Esther Eidinow (eds), *The Oxford Classical Dictionary (4th ed.)*, Oxford: Oxford University Press.
Augé de Lassus, Lucien (1914), *Saint-Saëns*, Paris: C. Delagrave.
Auhagen, Ulrike (2009), *Die Hetäre in der griechischen und römischen Komödie*, Munich: C. H. Beck.
Babbitt, Frank Cole (1928), *Plutarch Moralia Vol. II*, Cambridge, MA: Harvard University Press.
Babbitt, Frank Cole (1936), *Plutarch Moralia Vol. IV*, Cambridge, MA: Harvard University Press.
Babbitt, Frank Cole (1936), *Plutarch Moralia Vol. V*, Cambridge, MA: Harvard University Press.
Barker, Emma (2012), *Art & Visual Culture, 1600–1850: Academy to Avant-Garde*, London: Tate Enterprises Limited.
Bayard, Émile (1902), *Le Nu Esthétique*, Paris: E. Bernard.
Benner, A. R., and Fobes, E. H. (1949), *The Letters of Alciphron, Aelian, and Philostratus*, Cambidge, MA: Harvard University Press.
Berger, Jack (1972), *Ways of Seeing*, London: Penguin Books.
Blok, Josine (2017), *Citizenship in Classical Athens*. Cambridge: Cambridge University Press.
Blondell, Ruby (2013), *Helen of Troy: Beauty, Myth, Devastation*, Oxford: Oxford University Press.
Bond, Sarah E. (2022), "Why We Need to Start Seeing the Classical World in Color." *Hyperallergic*, 13 Jul. Available online: https://hyperallergic.com/383776/why-we-need-to-start-seeing-the-classical-world-in-color/.

Bonfante, Larissa (1989), "Nudity as a Costume in Classical Art", *American Journal of Archaeology* 93 (4): 543–70.
Bonfante, Larissa (1997), "Nursing Mothers in Classical Art", in Natalie Kampen, Ann O. Koloski-Ostrow, and Claire L. Lyons (eds), *Naked Truths: Women, Sexuality, and Gender in Classical Art and Archaeology*, 174–96, London: Routledge.
Borzello, Frances (1982), *The Artist's Model*, London: Faber and Faber Ltd.
Bowie, E. L. (1970), "Greeks and Their Past in the Second Sophistic", *Past & Present* 46: 3–41.
Bremmer, Jan (2019), "Religion and the limits of individualisation in ancient Athens: Andocides, Socrates, and the fair-breasted Phryne", in Martin Fuchs, Antje Linkenbach, Martin Mulsow, Bernd-Christian Otto, Rahul Bjørn Parson, and Jörg Rüpke (eds), *Religious Individualisation: Historical Dimensions and Comparative Perspectives*, 1019–32, Berlin: De Gruyter.
Cameron, Alan (1993), *The Greek Anthology: From Meleager to Planudes*, Oxford: Clarendon Press.
Campbell, David A. (1982), *Greek Lyric Vol. I: Sappho and Alcaeus*, Cambridge, MA: Harvard University Press.
Cantarelli, Luigi (1885), "Osservazioni sul processo di Frine", *Rivista di Filologia e di Istruzione Classica* 13: 465–82.
Cavallini, Eleonora (2001), *Il Banchetto dei Sapienti: Libro XIII Sulle Donne Ateneo di Naucrati*, Bologna: d.u. press.
Cavallini, Eleonora (2006), "Frine, Cortigiana Mediatica/Phryne: Cnidian Venus to Movie Star", *Quaderni di Scienza della Conservazione* 6: 215–36.
Cavallini, Eleonora (2014), "Esibizionismo o propaganda politica? Frine tra storia e aneddotica", in Umberto Bultrighini and Elisabetta Dimauro (eds), *Donne che contano nella storia Greca*, 127–52, Lanciano: Carabba.
Cavallini, Eleonora (2013), "Interview with Elena Kleus". Available online: https://www.yumpu.com/en/document/read/9092742/print-article-pdf-mythimedia-greek-myth-in-todays-culture.
Celli, Carlo, and Cottino-Jones, Marga (2007), *A New Guide to Italian Cinema*, New York: Palgrave Macmillan.
Champfleury, Ligaran (1872), *Souvenirs et portraits de jeunesse: Autobiographie et mémoires*, Paris: E. Dentu.
Chare, Nicholas and Contogouris, Ersy (2022), "On the Nude: Addressing Old and New Perspectives", in Nicholas Chare and Ersy Contogouris (eds), *On the Nude: Looking Anew at the Naked Body in Art*, 1–20, New York, Routledge.
Clark, Christina (2001), "The Body of Desire: Nonverbal Communication in Sappho 31 V: dis minibus Barbara Hughes Fowler", *Syllecta Classica* 12: 1–32.

Clark, Kenneth (1956), *The Nude: A Study in Ideal Form*, Princeton: Princeton University Press.
Cohen, Edward E. (2006), "Free and Unfree Sexual Work: An Economic Analysis of Athenian Prostitution", in Christopher A. Faraone and Laura McClure (eds), *Prostitutes and Courtesans in the Ancient World*, 95–124, Madison: University of Wisconsin Press.
Conquest, Robert (2000), "Phryne", *The New Criterion* 19 (2): 37.
Cooper, Craig (1995), "Hyperides and the Trial of Phryne", *Phoenix* 49 (4): 303–18.
Corpataux, Jean-François (2009), "Phryné, Vénus et Galatée dans l'atelier de Jean-Léon Gérôme", *Artibus et Historiae* 30 (59): 145–58.
Corso, Antonio (1997), "Love as Suffering: The Eros of Thespiae of Praxiteles", *Bulletin of the Institute of Classical Studies* 42: 63–91.
Corso, Antonio (2007), "The cult and political background of the Knidian Aphrodite", in Erik Hallager and Jesper Tae Jensen (eds), *Proceedings of the Danish Institute at Athens V*, 173–97, Aarhus: Aarhus University Press.
Couëlle, Colombe (2010), "Désirs d'Antique ou comment rêver le passé gréco-romain dans la peinture européenne de la seconde moitié du XIXè siècle", *Anabases* 11: 21–54.
Coutelet, Nathalie (2014), "Les Folies-Bergère: une pornographie « select »", *Romantisme* 163 (1): 111–24.
Crotty, Kevin (1994), *The Poetics of Supplication: Homer's Iliad and Odyssey*, Cornell: Cornell University Press.
Csapo, Eric G. (2000), "From Aristophanes to Menander? Genre Transformation in Greek Comedy", in Mary Depew and Dirk Obbink (eds), *Matrices of Genre: Authors, Canons, and Society*, 115–33, Cambridge, MA: Harvard University Press.
Čulík-Baird, Hannah (2022), *Cicero and the Early Latin Poets*, Cambridge: Cambridge University Press.
Cummings, Michael S. (2001), "The Early Greek Paraclausithyron and Gnesippus", *Scholia: Studies in Classical Antiquity* 10, 38–53.
Curnonsky, Maurice (1897), "Les Folies-Bergère. – L'Eldorado. – La Cigale.", *Revue d'Art Dramatique* I, Paris, 18 Rue Favart: 360–3.
Curtis, Todd (2014), "Genre and Galen's Philosophical Discourses", *Bulletin of the Institute of Classical Studies* Supplement 114: 39–59.
Dancy, Russell (2021), "Xenocrates", *Stanford Encyclopedia of Philosophy*, Stanford University, 27 March. Available online: https://plato.stanford.edu/entries/xenocrates/.
Davidson, James (1997), *Courtesans and Fishcakes: The Consuming Passions of Classical Athens*, Chicago: University of Chicago Press.
Davis, Holly (2013), "Defining 'Pimp': Working towards a Definition in Social Research," *Sociological Research Online* 18 (1): 71–85.

De Young, Justine (2011), "'Housewife or Harlot': Art, Fashion, and Morality in the Paris Salon of 1868", in Ilya Parkins and Elizabeth M. Sheehan (eds), *Cultures of Feminity in Modern Fashion*, 124–47, Lebanon, NH: University of New Hampshire Press.

Dillon, Sheila (2010), *The Female Portrait Statue in the Greek World*, New York: Cambridge University Press.

Donnay, Maurice (1894), *Phryné: Scènes Grecques Représentées au Chat Noir*, Paul Ollendorff (ed.), Paris: A. Michel.

Dover, K. J. (2016), *Greek Homosexuality; With Forewords by Stephen Haliwell, Mark Masterson and James Robson* (3rd ed.), London: Bloomsbury.

Du Pays, A. (1851), "Ecole des Beaux-Arts. Exposition des Grands Prix–Envoi des pensionnaires de l'Académie à Rome", *L'Illustration*, 9–16 October, 450 (18): 227–8.

Edmonds, John Maxwell (1959), *The Fragments of Attic Comedy After Meineke, Bergk, and Kock, Vol II*, Leiden: Brill.

Edwards, Walter Manoel, Browning, Robert, and Wilson, Nigel Guy (2012), "Athenaeus", in Simon Hornblower, Anthony Spawforth, and Esther Eidinow (eds), *The Oxford Classical Dictionary* (4th ed.), Oxford: Oxford University Press.

Eichholz, D. E. (1962), *Pliny Natural History Vol. X*, Cambridge, MA: Harvard University Press.

Eidinow, Esther (2010), "Patterns of Persecution: 'Witchcraft' Trials in Classical Athens", *Past & Present* 208: 9–35.

Eidinow, Esther (2016), *Envy, Poison, and Death: Women on Trial in Classical Athens* Oxford: Oxford University Press.

Elias, Camelia (2004), *The Fragment: Towards a History and Poetics of a Performative Genre*, Bern: P. Lang.

Elsner, Jaś (2007), *Roman Eyes: Visuality and Subjectivity in Art and Text*, Princeton: Princeton University Press.

Feldman, Martha, and Gordon, Bonnie (2006), "Introduction", in Martha Feldman and Bonnie Gordon (eds), *The Courtesan's Arts: Cross-Cultural Perspectives*, 3–26, Oxford: Oxford University Press.

Finglass, Patrick (2018), "Gazing at Helen with Stesichorus", in Alexandros Kampakoglou and Anna Novokhatko (eds), *Gaze, Vision, and Visuality in Ancient Greek Literature*, 140–59, Berlin: De Gruyter.

Frine, cortigiana d'Oriente (1953), [film] Dir. Mario Bonnard, Italy: Zeuss Film.

Funke, Melissa (2019), "Nostalgic Authority: Alciphron's Use of Visual Culture", in Michèle Biraud and Arnaud Zucker (eds), *The Letters of Alciphron: A Unified Literary Work?*, 138–56, Leiden: Brill.

Funke, Melissa (2022), "Epistolarity, Eroticism, and Agency: The Female Voice in Fictional Greek Love Letters", in Anna Tiziana Drago and Owen Hodkinson (eds), *Ancient Love Letters: Form, Themes, Approaches*, 223–6, Berlin: De Gruyter.

Garval, Michael D. (2012), *Cléo de Mérode and the Rise of Modern Celebrity Culture*, Farnham: Ashgate.

Gautier, Théophile (1861), *Abécédaire du Salon de 1861*, Paris: E. Dentu.

Gherchanoc, Florence (2012), "La beauté dévoilée de Phryné: De l'art d'exhiber ses seins", *Mètis—Anthropologie des mondes grecs anciens* 10: 201–25.

Gilhuly, Kate (2009), *The Feminine Matrix of Sex and Gender in Classical Athens*, Cambridge: Cambridge University Press.

Glazebrook, Allison (2006), "The Bad Girls of Athens: The Image and Function of *Hetairai* in Judicial Oratory", in Christopher A. Faraone and Laura McClure (eds), *Prostitutes and Courtesans in the Ancient World*, 125–38, Madison: University of Wisconsin Press.

Glazebrook, Allison (2021), *Sexual Labor in the Athenian Courts*. Austin: University of Texas Press.

Goldhill, Simon (2000), "Civic Ideology and the Problem of Difference: The Politics of Aeschylean Tragedy, Once Again", *The Journal of Hellenic Studies* 120: 34–56.

Goldhill, Simon (2001), "Setting an agenda: 'Everything is Greece to the Wise,'" in Simon Goldhill (ed.), *Being Greek Under Rome*, 1–27, Cambridge: Cambridge University Press.

Gow, A. S. F. (1965), *Machon The Fragments*, Cambridge: Cambridge University Press.

Granholm, Patrik (2012), *Alciphron, Letters of the Courtesans: Edited with Introduction, Translation and Commentary* (Diss. Uppsala).

Green, Peter (2004), "Occupation and coexistence: the impact of Macedon on Athens, 323–307", in Olga Palaia and Stephen V. Tracy (eds), *The Macedonians in Athens, 322–229 b.c.: Proceedings of an International Conference Held at the University of Athens, May 24–26 2001*, 1–7, Havertown: Oxbow Books.

Gutzwiller, Kathryn (2004), "Gender and Inscribed Epigram: Herrenia Procula and the Thespian Eros", *Transactions of the American Philological Association* 134 (2): 383–418.

Hall, Edith (1995), "Lawcourt Dramas: The Power of Performance in Greek Forensic Oratory", *Bulletin of the Institute of Classical Studies* 40: 39–58.

Hall, Edith (2006), *The Theatrical Cast of Athens: Interactions between Ancient Greek Drama and Society*, Oxford: Oxford University Press.

Hamel, Debra (1999), *Trying Neaira: The True Story of a Courtesan's Scandalous Life in Ancient Greece*, New Haven: Yale University Press.

Hartwig, Andrew (2014), "The Evolution of Comedy in the Fourth Century", in Eric Csapo, Hans Rupprecht Goette, J. Richard Green, Peter Wilson (eds), *Greek Theatre in the Fourth Century bc*, 207–27, Berlin: De Gruyter.

Haskins, Ekaterina (2018), "Reimagining Helen of Troy: Gorgias and Isocrates on Seeing and Being Seen", in Alexandros Kampakoglou and Anna Novokhatko (eds), *Gaze, Vision, and Visuality in Ancient Greek Literature*, 245–70, Berlin: De Gruyter.

Havelock, Christine Mitchell (1995), *The Aphrodite of Knidos and Her Successors: A Historical Review of the Female Nude in Greek Art*, Ann Arbor: The University of Michigan Press.

Haynes, Natalie (2017), "The 'It Girl' of the Ancient World." *BBC Culture*, BBC, 9 November. Available online: https://www.bbc.com/culture/article/20171108-the-it-girl-of-ancient-greece.

Henry, Madeleine M. (1988), *Menander's Courtesans and the Greek Comic Tradition*, Frankfurt: Verlag Peter Lang.

Henry, Madeleine M. (1995), *Prisoner of History: Aspasia of Miletus and Her Biographical Tradition*, New York: Oxford University Press.

Hicks, R. D. (1925), *Diogenes Laertius Lives of Eminent Philosophers Vol. II: Books 6–10*, Cambridge, MA: Harvard University Press.

Jensen, Christian (1917), *Hyperidis Orationes Sex Cum Ceterarum Fragmentis*, Stuttgardt: Teubner.

Jones, Christopher P. (2004), "Multiple identities in the age of the Second Sophistic", in Barbara E. Borg (ed.), *Paideia: the World of the Second Sophistic*, 13–21, Berlin: De Gruyter.

Kapparis, Konstantinos (1999) *Apollodorus "Against Neaira"[D. 59]*, Berlin: De Gruyter.

Kapparis, Konstantinos (2005), "Immigration and Citizenship Procedures in Athenian Law", *Revue internationale des droits de l'antiquité* 52: 71–113.

Kapparis, Konstantinos (2017), *Prostitution in the Ancient Greek World*, Berlin: De Gruyter.

Kapparis, Konstantinos (2021), *Women in the Law Courts of Classical Athens*, Edinburgh: Edinburgh University Press.

Kassel, R., and Austin, C. (1989), *Poetae Comici Graeci Vol. VII: Menecrates–Xenophon*, Berlin: De Gruyter.

Kassel, R., and Austin, C. (1991), *Poetae Comici Graeci Vol. II: Agathenor–Aristonymus*, Berlin: De Gruyter.

Keesling, Catherine (2006), "Heavenly Bodies: Monuments to Prostitutes in Greek Sanctuaries", in Christopher A. Faraone and Laura K. McClure (eds), *Prostitutes and Courtesans in the Ancient World*, 59–76, Madison: University of Wisconsin Press.

Kennedy, Rebecca Futo (2014), *Immigrant Women in Athens: Gender, Ethnicity, and Citizenship in the Classical City*, New York: Routledge.

Kennedy, Rebecca Futo (2015), "Elite Citizen Women and the Origins of the *Hetaira* in Classical Athens," *Helios* 42 (1): 61–79.

Kerley, Lela F. (2010), "The Art of Posing Nude: Models, Moralists, and the 1893 Bal des Quat'z-Arts", *French Historical Studies* 33 (1): 69–97.

Kerley, Lela F. (2017), *Uncovering Paris: Scandals and Nude Spectacles in the Belle Époque*, Baton Rouge: Louisiana State University Press.

Kermode, Frank (2000), *The Sense of an Ending: Studies on the Theory of Fiction with a New Epilogue*, Oxford: Oxford University Press.

Konstantakos, Ioannis M. (2006), "The Lady and the Loser: Aristodemos and Lynkeus on Love-Affairs of New Comedy Poets", *Hermes* 134 (2): 150–8.

Konstantakos, Ioannis M. (2011), "Conditions of Playwriting and the Comic Dramatist's Craft in the Fourth Century", *Logeion* 1: 145–83.

Kovacs, David (1995), *Euripides: Children of Heracles. Hippolytus. Andromache. Hecuba*, Cambridge, MA: Harvard University Press.

Kris, Ernst, and Kurz, Otto (1979), *Legend, Myth, and Magic in the Image of the Artist: A Historical Experiment*, New Haven: Yale University Press.

Kucharski, Janek (2012), "Vindictive Prosecution in Classical Athens: On Some Recent Theories", *Greek, Roman, and Byzantine Studies* 52: 167–97.

Kurke, Leslie (1997), "Inventing the 'Hetaira': Sex, Politics, and Discursive Conflict in Ancient Greece", *Classical Antiquity* 16 (1): 106–50.

Kurke, Leslie (2002), "Gender, Politics, and Subversion in the *Chreiai* of Machon," *Proceedings of the Cambridge Philological Society* 48: 20–65.

La Venere di Cheronea/Aphrodite, déesse de l'amour/Aphrodite, The Goddess of Love (1957), [film] Dir. Fernando Cerchio and Viktor Tourjansky, Italy: Rialto Film.

Lape, Susan (2003), *Reproducing Athens: Menander's Comedy, Democratic Culture, and the Hellenistic City*, Princeton: Princeton University Press.

Lathers, Marie (2001), *Bodies of Art: French Literary Realism and the Artist's Model*, Lincoln: University of Nebraska Press.

Lee, Mireille (2015), *Bodies, Dress, and Identity in Ancient Greece*, New York: Cambridge University Press.

Lee, Mireille (2015), "Other 'Ways of Seeing': Female Viewers of the Knidian Aphrodite", *Helios* 42 (1): 103–22.

Loddo, Laura (2022), "'Ἕως ἂν κατέλθωσιν εἰς τὴν αὑτῶν: Did the Athenians Reduce their Reception of Refugees in the Fourth Century BC?" *Pallas* 112: 199–230.

Loomis, William T. (1998), *Wages, Welfare Costs and Inflation in Classical Athens*, Ann Arbor: University of Michigan Press.

MacDonald, Dennis Ronald (1998), "The Breasts of Hecuba and Those of the Daughters of Jerusalem: Luke's Transvaluation of a Famous Iliadic Scene", in

Jo-Ann A. Brant, Charles W. Hedrick, and Chris Shea (eds), *Ancient Fiction: The Matrix of Early Christian and Jewish Narrative*, 239–54, Atlanta: Society of Biblical Literature.

MacDonald, Hugh (2014), "Lost Legacy", *Opera News* 78 (11). Available online: https://www.operanews.com/Opera_News_Magazine/2014/5/Features/Lost_Legacy.html

Macdonald, Hugh (2019), *Saint-Saëns and the Stage: Operas, Plays, Pageants, a Ballet and a Film*, Cambridge, UK: Cambridge University Press.

Maierhofer, Waltraud (2007), "Art, Fame, Sentiment, and Self: Constructions of Identity in Text and Image", in Tobias G. Natter (ed.), *Angelica Kauffman: A Woman of Immense Talent*, 18–31, Ostfildern: Hatje Cantz.

Mansfield, Elizabeth C. (2007), *Too Beautiful to Picture: Zeuxis, Myth, and Mimesis*, Minneapolis: University of Minnesota Press.

Marchant, E. C. (1923), *Xenophon Vol. IV: Memorabilia. Oeconomicus. Symposium. Apology*, Cambridge, MA: Harvard University Press.

McClure, Laura K. (2003a), *Courtesans at Table: Gender and Greek Literary Culture in Athenaeus*, New York: Routledge.

McClure, Laura K. (2003b), "Subversive Laughter: The Sayings of Courtesans in Book 13 of Athenaeus' *Deipnosophistae*", *The American Journal of Philology* 124 (2): 259–94.

Miles, Sarah (2016), "Greek Drama in the Hellenistic World", in Betine van Zyl Smit (ed.), *A Handbook to the Reception of Greek Drama*, 45–62, Chichester: Wiley and Sons.

Montel, Sophie (2010), "The Architectural Setting of the Knidian Aphrodite", in Amy C. Smith and Sadie Pickup (eds), *Brill's Companion to Aphrodite*, Leiden, Brill: 251–68.

Morales, Helen (2011), "Fantasising Phryne: The Psychology and Ethics of Ekphrasis", *Cambridge Classical Journal* 57: 71–104.

Mori, Anatole (2015), "Literature in the Hellenistic World", in Martin Hose and David Schenker (eds), *A Companion to Greek Literature*, 89–111, Chichester: Wiley and Sons.

Mulvey, Laura (1975), "Visual Pleasure and Narrative Cinema", *Screen* 16 (3): 6–18.

Naiden, Fred (2006), *Ancient Supplication*, Oxford: Oxford University Press.

Nead, Lynda (1992), *The Female Nude: Art, Obscenity, and Sexuality*, London: Routledge.

Nervegna, Sebastiana (2013), *Menander in Antiquity: The Contexts of Reception*, Cambridge: Cambridge University Press.

Nesselrath, Heinz-Günther (1997), "The polis of Athens in Middle Comedy", in Gregory W. Dobrov (ed.), *The City as Comedy: Society and Representation in Athenian Drama*, 271–88, Chapel Hill: University of North Carolina Press.

Nitka, Maria (2020), "Naked Truth and Beauty of the Nude in Heinryk Siemiradzki's *Phryne*", in Maria Nitka and Agnieszka Kluczewska-Wójcik (eds), *Henryk Siemiradzki and the International Artistic Milieu in Rome*, 135–54, Roma: Accademia Polacca Roma.

Normandy, Georges (1909), *Le nu à l'Eglise, au Théâtre et dans la Rue*, Paris: G. Normandy.

O'Neill, K. (1998), "Aeschylus, Homer, and the Serpent at the Breast", *Phoenix* 52 (3/4): 216–29.

Olson, S. Douglas (2010), *Athenaeus, The Learned Banqueters, Vol. VI*, Cambridge, MA: Harvard University Press.

Osborne, Robin (1994), "Looking on—Greek style: Does the sculpted girl speak to women too?", Ian Morris (ed.), *Classical Greece: Ancient histories and modern archaeologies*, 81–96, Cambridge: Cambridge University Press.

Osborne, Robin (2011), *The History Written on the Classical Body*, Cambridge: Cambridge University Press.

Pasler, Jann (2012), "Saint-Saëns and the Ancient World: From Africa to Greece", in Jann Pasler (ed.), *Camille Saint-Saëns and His World*, 232–59, Princeton: Princeton University Press.

Paton, W. R. (1916), *The Greek Anthology Vol. I: Books I–VI*, Cambridge, MA: Harvard University Press.

Paton, W. R. (1918), *The Greek Anthology Vol. V: Books XIII–XVI*, Cambridge, MA: Harvard University Press.

Pavel, Thomas G. (1986), *Fictional Worlds*, Cambridge, MA: Harvard University Press.

Payne, Mark (2007), *Theocritus and the Invention of Fiction*, Cambridge: Cambridge University Press.

Pérez-Prendes Muñoz de Arraco, José Manuel (2005), "El mito de Friné: nuevas perspectivas", *Anuario Real Academia de Bellas Artes de San Telmo* 5: 27–46.

Peterson, Anna Irene (2022), "What is Athens without Menander? The Comic Poet, the Courtesan, and the Production of Space in Alciphron's *Letters*", *Arethusa* 55(2): 177–207.

Phillips, David D. (2013), *The Law of Ancient Athens*, Ann Arbor: University of Michigan Press.

Renaud, Robert (1992), "Ars regenda Amore. Séduction érotique et plaisir esthétique: de Praxitèle à Ovide", *Mélanges de l'école française de Rome* 104 (1): 373–438.

Ridgway, Brunilde Sismondo (1987), "Ancient Greek Women and Art: The Material Evidence", *American Journal of Archaeology* 91 (3): 399–409.

Rösch, Yvonne (2019), "Close Encounters with the *hetaira*: Reading Alciphron's Book 4", in Michèle Biraud and Arnaud Zucker (eds), *The Letters of Alciphron: A Unified Literary Work?*, 224–43, Leiden: Brill.

Rosenmeyer, Patricia (2001a), "(In)versions of Pygmalion: The Statue Talks Back", in André Lardinois and Laura McClure (eds), *Making Silence Speak: Women's Voices in Ancient Greek Literature and Society*, 240–60. Princeton: Princeton University Press.

Rosenmeyer, Patricia (2001b), *Ancient Epistolary Fictions*, New York: Cambridge University Press.

Rowden, Clair (2009), "Opera, Caricature and the Unconscious: Jules Massenet's Thaïs, a Case Study", *Music in Art* 34 (1/2): 274–89.

Roworth, Wendy Wassyng (1983) "The Gentle Art of Persuasion: Angelica Kauffman's *Praxiteles and Phryne*", *Art Bulletin* 65: 488–92.

Roworth, Wendy Wassyng (2007), "Angelica in Love: Gossip, Rumor, Romance, and Scandal", in Tobias G. Natter (ed.), *Angelica Kauffman: A Woman of Immense Talent*, 42–51, Ostfildern: Hatje Cantz.

Salomon, Nanette (1997), "Making a World of Difference: Gender, asymmetry, and the Greek nude", in Natalie Kampen, Ann O. Koloski-Ostrow, and Claire L. Lyons (eds), *Naked Truths: Women, Sexuality and Gender in Classical Art and Archaeology*, 197–219, London: Routledge.

Sandner, Oscar (2007), "Angelica K. or the Ward Who Would be Guardian: The Early Years 1762–75", in Tobias G. Natter (ed.), *Angelica Kauffman: A Woman of Immense Talent*, 32–41, Ostfildern: Hatje Cantz.

Schmitz, Thomas A. (2004), "Alciphron's Letters as a Sophistic Text", in Barbara E. Borg (ed.), *Paideia: the World of the Second Sophistic*, 87–104, Berlin: De Gruyter.

Seaman, Kristen (2004), "Retrieving the Original Aphrodite of Knidos", *Atti della Accademia Nazionale dei Lincei, Rendiconti Classe di scienze morali, storiche e filologiche* 9 (15): 531–94.

Searby, Denis Michael (2019), "The Fossilized Meaning of *Chreia* as Anecdote", *Mnemosyne* 72 (2): 197–228.

Semenov, Anatol (1935), "Hypereides und Phryne", *Klio* 28 (28): 271–9.

Silver, Morris (2017), *Slave-Wives, Single Women and Bastards in the Ancient Greek World: Law and Economics Perspectives*. Philadelphia: Oxbow Books.

Simon, Erika (1983), *Festivals of Attica: an archaeological commentary*, Madison: University of Wisconsin Press.

Smith, Alison (1996), *The Victorian Nude: Sexuality, Morality, and Art*, Manchester: Manchester University Press.

Sommerstein, Alan H. (2009), *Talking about Laughter and Other Studies in Greek Comedy*, Oxford: Oxford University Press.

Spivey, Nigel (2013), *Greek Sculpture*, Cambridge: Cambridge University Press.

Squire, Michael (2011), *The Art of the Body: Antiquity and its Legacy*, London: I.B. Tauris and Co.

Stewart, Andrew (1997), *Art, Desire, and the Body in Ancient Greece*, Cambridge: Cambridge University Press.

Stonard, John-Paul (2010), "Kenneth Clark's 'The Nude. A Study of Ideal Art', 1956", *The Burlington Magazine* 152 (1286): 317–21.

Ténarg (1897), "Folichonneries Théâtre", *Folichonneries*, 4, 28 février.

Thorsen, Thea Selliaas (2012), "Sappho, Corinna and Colleagues in Ancient Rome. Tatian's Catalogue of Statues (*Oratio ad Graecos* 33-4) Reconsidered", *Mnemosyne* 65 (4–5): 695–715.

Todisco, Luigi (2020), "Frine a Delfi: Una postilla", *Quaderni di storia* 91: 209–18.

Tuplin, C. J. (1986), "The Fate of Thespiae during the Theban Hegemony", *Athenaeum* 64: 321–41.

Van Gogh Museum (1996), "Catalogue of acquisitions: paintings and drawings July 1994—December 1996", *Van Gogh Museum Journal*. Available online: https://www.dbnl.org/tekst/_van012199601_01/_van012199601_01_0015.php

Von Ostini, Fritz (1890), *Münchener Neueste Nachrichten* 279.

Vox, Onofrio (2019), "Women's Voices: Four of Five Women's Letters by Alciphron", in Michèle Biraud and Arnaud Zucker (eds), *The Letters of Alciphron: A Unified Literary Work?*, 107–25, Leiden: Brill.

Walz, Christian (1833), *Rhetores Graeci* Vol. IV, Black, Young & Young: London.

Walz, Christian (1833), *Rhetores Graeci* Vol. VII. Pars I, Black, Young & Young: London.

Webb, Ruth (2009), *Ekphrasis, Imagination and Persuasion in Ancient Rhetorical Theory and Practice*, Farnham: Ashgate.

West, Martin L. (2003), *Homeric Hymns. Homeric Apocrypha. Lives of Homer*, Cambridge, MA: Harvard University Press.

Whitehead, David (1977), *The Ideology of the Athenian Metic*, Cambridge: Cambridge Philological Society.

Whitehead, David (2000), *Hypereides: The Forensic Speeches*, Oxford: Oxford University Press.

Whitmarsh, Tim (2002), *Greek Literature and the Roman Empire: The Politics of Imitation*, Oxford: Oxford University Press.

Witzke, Serena S. (2015), "Harlots, Tarts, and Hussies? A Problem of Terminology for Sex Labor in Roman Comedy", *Helios* 42 (1), 7–28.

Index Locorum

Aelian
  Varia Historia
  9.32 72

Aeschylus
  Libation Bearers
  896-99 91

Alciphron
  4.1 8, 61–3
  4.3 81–2, 99
  4.4 82
  4.8.4 40
  4.8.6 40
  4.15 100

Alexis
  The Woman from Knidos/The Knidian Goddess 47, 66

Anaxilas
  Neottis
  fr. 21 K-A 27
  fr. 22 K-A 4, 44–6

Andocides
  On the Mysteries
  1.110 94

Anonymous Seguerianus
  Ars Rhetorica
  215 80

Antiphanes
  Country-Dweller
  fr. 2 K-A 42
  The Birth of Aphrodite/Aphrodite's Offspring 47

[Aristotle]
  Constitution of the Athenians
  43.6 94

Athenaeus
  13.557f 78
  13.567a-b 149 n. 27
  13.568a-d 78
  13.568e 78
  13.569a 15
  13.569b 78
  13.571c 28
  13.571d 28
  13.583c 4
  13.585f 68
  13.588f 40
  13.590c 36
  13.590c-d 84
  13.590d 84
  13.590e 93, 98
  13.590e-f 80, 81
  13.590f 5
  13.590f-591a 54
  13.591a 5, 60, 67
  13.591a-b 57
  13.591b 5, 71
  13.591c 147 n. 4
  13.591d 6
  13.591e 83, 161 n. 4
  13.591e-f 82–3
  13.591f 147 n. 3
  13.599b 153 n. 49
  Epit. 2.2.117 87

Clement of Alexandria
  Protrepticus
  4.35 67

Demosthenes
  Against Aristogeiton
  25.79-80 162 n. 31
  Against Euboulides
  57.34 36
  57.35 36
  On the Crown
  18.260 89

[Demosthenes]
Against Neaira
59.13 30
59.18 30
59.19 30, 31
59.22 31
59.24 31
59.26 152 n. 28
59.29 31, 152 n. 31
59.30 32
59.33 95
59.122 24

Dio Chrysostom
Corinthian Discourse
37.28 71

Diogenes Laertius
4.2.7 41
6.2.60 71

Epicrates
Anti-Lais 43

Euripides
Andromache
628-531 92
Trojan Women
1052-59 92

Fragmente der griechischen Historiker
405 F 1 29

Galen
Protrepticus
1.26 52

Gorgias
Encomium of Helen 98

Greek Anthology
6.260 59–60
16.160 66
16.203 58
16.204 60
16.205 59
16.206 58

Herodas
2.69-70 95

Homer
Iliad
3.442 96
22.79-83 91

Homeric Hymn to Aphrodite
52-66 96
90 96
93 96

Hypereides
Against Aristagora 36
Against Autocles for Treason
fr. 1 87
In Defense of Phryne
fr. 67 84
fr. 176 84
fr. 177 80

Isaeus
On the Estate of Philoctemon
6.19 33
6.20 33
6.21 33
6.50 34

Longinus
On the Sublime
34.3-4 83

[Lucian]
Erotes
13 97
13-14 68
14 97
15 98
16 68, 98

Ovid
Metamorphoses
10.243-97 69
10.294 69

Pausanias
1.20.1-2 57
2.2.4-5 40
10.15.1 71

Pliny the Elder
Natural History
34.70 70

35.86-87 107
35.125 56
36.20-21 64

Plutarch
Cimon
4.5 56
Mor.
125a 5
336d 71
389a 89
401a 4, 52, 71, 72
401c 71, 75
401d 71
753f 60
848e 85
849a 85
849e 5, 81, 86
Per.
32 87

Posidippus
The Ephesian Girl
fr. 13 K-A 47–8, 82–3

Quintilian
2.15.8 95
2.15.9 80
10.5.2 83

Rhetores Graeci (Walz)
4.414 92
7.335 92

Sappho
fr. 31 1.7-16 96–7, 98

Stesichorus
fr. 106 F 98

Timocles
Delians
fr. 4, l.7 85
Icarians
fr. 17 85
Neaira 43
fr. 25 K-A 4, 31, 46–7
Orestautocleides
fr. 27 K-A 43–4

Valerius Maximus
4 ext. 3a 41

Xenophon
Apology
14.3 87
Memorabilia
3.11.4 39

Index

Alciphron 5, 8, 40–1, 60–3, 68–9, 74–8, 144
   Phryne's trial in the *Letters* 79–83, 92, 96, 99, 101, 156 n. 24
Alexander the Great 6, 7, 52, 85, 107, 137
Alexandria 4, 7–8, 9, 11–13, 49, 144
Alke 28, 32–5, 43, 152 n. 33
Altri Tempi (film) 105, 133, 134
anecdote (literary genre) 1–2, 4, 8–9, 11–14, 16, 18, 38–41, 55–6, 86
Apelles 5, 38, 47, 52, 54, 56, 68, 74, 76–7, 80, 93, 107, 160 n. 89 and 97
   modern painting 111, 114, 129
Aphrodite (goddess) 59, 68, 69, 75, 93–4, 96, 99
Aphrodite Anadyomene 53, 115, 129, 166 n. 24
Aphrodite of Knidos/Knidia 3, 5, 51, 47, 54, 56, 64–70, 73–5, 97–8, 114–15, 140, 158 n. 56
Apollodorus (Athenian orator/speechwriter) 23, 32, 95, 100–1
Aristagora 36–7, 84, 86, 153 n. 41
Aristodemus 8–9, 12, 144, 148 n. 12
asebeia 79, 81, 87–8, 90
Aspasia 20, 87–8, 162 n. 28
Athenaeus 3–4, 8, 9, 14–17, 28, 40, 52–6, 144, 157 n. 21
   Aphrodite of Knidos and Praxiteles 67–72, 75–8, 127, 129–30
   Aspasia's trial 87
   Phryne's trial 80–6, 91–7, 115
Athens
   Classical/fourth-century 2, 4, 6–7, 24, 33
   literary version 3, 8, 12–18, 63, 77, 103
atticizing 9, 16

Bal des Quat'z'Arts 120
Blasetti, Alessandro 105, 136
body as metaphor 76, 96
Bonnard, Mario 105, 169 n. 66

Boulanger, Gustave 112–14, 119, 131, 165 n. 16

Champfleury (Jules François Felix Fleury-Husson) 116–18
chreia(i) 12–13, 148 n. 25
Clytemnestra 91–3
Comedy
   fourth-century 7–8, 10–11, 42–3, 53, 82, 143
   Old 10
Corinth 12, 30, 32, 40, 148 n. 21, 152 n. 26
Cynculus (character from Athenaeus) 15–16, 52–3, 78

de Mérode, Cléo 126–7
Demosthenes 7, 30, 38, 83–5
Diogenes (Cynic philosopher) 38, 40, 71
Donnay, Maurice 122–3

ekphrasis 54–5, 76
enargeia 17, 52, 55
epigram 51, 55, 57–68, 73, 76, 108
eros (desire) 58, 60, 63, 96, 98
Eros (statue by Praxiteles) 5, 52, 56–63, 107–9, 156 n. 18
Euthias 4, 79–82, 84, 87–9, 99

Falguière, Alexandre 115, 126–7
femmes nues 105, 120
fictionalizing 8–9, 13, 15–18, 20, 55, 80, 120, 143
Folies Bergère 127
fragments (literary) 3, 9–15, 17, 104
   coercive fragments 14, 67
Frappa, José 130–1, 168 n. 61
Frine, cortigiana d'Oriente 136–8

Gérôme, Jean-Léon 105, 111, 114–16, 118, 119, 123, 128, 130, 166 n. 23, 167 n. 40

Glykera 56, 123, 155 n. 12
graphē (public lawsuit) 37, 80, 90, 100
Greek literature in the Roman Empire (Second Sophistic) 2, 8, 13, 15–17, 76

Hecuba 91–4
Helen (of Troy) 91–4, 96, 98–9, 155 n. 8, 163 n. 50, 164 n. 61
Hellenistic literature 7–8, 11–13, 41, 144
Herpyllis 39, 150 n. 5
hetaira(i)
    artists 51, 56, 67
    category of sex worker 2, 4, 8, 24–6, 28
    comedy 10–11, 42–8, 148 n. 19, 153 n. 57
    Hellenistic literature 11–13, 38, 149 n. 27
    Imperial literature 13, 16, 18, 38, 76–8
    legal oratory 10, 79
    philosophers 39–42, 71
Hypereides 4–6, 36–7, 72, 161 n. 20 and 21
    film 134–5
    modern painting 114, 130
    Phryne's trial 80–7, 89–93, 95, 99
    stage 123

Idomeneus 81, 83–5, 91–2
Isodaites 80, 89

Kauffman, Angelica 106–11, 141, 165 n. 6
Kleus, Elena 136–8, 141, 142, 169 n.67

La Venere di Cheronea/Aphrodite, déesse de l'amour/Aphrodite, The Goddess of Love 106, 134, 138–40
Lais 38, 40–1, 43, 43, 123
Le Chat Noir cabaret 121–3
Lee, Belinda 133, 139–41, 142
Leroux, Marie-Christine 116–17, 118, 127, 141
Leontium 39, 153 n. 47
Lollobrigida, Gina 105, 133–6, 140–1, 142, 169 n. 63
Lyceum 4, 80, 87–9, 162 n. 36
Lynceus of Samos 11–12, 14, 144

Machon 8, 12–14, 38, 144, 148 n. 24 and 25
maggiorata fisica 134–5, 142

Marchal, Charles-François 118–19, 166 n. 30
Margyl, Jane 127
Menander 7, 10–13, 16, 43, 148 n. 11, 149 n. 28, 155 n. 12
metic 35–7, 85, 87, 90, 94, 99, 120
Mnesarete (Phryne's original name) 1, 4, 29, 71, 147 n. 2, 159 n. 70
Myrtilus (character from Athenaeus) 15–16, 28, 52–3, 78

Nadar (Gaspard-Félix Tournachon) 116, 117, 126, 127
Neaira 23, 29–32, 35, 43, 46, 83, 100–1, 151 n. 24
Néo-Grec movement 111–12, 114–15
nostalgia 2, 8, 17–18, 51, 55, 76–8
nudity
    nudity and the Aphrodite of Knidos 64–6
    onstage nudity 105, 120–2, 126, 128
    Phryne's nudity at Eleusis 53–4, 67, 69, 72
    Phryne's nudity at trial 92–3, 95–6, 98, 102
    the Nude in art 73–4, 77, 105, 112–15, 118

paideia 16
pallakē/pallakia 24, 27–8, 36–7, 39, 150 n. 4 and 5
Parreiras, Antonio 131, 133
phthonos ("envy/ill-will") 87–8
pornē 16, 24, 27, 39
Pradier, James 112
Praxiteles
    character in Alciphron's *Letters* 61–4
    creator of Aphrodite of Knidos 64–8, 69–70, 74–5, 96
    epigrams 57–60, 66
    film 106, 137–40
    modern painting 107–9, 111, 115
    portraits of Phryne 70–2, 82, 104
    relationship with Phryne 3, 5, 8, 38, 47, 51–2, 54–7, 70–2
    stage 126

Plutarch 3–4, 8, 9, 52, 55, 115
  biography of Hypereides 80–1, 85–6
Pygmalion 19, 69, 166 n. 23
Posidippus 47, 49, 82–3

Rosa, Salvator 109–11, 165 n. 9

Saint-Saëns, Camille 124–5, 167 n. 42 and 43
Sanderson, Sibyl 124–5, 142, 168 n. 47
sexual labor 23–4, 25, 27–9
Siemiradzki, Henryk 129–30, 168 n. 56
social mobility of sex workers 33–4, 47, 49, 199
Socrates 39, 87–9, 162 n. 25
supplication 80, 90–4, 95, 99, 163 n. 53

Theodote (character from Xenophon's *Memorabilia*) 39, 41

Thespiai 4, 5–6, 29, 35, 67, 71–2, 104, 144, 151 n. 22 and 23
  Sanctuary of Eros 57–61, 63, 156 n. 18, 19, and 22
Timocles 4, 10, 31, 43–4, 46, 85, 154 n. 62, 162 n. 23

visualization/visual erotics 51–2, 62–3, 69, 75, 93, 97
  Laura Mulvey and the cinematic gaze 62
  John Berger on women in art 62–3, 73
von Stuck, Franz 131, 132

Winckelmann, Johann Joachim 106, 107, 112, 132

Xenocrates 38, 40–1, 109–11

www.ingramcontent.com/pod-product-compliance
Lightning Source LLC
Chambersburg PA
CBHW052119300426
44116CB00010B/1723